THE AUTHOR: Nels F. S. Ferré was born in Lulea, Sweden in 1908 and came to this country alone at the age of thirteen to work for an education. He was graduated from Boston University in 1931 and from Andover Newton Theological School in 1934, with high honors in both instances. His M.A. degree was earned at Harvard in 1936 and his doctorate in 1938, following a year spent in Europe as a Sheldon Travelling Fellow. In the fall of 1937 he joined the faculty of Andover Newton and was later appointed Abbot Professor of Christian Theology. In 1950 he became Professor of Philosophical Theology at Vanderbilt University.

His first book *Swedish Contributions to Modern Theology,* which grew out of his studies at Upsala and Lund Universities, 1936-1937, was published in 1939. Among the other books which followed are: THE CHRISTIAN FELLOWSHIP, RETURN TO CHRISTIANITY, THE CHRISTIAN FAITH, FAITH AND REASON, EVIL AND THE CHRISTIAN FAITH, STRENGTHENING THE SPIRITUAL LIFE, THE CHRISTIAN UNDERSTANDING OF GOD, and THE SUN AND THE UMBRELLA.

Christian Faith and
Higher Education

Other Books by Nels F. S. Ferré

Christian Faith and Higher Education

by NELS F. S. FERRÉ

Professor of Philosophical Theology
Vanderbilt University School of Religion

Harper & Brothers *Publishers* *New York*

Library of Congress catalog card number: 54-8949

To My Teachers

Warren O. Ault

Julius Seelye Bixler

Edgar S. Brightman

Winfred Donovan

Daniel Evans

William Ernest Hocking

Anders Nygren

Alfred North Whitehead

Contents

Contents

Preface

"It can be said without danger of exaggeration that that ideology which captures the higher education of a nation will ultimately determine its mind and soul."[1] Those of us who believe in the Christian faith as universal truth are concerned to exhibit its educational adequacy. Education should teach nothing but truth; truth is its only authority. Our task is to find the best way to teach religion in higher education. Religion has no right at all, however, to demand to be taught unless it can vindicate its truth in the open court of knowledge. Certainly public education is well rid of whatever cannot stand some appropriate test of public verification. General education, at least, has a duty to reject the teaching of all that cannot be generally understood and accepted.

The integrity of education demands that it scrutinize the claim of religion to be a legitimate subject for public instruction. Education has to safeguard its inviolate duty to teach nothing but the truth from the assumption that religion is the complete master, not the servant, of education. All too easily education may lose to religious dogmatism not only its freedom but its very life in truth.

At the same time, to a large extent, all over the world higher education "floats rudderless on the changing tides of force."[2] Today

[1] Howard Y. McClusky, "The Development of Religious and Moral Values," in *Liberal Learning and Religion*, Amos N. Wilder, ed. (New York, Harper, 1951), p. 237.

[2] Eivind Berggrav, *Man and State* (Philadelphia, Muhlenberg Press, 1951), p. 47.

9

educators are searching their own hearts not only with respect to guilt for the condition of the world—for growth in education was supposed to remedy that condition—but also with regard to what can actually be done to improve education. Responsible educators carry a heavy burden in their hearts. Sir Walter Moberly says that "in plain language, we need to repent."[3] Repentance, however, beyond regret over past failures, must be mostly a matter of reorientation and reconstitution. The purpose of this volume, accordingly, is constructive. We have many excellent volumes that analyze our modern predicament and suggest a reconstruction of education in terms of values, purpose, or religion. Our main task is to propose a relation between education and religion in terms of the Christian faith that protects the integrity of both, while also joining them organically for mutual discipline and service.

This volume has come to be written because of invitations to speak on the subject first at Green Lake, Wisconsin, for the Northern Baptist Educational Society, and then at Montreat, North Carolina, for the Presbyterian Educational Association of the South; sponsoring a Pan-Presbyterian and Reformed Educational Conference. At the latter occasion there were present members of the Commission on Religion in Higher Education of the National Council of Churches who requested that I undertake to write this volume. Help was sought from the Danforth Foundation, which gave me the honor to deliver the first Danforth Lectures on this subject at Boston University. I cannot be sufficiently thankful to men like Hunter Blakely, John Gross, and Paul Calvin Payne for getting me started on this project. Kenneth I. Brown of the Danforth Foundation has stood behind me throughout. Raymond MacLain, executive director of the National Council Commission, has been an encouraging friend. In addition to these two, the following people have read the manuscript and offered constructive suggestions: Dean Leonard Beach, Dean John Keith Benton, Dr. Edwin Mims of Vanderbilt University, Dr. John Gross, executive secretary of the Methodist Commission of Educational Institutions, Dr. John Q. Schisler, executive secretary, Division of the Local Church, Board

[3] *The Crisis in the University* (London, S. C. M. Press Ltd., 1949), p. 212.

of Education, Methodist Church, and Dr. Nathaniel Micklem, formerly Principal of Mansfield College, Oxford, England. I am thankful to them for improvements in thought and style. Finally, however, I have had to make my own decisions, and have to assume responsibility for any faulty emphasis, expression, or other error in the text. The substance of Chapter Ten has appeared in the *Journal of Religion.*

As always, my wife has been my main critic and helper. Our faculty secretary, Miss Lorine Martin, has had to labor hard and long over many drafts. One draft was typed by Mrs. James N. Nesmith. Dr. Kuhlman, director of the Joint University Library, has made available not only excellent working conditions, but also suggested special books and pamphlets to enrich the background of preparation. Mr. Frank Grisham, the librarian of the School of Religion, has been helpful at every point of need. Mr. Harold Hinderliter, our Carré Fellow and my assistant, has checked the notes for me. As ever it is a privilege to work with the Religious Book Department of Harper & Brothers. When professional relations are fulfilled in personal friendship, life becomes easier and work more pleasant.

I consented to write this book because of an obvious need. Whatever service I may have rendered is mostly by making marginal notes on education from the point of view of a theologian. The final test of what has been done will be truth and time; what seems to me now to be the most important issue may not be central in the future. History humbles us all by making its own selections. On the other hand, each worker must trust that the vision that is given him neither originates nor ends with him. The final issue lies with God.

NELS F. S. FERRÉ

Nashville, Tennessee

Christian Faith and Higher Education

Chapter I

What Is Education?

EDUCATION is the assisting of seekers for more truth and a better life to appropriate for themselves what is real, important, useful, and satisfying. It is offering to others, with discrimination, what we are, know, and believe, the more mature members sharing with the less mature.[1] Such education consists of three interrelated processes: discriminating transmission of our cultural heritage; provision for conditions which promote creative discovery; and inner development of persons, both as individuals and as a society. All these processes are, of course, ideal goals or directives and the more nearly they are attained the more nearly successful is education.

A discriminating transmission of our cultural heritage is a primary task for education. Richness and depth depend on historic background and mastery of detail. Gardner Murphy finds rich individuality possible only because it is superimposed, "as a very complex end result, upon a developmental continuity."[2] The ages live

[1] Cf. education is "an activity or endeavor in which the more mature of human society deal with the less mature, in order to achieve a greater maturity in them and contribute thereby to the improvement of human life." J. Donald Butler, *Four Philosophies and Their Practice in Education and Religion,* (New York, Harper, 1951), p. 10.

Cf. also, "Education knows no limits but the limits of life itself. It is as broad as experience. Therefore to restrict it in thought—it cannot be restricted in practice—to the public school is a tragic neglect of responsibility for the shaping of vital areas of the child's personality and character." Frank E. Gaebelein, *Christian Education in a Democracy* (New York, Oxford, 1951), p. 92.

[2] *Personality: A Biosocial Approach to Origins and Structure,* (New York, Harper, 1941), p. 63.

15

in us; we are the social stream, rippling out at a point of understanding and response. Knowledge is an overwhelmingly social act. Its most important aspect is not what we think *on*, but think *with*— what Whitehead calls "the background of ignorance." But as far as possible we should become consciously aware of these depths, and learn to discriminate their wealth of material.

For mere knowledge is of little avail. Suppose, for instance, that a person became aware of his total historic heritage. Such collective experience by itself would do him no more good than the mixture and confusion of drives and insights it has already produced. He would be like his actual world, which is the very object of reconstruction at the hands of education. Our main problem is not quantity of knowledge, but selectivity—quality of insight. Arnold Nash graphically compares trust in more facts to the saving of a drowning man by increase of water.[3] To be sure, without sufficient data from history, literature, and scientific development, education becomes superficial; but what matters most to education is the power to extricate the relevant, the important, the useful.

This insight is particularly needed, because no one ever does appropriate the total heritage of mankind. Generally we absorb and reflect the behavior patterns of our own community in what we do. Sociology tends to make man a social granule who is, merely or mostly, "a cross section of his community, a wholly dependent unit of group culture."[4] Apart from a small, creative minority, man is rightly described in such a way. Group cultures, however, are themselves partial enactments of man's total heritage; but even the to-

---

Cf. also, "The action of the individual only gains historical significance through his relation to the life of a social group. This is true even when his action takes the form of *separation* from the social group. Even the hermit in his denial of society is related to society. And only through this relation does the life of the hermit as a whole gain historical significance." Paul Tillich, "The Kingdom of God and History," in *The Kingdom of God and History*, The Official Oxford Conference Books (New York, Harper, 1938), Vol. III, p. 109.

[3] "The search for more facts as the cure for our present ills in the social sciences is like suggesting that the remedy for indigestion is more food, or, for a drowning man, more water." *The University and the Modern World* (New York, Macmillan, 1943), p. 139.

[4] Denison M. Allan, *The Realm of Personality* (Nashville and New York, Abingdon, 1947), p. 34.

tality of culture is in itself no guide to what is real, significant, and useful. The nub of our problem is, therefore, how to judge with considered care both the total heritage in so far as we can appropriate it, and our own group culture. What we need is some standard of significance in terms of which we can judge both our general and specific heritage. We have to determine some principle or principles for selecting what is significant. Naturally, therefore, the Harvard Report on *General Education in a Free Society* amazes us by declaring that a teacher's value and truth *"ultimately* depend on how complete this truth is *as judged by the only standards by which it can be judged; namely, the traditions of his nation and culture"*[5] (our italics). Such standards, considered in the light of our world conflict and our own obvious shortcomings, are not only partial, but invidious and divisive. Education, if possible, should rather be governed by a universal, inclusive, co-operative principle of significance.

Another reason for the utmost discrimination in the transmission of our cultural heritage is what Ortega y Gasset calls "the principle of economy in education."[6] Many educators are up in arms about the continual crowding of the curriculum and the packing of courses. Robert Ulich believes that theological education, for instance, because of this basic folly makes "grinds" of its students rather than men of God. The Harvard Report complains that too many "have learned too little about too much."[7] There seems to be nearly general agreement that reform is necessary at this key point. But if less is

[5] (Cambridge, Mass., Harvard University Press, 1945), p. 104.

[6] *Mission of the University* (Princeton, Princeton University Press, 1944), p. 70. Cf. also, "Only so much must be taught as can truly be learned. On this point we must be unshakable though the line of action which issues from it is drastic." *Ibid.*, p. 72.

Cf. also, "The good schoolmaster is known by the number of valuable subjects that he declines to teach." Sir Richard W. Livingstone, *The Future in Education* (Cambridge, Eng., The University Press, 1941), p. 28.

Cf., "As Mr. Whitehead has said, a student should not be taught more than he can think about. Selection is the essence of teaching. Even the most compendious survey is only the rudest culling from reality. Since the problem of choice can under no circumstances be avoided, the problem becomes what, rather than how much, to teach; or better, what principles and methods to illustrate by the use of information. "Harvard Committee, *General Education in a Free Society*, p. 63.

[7] *Ibid.*, p. 147.

to be taught about our vast heritage, the method of selection becomes even more important.

Education as the transmission of culture is not only a social act but is a deliberate social decision. Out of multitudinous social facts, contained in libraries, records, institutions, as well as in memories, education becomes living knowledge by means of a social act. The facts of knowledge must become personally and socially appropriated if they are to gain relevance, present power, and living meaningfulness. Most knowledge becomes perpetuated, anyway, because of its importance for life; what is not relevant is either forgotten, neglected, or made into a curio. Such facts become external to living history. But beyond knowledge as such a social *act*, lies knowledge as a social *decision*; as the deliberate selection of one set of facts or one kind of context rather than other possible choices. Education is under constant obligation to pass on with discriminating care whatever is most useful and satisfying to society.[8] For this reason the principle of significance in education becomes strategic to its entire task. Education is necessarily selection; therefore the standard for selection and the manner of selection are critical questions for any adequate education. Culture must be transmitted from one generation to the other with discriminating care.

In the discriminating transmission of our total heritage the first test should be truth; genuineness is a requirement of all true education. Our ideas should correspond descriptively with the actual facts, and prescriptively with what can actually become a desirable set of facts. Facts, as far as possible, should be critically established, correctly interpreted, and adequately communicated. No canons of criticisms can be too severe in their demand on intellectual integrity, thoroughness of research, patience in interpreting, care in communication. Constant and critical checking is required.

Each person and group, moreover, has interests that influence his seeing. Secondhand reporting, even when meant to be objective, dis-

[8] "Though it is not within our power to discern certain knowledge we do well to act decisively on the basis of whatever probability attends the object of our faith." Gordon W. Allport, *The Individual and his Religion* (New York, Macmillan, 1950), p. 138.

torts truth. We tend to idealize however, whatever in the past pleases us, and "debunk" whatever we dislike. Out of limited loyalty we are even prone to such "transformations" of truth. Thus, instead of learning from the past, we frequently use it to confirm our prejudices. To know what actually happened in history, to understand what others felt in literature, to enter into the experience of the whole person as he sought for certain knowledge, is hard beyond general belief. Nevertheless, such correspondence with facts, as far as possible, is an inescapable demand on any adequate education.

What we see depends more than we think on what we are. Even though we vary in our capacity for objective knowledge, even verification depends in some degree on the angle of vision, on focus and perspective. Perspective, moreover, depends largely on dominant motivation. Purpose is important to investigation, and ought therefore to be an open, not a hidden, factor in knowledge. Nevertheless our own interest need not wholly determine what we actually see; we have some capacity to abstract beyond immediate interest. Reason can entertain a consistency of context in terms of which we can become corrected. Our spirit, to be sure, is driven by self; but the self can see himself wrong, and thus allow for regret, change of heart and mind, growth, and decisions for the greater good or fuller truth. Thus to an effective extent pressures by society can be held off, facts can be found, past feelings felt, and previous experiments entered into more than mechanically. Even on the part of communities there can be similarly constructive regret and corrective growth. Whatever power makes such transcendence of self and society real, is by that very fact "the clue to education."[9] Even though we are later to discuss in fuller detail the criteria of truth, be it noted at once that effective education cannot afford to neglect the attitudinal side of experience.[10]

Particularly important for the establishing of fact is correctness of context. Facts are relational in nature; they are fully what they are

[9] Cf. Randolph C. Miller, *The Clue to Christian Education*, (New York, Scribner, 1950).

[10] "Hence everything finally depends on the teacher's quality of mind and spirit." The Harvard Committee, *op. cit.*, p. 24.

only within their true context of relationships and meanings. Facts are constituted largely by their context. We all know what mischief can be done by the presentation of mere fact, completely true as far as it goes, while the full context which would actually change the nature of that fact is withheld. We call such dealing with fact misrepresentation. Yet when each present generation reinterprets the past it tends to select facts to endorse what it is doing, and neglects —mostly subconsciously—to include the very facts that would judge its prejudices and mistakes. Our total heritage can be misrepresented through glorification, "debunking," falsification. Inclusiveness as well as correspondence is therefore a criterion; there is need not only to test fact as fact, but, much more, to unlock fact by total context. Such whole-seeing is a major task for adequate education.

Correspondence to fact and inclusiveness of context in dynamic cooperation contribute moreover a vital part of effective coherence. Correspondence needs to be checked, even for its factuality, by means of a deep and proportioned coherence. We need ever to be aware of our scope. Inclusiveness and correspondence should be examined in the light of proportion, appropriateness, and pattern of context. Whether in history, literature, or the development of science, the truth of our total heritage can be taught with considered care only by those who have lived deeply, who have great, open spirits, and who have also the ability to take pains. Great living, depth of concern, competent training, disciplined minds are necessary to communicate our total heritage. What is needed is the best possible combination of the factual, the contextual, and the attitudinal aspects of life and knowledge.

Relevance is another test. The principle of economy, which demands that students be taught no more than can be richly appropriated, requires that we select severely only what is most relevant to our own age. This standard is, however, full of danger, for it is open to constant abuse through rationalization. Relevance pertains to depth of interest. Each age seeks answers from the past to its own distinctive problems. Interest centers in decision. Education is often dull and unprofitable because subjects are taught as fields of general content without regard to the necessity of selective relevance. Naturally, the context must not be distorted by disproportioned presentation or by the misrepresenting of omissions; but the pattern of selection must be the question of relevance, and the background must yet be kept proportionate, appropriate, and inclusive.

Significance is a criterion of basic importance. Significance resides in the nature of things. It consists of the fullest possible actualization of all the constructively harmonious and satisfying potentialities *for* and *in* experience.[11] Whatever is important for life is not incidental. Experience is not subject to significance, nor significance to experience; significance is both a quality of experience and the conditions for experience; it is a possible relation of experience to environment. Only as educators discover the true nature of things, and how to release its constructive and creative potentialities for experience, can education become significant. To do so they must understand the total scope of human needs, and the wide reaches of reality which exist for the fulfilling of those needs. To communicate our total heritage with discriminating care is to use the criterion of significance as a basic standard. To determine the nature of significance—which constitutes our principle for selection from our cultural heritage—we shall need a later, separate discussion on the nature of religion and reality. In any case, significance is solidly embedded in truth —not only in the truths of experience, actual and possible, but in the very nature of reality.

Another valid test is satisfaction. Human life and civilization have the right to become satisfied at their deepest levels of meaning and of aspiration. Whatever is false fails organically and lastingly to satisfy. It can be wanted and cherished, but it cannot constitute a diet that produces health and happiness. A narcotic may be very much desired, but it cannot satisfy the organic needs of either body or mind—much less the level of purpose or meaningful existence. Satisfaction and significance are correlative terms: both are determined by the nature of things, by what is organically required, by what is creatively potential, by what is constructively essential. Only the significant can

[11] On this level of analysis, at least, I agree with the Harvard Report that we must be concerned "Not with the thousand influences dividing man from man, but with the necessary bonds and common ground between them" (p. 12).

offer lasting satisfaction; but significance precedes and outstrips satisfaction, as the nature of things precedes and outstrips human experience. If education is blind at this point it cannot avoid failing in its basic task. Partial or unbalanced, perverted or misdirected satisfactions, by failing of significance, exact appropriate penalties. In some real sense, virtue is its own reward.[12] Virtue is behavior in tune with creative and increasing common good, including the agent of behavior. Experience can never be satisfied by completion; only by appreciation of the present good and expectation of more good to be achieved and enjoyed. Satisfaction as the enjoyment of significant experience is a secondary yet sturdy test of truth.

To summarize, may we then understand that to pass on our total heritage with discriminating care and with studied relevance is always one primary aim of education.[13] Fact, context, coherence, relevance, significance, and satisfaction are criteria for judging the past in the selection of what can be taught according to the principle of economy. These standards are themselves relative to the nature of things, to the need of life to be organized in right relation to the total environment, and to the question of effective motivation. Education is the discovery and implementation of significant truth. Education is not merely the transmission of our heritage, but its transmission with creative and critical care; it is the discriminating transmission of culture.

Besides such transmission of culture, education, in the second place, should also live by creative discovery.[14] The past is never

[12] "We are inclined to avert uncomfortable questions about educational aims by saying that we want to produce, not people adapted to a given environment but people of maximal adaptability. . . . This chaos of values is the most serious feature of our present crisis; for when intellectual and moral values drift, man himself loses personal stature. The disintegration of the world-view inevitably involves the disintegration of the personal; the breaking up of thought and knowledge into separate systems means also the dissolution of man himself into a group of functions." M. V. C. Jeffreys, *Glaucon: An Inquiry into the Aims of Education* (London, Sir Isaac Pitman & Sons, Ltd., 1950), p. 53.

[13] For a first-class discussion of this aspect of education cf. Jeffreys, *Glaucon*. It is especially recommended as collateral reading for this whole book.

[14] Cf. *ibid.*, p. 7.

Also, "Our greatest schools had been founded precisely in order that the young enough; transmission must be supplemented by discovery. The past lives in human history only within the present; the present is the occasion for the reorganization of the past for the sake of new needs— it is the opportunity for creative advance. But such creative discovery cannot be bidden; it refuses to follow mere historic and analytic preparation, however thorough. Although there must be background knowledge, creative discovery seems almost to happen rather than to be caused. The creative spirit blows where it lists, irrespective of observable and controllable prediction. Necessity is not the mother of invention, but its midwife; it helps to deliver the new thought, but cannot of itself bring it into being. It provides the occasion for creative advance, which when wed to competent preparation produces the condition for creativity. The new, however, has a way of arriving in unexpected personalities and in unpredictable directions. Yet that new does fulfill the old, even perhaps by the providing of a changed perspective on it or context of meaning for it.

Education, though it cannot causally control creative discovery, is nevertheless responsible for providing the conditions for creativity, for fostering receptive attitudes toward its findings,[15] and for preparing channels for their widest possible communication and application. Humdrum impartation of knowledge should be relieved by the chance for creative adventure; skill should be allowed to result in vision; knowledge should pass through wisdom in order to become creative insight.

Opportunity for concentration is a necessary condition for creative daring. The mind burdened by secondary cares may be creative in

would not be content to adjust themselves to society, but would set about with vigor and courage to adjust society where they saw it in need of change." Gordon Keith Chalmers, *The Republic and the Person* (Chicago, Regnery, 1952), p. 30.

Also, "Of the two purposes of education—to make a person fit for the world as it is and to make him able to change it—the second is the more important. But an education for changing the world would be very different from any that we have inherited: for all education hitherto has been a method of moulding the new generation into the shapes admired by the old: and the old generally prefer things as they are." As quoted from C. Delisle Burns, *Challenge to Democracy* (New York, Norton) by Gilbert A. Beaver, *Christ and Community* (New York, Association Press, 1950), p. 199.

[15] "The student is apt to arrive at the university with his mind already set in an attitude of incuriousness outside his own restricted field." Moberly, *op. cit.*, p. 58.

part, driven by necessity and drawn by ideal attainment, but it cannot deliver its maximum contribution. The creative person is himself responsible for letting himself become deflected from original thought, and prevented from creative production by externals or by personal anxieties. Personal ambitions, or fears about professional status and material needs, can so oppress the mind that it cannot rise from its weight of anxiety to consider primary matters. No provision for physical needs and no amount of leisure can remove the obstacles to creativity that come from within.[16] Nevertheless, the creative mind needs the chance for concentration that is given by the removal of unnecessary physical cares and by the provision of proper leisure from routine tasks.

Education, too, can prepare a receptive attitude toward the new and better insight. Too much attention to the transmission of the past can result in its becoming an ideal; the highest standard of the past becomes sacred, to the point that the best scholarship is supposed to be its interpretation and emulation. In such a way the creative spirit is treated as a shallow, evident intruder in the realm of truth. Personal envy also often combines with a false worship of the past to reject and resent the new. People who are not themselves creative often become proved traditionalists, who out of envy belittle or warn against the creatively new. Creative discovery also threatens old securities; fear then results in hatred, or in opposition to the new or studied ignoring of it. The more the new insights relate to personal and social values, and not merely to the description of facts, the more true it is that a primary task of great education is to foster appreciative and receptive attitudes toward the creative discoveries of pioneering minds.

An essential objective of education is therefore to prepare wide channels for the communication and application of the new; the

[16] "The vision of the highest is not always the reward of intense intellectual contemplation; indeed that discipline is often the mother of pride, and at the approach of pride the vision is at once blotted out. That is why the path of a student is so hard beset with special temptation. The vision is a gift, and it comes to those whom we would not expect to receive it, as well as to others whom we would—and to all in ways past predicting or tracking out." Spencer Leeson, *Christian Education* (London, Longmans, 1948), p. 46.

transmission of the past must always be for the sake of the better future. Education should be Messianic in spirit, ameliorative in attitude; it ought always to be expectant, on tiptoe, urgently oriented toward creative discovery in terms of which to redefine and reconstruct the old. Possibly one section of the teaching staff, ideally speaking, should devote itself to teaching, in the common sense of the word, and one emphasis in the curriculum should be descriptive and analytic; another should definitely be creative research; a third should be the interpretation and application of the creative new. The nature of things is full of untapped possibilities. Though skill needs to be stressed, therefore, as the achievement of descriptive and analytic competence, and though knowledge is a prerequisite for any adequate pedagogy, yet vision and creative discovery need to relieve skill of its dullness and routine. They can enliven and transfigure the meaning and the use of knowledge. There is need for persons to be specially trained to relate vision to skill, creative discovery to matured and general wisdom. Since good will without organization is generally fugitive and ineffective, there ought to be special training in sifting the new insights with a view to the illumination and transformation of the old.

Creative discovery has at least three sources. One is the investigation of nature or science. Scientific studies are obviously not confined to mere description, analysis, or prediction: science at its forefront is creative struggle with darkness. Obviously the new stress in the social sciences has long since abandoned and long since outstripped such narrow limits. This stress accentuates values and nonmetrical measures; it seeks dynamic interconnections among events in nature. "Proportion of configuration, irrespective of dimensions, magnitude or quantity"[17] cannot be reduced to exact mathematical measurement. The social sciences have the capacity both to predict generally and to "engineer" social patterns by the careful investigation of the social laws that condition human behavior. Human freedom and social decisions are not unmotivated, or without understandable organic contexts. Field theories of freedom can help to shed much light on

[17] Laura Thompson, *Culture in Crisis: A Study of the Hopi Indians* (New York, Harper, 1950), p. 17.

social decisions, and cybernetics can assuredly illumine many aspects of human purposing. Research in the fields of the social sciences can lead to vital creative discovery, and is one of the basic needs of modern education. But research here as well as in the natural sciences should be solidly based on description, observation, and insight into actually operating phenomena.

Neither the natural nor the social sciences, of course, need be tied to the past. Both are creative; both depend on insight that results in creative hypotheses, which help to explain the workings of nature and to extend man's knowledge of it. Creative thinking in the sciences results in new presuppositions, new contexts of meaning, new perspectives from which to interpret facts that both alter and fulfill what was previously considered to be true. There are creative philosophers or seers in science, as well as analysts and fact-finders; science, for one part, is a creative enterprise. The results of science also establish new facts and new relationships that affect thinking in other fields: scientific relativity in the natural sciences has vitally affected historiography, philosophy, and religious interpretation. Instead of dreading the results of science in a dangerous modern world, we should accept with genuine gratitude its creative drive and its new discoveries—not only for our physical welfare but for our total educational process. As the sciences pass from the stage of "concepts by inspection" to the stage of "concepts by postulation,"[18] they will combine increasingly the two aspects of descriptive knowledge and creative discovery that facilitate their integration within man's total inquiry.

There is also creative discovery through philosophy proper, or through the theoretical reason as such. Speculation, in today's practical world, is under a black cloud; but no one can know the history of thought—even of science—without realizing how much we owe to those who have developed the implications and involvements of the theoretical reason. Philosophy and mathematics are organically related to empirical inquiry. Their physical counterparts can even occasionally be suggested by the theoretical—theoretical truth often varying with the empirical and vice versa; theoretical thinking has

[18] *Ibid.*, p. 18.

actually led to empirical discovery. Since the discovery of Uranus in 1844 by means of mathematical calculation, and now with the theoretical nature of modern science with its postulational concepts of genes and atoms, there is more understanding of the vital place that the development of the theoretical aspect of knowledge plays in creative discovery. The philosophy of science, the philosophy of education, the philosophy of history, the philosophy of social relations, and particularly metaphysics, should be vital evidences of the method of creative discovery.

Most important for education, however, are the creative discoveries made by the great religious seers. The prophets of the Old Testament helped to mold, guide, and develop the great Jewish creative discoveries in religious and social relations. Socrates combined the philosophic vision with the religious vision, and thus set the stage for growth both in knowledge and in education. The histories of education, science, philosophy, and religion began together; education needs to keep them together. Great social scientists today, like Karl W. Deutsch, dare to acknowledge that Jesus' understanding and love of human nature is still ahead of the men of empirical methods —helping them, to be sure, but as a daring light in their van. Gandhi was both a religious seer and a social engineer. Schweitzer shows both an intuitive grasp of social issues and a personal religious example that can help a confused world.[19]

We must deal concretely, in the chapters that follow, with the meaning and relevance of religion. But even here we must take note of the fact that great spirits—whom Toynbee calls "charismatic" personalities—are often the channels for creative discovery. In some way, if education is to become adequate, it must know how to direct others toward creative life, to prepare concrete channels for communicating and implementing the constructively new, and to foster receptive attitudes for its appropriation.

We have thus seen that education deals (1) with the transmission

[19] "Nobody can inspire who does not have deep convictions. They are the results, but also the feeders of the spirit." Robert Ulich, "The Preparation of Teachers," in *Religious Perspectives in College Teaching,* Hoxie N. Fairchild, ed. (New York, Ronald Press, 1952), p. 451.

of our cultural heritage, and (2) with creative discovery. These two aspects of education point out toward the outer, objective world. But the objective stress should not obscure the place of the subjective; full emphasis must be placed on the third aspect of education, namely (3) the inner development of persons, both as individuals and as a society. What comes from the past or is discovered as new exists, after all, if not altogether for experience, nevertheless with reference to experience. As far as education goes, in any case, the inner development of the student is an indispensable aspect of all good teaching. If we can no longer hold that to educate is merely to lead or to draw out of a student what is already latent within, there are nevertheless human potentialities to be matured in relation to the outside world. Thus inner development is the third main factor in education.

For purposes of clarity we shall develop this point under three headings. The first is the inner development of practical or professional capacities. Work is normal to satisfactory living. However much machines may replace human labor and skill, and however much they may shorten man's working time, every person, in order to become his true self, needs to develop practical competence and become engaged in meaningful labor. Cultural attainments must flower from the main branch of the working efficiency of any civilization. John Dewey and his school rightfully have called into question the study of "cultural" subjects to the neglect of thorough training in the arts of living that pertain to all men within the glory of their common humanity.

The modern movement of general education is significant at this point.[20] General education can help carry the burden of relating the academic to the practical. Besides broadening man's cultural vision and integrating his knowledge, general education can provide for significant practical training in the universities,[21] up through the

---

[20] "The new horizon is that of an educated and self-educating adult democracy." M. L. Jacks, *Modern Trends in Education* (London, Andrew Melrose, Ltd., 1950), p. 39.
[21] "The Harvard Report distinguishes three main fields—the Humanities, the Social Sciences and the Natural Sciences. It proposes not to abolish specialization, but to supplement it. Out of sixteen courses necessary for the degree, no less than six

highest reaches of graduate study. General education can also be run separately from the university as such, and provide a different kind of graduate training.[22] Every person, in any case, should have more than one basic skill; people should be somewhat acquainted with all the basic aspects of working life. The more such acquaintance can come from actual experience the better. Whitehead in *Aims of Education* has pointed out how very much manual skill adds to intellectual creativity. In a world of gadgets, mechanized homes, and automobiles, people should be at least somewhat trained in their operation. In a world of industry the attitudes, tempo, and actual workings of factory life should be part of the educated consciousness. City dwellers should live at some time in the country and thus gain firsthand experience of country life. Education has a task to make our complex world intelligible to the whole citizenry.

Part of this experience could come through reading and audiovisual education. Part could come through field trips. Part could come through such projects as students in industry, part-work-part-school programs, and summer on the farm. Part could come through some thoroughgoing adult education. With increasing leisure time[23] on account of shorter hours—if we would create positive economic goods and organize the body politic for peace—there will be abun-

---

must be in 'general education,' that is, directly concerned with general relationships and values, with 'what needs to be done and to what ends' rather than with 'what can be done and how to do it.' Both in Humanities and in Social Science one particular course is compulsory for all." Moberly, *op. cit.*, p. 187.

Cf. also, "General education means the whole development of an individual, apart from his occupational training. It includes the civilizing of his life purposes, the refining of his emotional reactions and the maturing of his understanding about the nature of things according to the best knowledge of our time.

"In this sense general education is the fundamental problem of modern society." Ortega y Gasset, *op. cit.*, p. 1.

[22] "The researches which appeal to scholars and students do not interest and only indirectly concern the ordinary man, and to teach these subjects to him as they are taught in universities or in the higher forms of schools is like talking a foreign language to people who neither know it, nor have the wish or need to understand it." Livingstone, *op. cit.*, p. 78.

[23] "Aristotle may have gone too far when he said that the object of education was to help men to use their leisure rightly. But we have treated the majority as if they were to have no leisure, or as if it did not matter how they used what leisure they had." *Ibid.*, p. 4.

dant time not only for adult education in "folk schools" like the Danish, but for daytime and evening cross-fertilization of occupations.[24] Wherever practicable, creative civilization will never neglect the basic practical-professional training, technical and vocational. Besides thorough training in one skill and basic acquaintance with some other for the sake of social mobility, such a society will also find ways of technically orienting all educated people; more and more the creative training for democracy will require such a practical enrichment of education. Work is an organic integral part of all noble and meaningful living. Not to work, if one is able to do so, is to become a parasite, and to lose an essential part of his inner development. Only by doing the work of the world can we learn its way and our own place in it.

A second facet of inner development is social becoming. This is one of the hardest tasks of education, because it has to do with the total being of man or the inner heart of group relations. Many people can be highly learned, yet cannot contribute what they should because of their lack of the mastery of social relations. Yet man is organically related to men; no one can find solitary satisfaction. To be human is to be social, by the very fact of the heritage of one's experience, and by the social nature of all experiential reference. To fail at this point is to fail at the center of education. Education is neither primarily training in skill nor impartation of knowledge; it is principally the development of persons in all their relationships.[25]

Counseling and juvenile and adult penology are at best curative; they are needed as educative measures. But they are at best the arresting or curing of abnormal, injurious, or destructive tendencies. Education for social adjustment should be constructive from the start. It should be preventive social medicine. The problem here is how to combine adequate meaning and motivation from the earliest childhood on through life; home, community, and school are all involved in this task.

[24] "This Danish national education has three secrets of success: it is given to adults; it is residential; it is essentially a spiritual force." *Ibid.*, p. 47.

[25] "But subjects are not taught in a vacuum; teaching that would lay any claim at all to distinction, if not to actual greatness, is the influence of personality upon personality, rather than the mere imparting of a set of facts." Gaebelein, *op. cit.*, p. 48.

It is at this point particularly that religion must be tested. *The field of religion combines meaning with motivation.* The question involves therefore the whole place of religion in education, and it must be discussed in its proper place. Certainly the school can help to socialize the students; but we must even now put in question the adequacy of such socialization. The social processes of the school and the competent teaching of social relations, from family to international life, are of course significant instruments for socialization. We shall, however, see that the whole question of human nature, and of the meaning of social life as a whole, are involved in this decision as to the kind of education that will truly be more than the mere arrest or cure of unsatisfactory social behavior.

Inner development requires much more, however, than the releasing of practical vocational capacities and the freeing and growing of social outreach; it demands inviolably that the deepest self of each person be unfolded, "to educe the man." Modern man is too hollow; instead of being a person he is a nodule. He lives "playing a role," whether in work or in social relations. He is afraid to be long alone; he dreads self-examination, or the serious searching of the meanings and satisfactions of his own life. Somehow education must mean the continual enrichment of the inner man; the accumulation of spiritual resources; the deepening of personal meanings; the vitalization of individuality. Society comprises necessarily the content and context of life; but the way in which that content and context are appropriated by each person determines his kind and depth of satisfaction; and the way he responds to them determines his creative contribution to society.[26]

Life is rich in individuals; and rich individuality is essential to vital community. The education that forfeits adequacy at this point is totally at fault. The whole cannot be good without satisfied, virtuous, and creative members of the community. Religion should contribute not only to social completion but also to individual fulfillment. The place of religion in education, and the kind of religion

[26] "The purpose of all education is to help students live their own lives. The appeal to heritage is partly to the authority, partly to the clarification of the past about what is important in the present." The Harvard Committee, *op. cit.,* p. 43.

we need, are questions to be determined chiefly at these two points of social completion and individual fulfillment. A new era with abundant opportunity for creative leisure makes specially urgent inner richness. In its early, formative years life now has a longer period of general education; in its middle years it has more leisure time; in its later years it has a lengthening span of retirement; thus education should provide depth, richness, and vitality of the inward life. Part of this can come from the dramatic understanding of history, part from the possession of literary resources[27]—readily available within—part from the knowledge of vocational life, and part from generous interest in contemporary decisions, events, and social processes; but man is still hollow without a vital organizing self as his creative center within.

Two things should be said at once. Our education has been weak in its appropriation of its best past, and in its creative appreciation of it and enrichment by it. We are deeply guilty of superficiality and pretense; we skim, not heavy cream, but light milk. There are two ways to remedy the situation: memorization and meditation.

Learning by heart need not mean learning by rote. Memorization of the best past enriches the present within some definiteness of grasp. We suffer from vagueness; we are frustrated by confusion. Group dynamics, or learning through group discussion, can release creativity only when the group can presuppose individuals with disciplined minds that command specific knowledge. William James rightly warned us against the danger of generalization where specific knowledge is wanting. Thoroughness about a few main things is a prerequisite for the rightful and confident decision to court creativity. If knowledge in every area is a social act, the history of every subject should be known in some concrete outline. Certain key events of history, and some classical expressions of human faith, hope, and wisdom, ought to be known with a good deal of precision. From our earliest training on, a few things ought to be learned, in common with such intensity of memorization and such urgency of

[27] "Hence the value of a practice too much neglected in modern education, the habit of learning great literature by heart and so storing up a treasure which later life may enable us to use." Livingstone, *op. cit.*, p. 24.

repetition that they form the background of every educated person. T. S. Eliot is quite right in his insistence that no civilization can be strongly educated if it lacks such a community core of learning.

Certain foundations of scientific development and theory, for instance, ought to be not only generally explained but also committed to exact memory and to lasting possession. We throw book after book at people, who become increasingly superficial. In the same way a few great pieces of literature ought to be known thoroughly, and the peak passages known by heart.[28] We do too much and gain too little; we teach too much and learn too little; we work too hard to too little advantage. We scan the whole world of knowledge at the expense of true seeing. A false practicality about the present, and a foolish fever for education in the large, have made us forfeit the solid base of learning, step by step, which should be built into the rock of solid appropriation until we can look with some clarity and concreteness on the history of thought and on whatever is selectively best in the past.

No amount of memorization, nevertheless, can by itself make a person educated: memorization needs to be steeped in meditation. Learning by heart becomes learning by rote, as John Dewey charged, unless the heart is readied for personal appropriation. Group dynamics, may—and perhaps should—both precede and follow such individual meditation; but it can never take the place of it. True solidarity presupposes true solitariness. The rich individuals are those who in secret turn over the nature and meaning of what they learn, until the content of knowledge becomes personal vision.[29]

[28] ". . . The importance of learning poetry by heart and of learning the right poetry. There are few greater treasures to be acquired in youth than great poetry— and prose—stored in the memory. At the time one may resent the labour of storing. But they sleep in the memory and awake in later years, illuminated by life and illuminating it. I doubt if anything learnt at school is of more value than great literature learnt by heart." *Ibid.*, p. 120; see also p. 24.

[29] "To the extent that it [knowledge] is abstract, it is valuable. But its value is lessened if the discoverer of knowledge too long forgets the concrete ground from which abstractions are made. Knowledge can be and too often is purchased at the price of wisdom. And today one of the decisive questions that confront the university mind is the problem as to whether this is too great a price to pay for knowledge." Bernard M. Loomer, "Religion and the Mind of the University," in Wilder, *op. cit.*, pp. 156–57.

Whitehead has said that the deepest of all knowledge is like that of Mary, who pondered in her heart the things she heard. Education cannot make persons meditate; teachers may let the students have the chance to meditate, but they cannot make them do it. Meditation requires both space and time and both can be provided. Such opportunity to meditate will no doubt always be abused; but so will all aspects of education.

The few who grow deep and rich will be the leaders of society; therefore the right opportunity ought to be provided. The seeding should not be governed by the poorest soil; the good soil will abundantly repay those who have respected its nature. Meditation involves not only space and time, but the right attitude on the part of the administration and the faculty. Shallow lives cannot instruct other lives without tempting them to superficiality; lives that are centered in external standards will make for an externalistic education. Administration and teachers alike, therefore, should find space and time for meditation. Thoughtful understanding requires fullness of thought; and, as we shall soon see, no thought can go deep that does not touch the hidden springs of the mystery that is the source of creativity.

For the *discriminating appropriation of the past, and for the discovering of the conditions for creativity,* therefore, we recommend both memorization and meditation—not apart, but together; and we recommend that, however late in life, teachers themselves start by slowing down in the rat race of so-called education in order to know, and to impart with all possible definiteness, some things that are capable of concrete memorization and repeated use, in order to live quietly and concernedly until they themselves are touched by springs of creativity. Vision needs to be added to skill; not only chronologically, but as the ever-accompanying meaning that gives zest to knowledge and vividness to life.

The personal and social development *of the inner life* need these two main means to education, which help to enact the discriminating transmission of our cultural heritage and the creative discovery of the meaning both of knowledge and of life. Only by an intense and relaxed cultivation alternately of these two paths to significant knowledge, and the insightful understanding of it, can students gain the capacities that the Harvard Report found essential; namely, "to think effectively, to communicate thought, to make relevant judgments, and to discriminate among values."[30] Only thus are combined concrete and definite knowledge with depth of background, personal understanding, and capacity for significant judgment.[31]

We have thus discussed some tasks and foci of education as such. We have not yet defined religion. One thing is certain: education has as its responsibility the discovery, impartation, and maturation of truth. In higher education the *meaning* of its total task, and the *power* with which it can reach its goal, become ever more important. Unless religion, therefore, is of such a nature as to provide organically a meaning and motivation to education it is an intruder. Education lives by the needs of actual people to know and to practice the truth.

Truth is its only standard; making truth effective is its only goal; teaching truth is its only mandate. Only as the nature of man, history, and reality require religious truth should it become part of education. A discussion of the nature of religion in general, and of the Christian faith in particular, should show whether education should teach religion, whether it can do without it, or whether, in fact, education itself is by its very nature through and through religious. We therefore turn to a general discussion of religion in order to show the relation of religion to education.

[30] Harvard Committee, *op. cit.*, p. 65.

[31] "It is these two points of reference that we have tried to establish so far. The first is a view of society as depending on both heritage and change. The second is a view of students as both united and divided: united as heirs of a common past and agents in a joint future; divided, as varying in gifts, interest, and hopes. From these premises comes an idea of education as, for all and at all stages beyond the earliest, both general and special." *Ibid.*, p. 103.

Chapter II

What Is Religion?

On the answer to this question depends, of course, the relation of religion to education. Education should deal only with verifiable truth; whatever in religion cannot qualify as tested knowledge should not be taught. Our thesis, however, is that religion as such is an inseparable part of education. If so, religion must have truth that can be publicly tested. Such a claim must, of course, be vindicated; many are convinced that our view of religion stems from special pleading. If we can prove our case, however, the question will no longer be whether, but what kind of, religion should be taught, and how.

What is religion? *Religion is man's response as a whole to what he considers most important and most real.* The word "religion" is probably derived from one of two Latin words: *religare* or *religere*. *Religare* in its more literal usage means "to bind back" or "to fasten"; and, in its freer use, "to bind" or "to chain." Many consider this to be the most likely meaning of the word "religion" in its primary sense—namely, the way in which the universe binds us up, or in which we are fastened to reality, or the way in which we become chained to life. Religion is then our *inescapable relation to reality*. If, as some think, the second word, *religere,* gives us a clue to the root meaning of religion, religion is what we "gather together," "collect again," or the threads we "rewind," the territory we "travel over again," the books we "reread," the thoughts we "repeat." The figurative idea of "going over again" is very strong in *religere*. Religion is what we accept after deep reflection; what we conclude after repeated experience; what we decide after we have retraced our lives.

We might, of course, rest content with learning the Latin word for religion, *religio,* which came to express the sense of right, what is obligatory, our conscientious duty, and, more loosely, a regard for sacred things, reverence. The root meaning seems in any case to indicate man's serious relation to his own experience of the world within which he is bound up. All these meanings, moreover, converge on the thought of our definition. Naturally we cannot put too much weight on a word, particularly if the history of the word is neither definite nor precise; nevertheless, the general meanings indicate what has been commonly understood by the word. Our definition is also not only in line with the meanings of all the words, but at their center.

Religion is "man's response." This phrase is a general statement about man's relation to reality. We are not defining religion in terms of those who consciously are seeking religious truth and satisfaction; all men, rather, are religious, by the nature of their human situation; all men, in order to live, must keep responding to reality in some way.[1] For this reason religion was not defined as the quest of some men for reality, or of other men for optional aspects of experience. Experience is essentially religious; but not every response to reality is religious. Religion is not the same as life. Religion is not merely a matter of our responses to reality; it is always a selective response—not in the sense that man is free to select religion, but in the sense that religion is the decision as to what for the chooser is the most important and the most real.

Religion is *man's* response. Consequently it is not to be equated with truth, or with the real, or with the important, or with the good. All these, as we shall show later, are basically part of the reality to which we respond. Man's response, however, may be good, bad, or a mixture of both. It may be ignorant or enlightened, wise or foolish, important or trivial. The response may be misguided, or may spring

---

[1] "Faith is not the product of search and endeavor, but the answer to a challenge which no one can forever ignore." Abraham Joshua Heschel, *Man Is Not Alone: A Philosophy of Religion* (New York, Farrar, Straus & Young, Inc., 1951), p. 76.

from ill will. It may be directed by fear or by faith. This being so, religion in itself is neither good nor bad. Religion is not to be judged as representing reality, but rather as showing man's understanding of it and his relation to it. Religious thoughts, acts, and institutions are all a matter of man's response.

No claim can therefore be made legitimately to the effect that to teach religion is good for education, or that to support a religious institution is good for a community. Whether religion is good or bad for man, whether religion is helpful or harmful for education, whether religion is beneficial or detrimental for a community, all depend on the kind of religion involved. Religion may do what is claimed for it by its devotees, yet be a serious obstacle to truth and a high barrier to effective community.

Nevertheless, there can be no question as to whether man is to have religion, whether religion should be taught, or whether it is needed by the community: there can be no more freedom from religion than from reality. Man is never free from responding to reality; the very running from it is a response, as well as the facing of it. Religion is existential in the sense that relation to reality is non-optional: man is forced to respond freely. In some real measure, too, the response itself—as to whether to face reality, and how to face or to evade it—both requires and represents real freedom. From such freedom, however, man cannot flee; it is forced on him. Man must choose from among the choices that confront him what for him is most important and most real.

Unless man is morally diseased and intellectually irresponsible, moreover, he cannot help developing some rough pattern of response. Repeated responses on the part of a maturing individual become shaped; they take on form. However little an individual may consciously choose what is most important and most real, in actual practice for him to live is to become tied in with the universe in some certain way; even the attempt to avoid reality shows a definite mold. However much the responses may change—unless a man is hopelessly ill—his life always contains some core of unity. The experience of self-decision—how to accept oneself in the light of experience as a whole—is common to all men. The way in which one interprets and evaluates himself in the light of what he experiences becomes a configuration of life; thereupon one's response to new experiences from within such a configuration becomes a constant steering of life with reference to the chart and compass of one's previous findings and decisions.

The total shape and pattern of one's configuration discloses what he considers to be most important and most real—not primarily in theory, but within the actual choices of the self.[2] Religion thus embodies man's relation to reality in terms of what he considers to be most important and most real; it is not only the way he happens to become "bound up" with the universe, but the way in which he himself "rereads" and repeats his experiences. If we should also bring in the third word derivation for our definition, religion is what within these responses is deemed to be obligatory and sacred: it is the "appropriate" or "right" way to become "bound up" with life, "to repeat" the responses we are free to make—but not to avoid—because they are true and worthy of acceptance. Religion is thus *man's response* to the reality that he inevitably confronts; not his total response, but the way he interprets, accepts, or shuns reality.

Religion is man's response *as a whole*. The phrase "as a whole" is ambiguous; it has at least two meanings. It may mean man as a total being in the inclusive sense, or it may mean man as a completely integrated self. A sick man goes to the hospital as a whole to be made whole. He cannot leave at home his mind, spirit, will, or any of his parts; all of him must go. Yet, though he must go as a whole, he also goes in order to be made whole. Or a man about to propose marriage may be divided in mind and heart regarding the step he is about to take. When he goes to propose, however, not only his physical self, but his whole self must go along; even though he is not wholly certain of his action, his whole self has to respond to the situation at hand. Similarly, when we make a religious response our total self must participate, even though it may be far

[2] "If all relations in the polar world can be reduced to a single cosmic formula, then all the problems of life and of knowledge of the world can be summed up in the single question: What is our attitude to the underlying principle by which this entire world is dominated?" Karl Heim, *Christian Faith and Natural Science* (New York, Harper, 1953), p. 159.

from unified; the entire self is organically involved in its response to what is most high and most real; mind, will, and emotions are all involved in the response on the part of any self. That self, however, may be far from entire in the sense of physical, mental, social, or spiritual wholeness.

Man *must* respond as a whole, in the inclusive sense, to what he considers to be most important and most real; he *should* respond as a whole in the sense of his being organically and personally integrated. In order to know reality correctly, and to be in right relation with it, *he must respond as a whole in both senses of the phrase.* This further assertion may not seem to follow from the definition we have given; it may appear to be smuggled in. Our definition has been descriptive, not normative; it has been situational, circumstantial, or existential, rather than ideal or directive. Nevertheless, a thorough analysis will show that right relation to reality demands an organically integrated response on man's part; only a unified response appropriately receives and relates itself to reality.

The need for an integrated whole response stems from man's nature. Not only is it actually true that when man responds he does so as a whole, in the sense that all basic factors of his make-up are included; but it is also a fact that no basic part can find its true and full function except in organic co-operation with all the other factors. We have already indicated the truth that when the mind thinks, the will is affected by the process, however dimly or strongly; and the feelings also are involved. Similarly, when a man wills he does so only in relation to some thought, and in connection with some emotions. All these functions, too, are in relation to the body via the brain; they affect it and are affected by it. As a matter of fact, any intellectual analysis fails to picture the intimate and immediate interaction of the self as a whole. The fact of man's organic wholeness entails the fact that man must respond as an inclusively involved self to what is most important and most real as a whole. The further fact, however, is that no basic part of man functions correctly unless it does so within the unity of organic wholeness. The first kind of whole response is a natural necessity; the second is conditional. If man is to find "personal wholeness," he must respond as an integrated whole. Such unitive response, as we shall now proceed to illustrate, is necessary in order to relate oneself correctly to the environment from the very beginning of personal life.

The earliest or lowest form of positive intellectual judgment is "this is this,"; the most basic or original negative judgment is "this is not this." Judgments, however, are not purely intellectual.[3] The organism seeks to satisfy all its drives; the person craves fulfillment as a total self; the intellect is an instrument of the self in this search for fulfillment. The earliest judgments are therefore not speculative, but practical. Connected with the awareness that "this is this" whereas "this is not this" comes an evaluative judgment, to the effect that either "this is better than this" or "this is worse than this." Such a phrasing of the primitive evaluating judgment may, however, be too abstract. The organism may respond in terms of "this feels more pleasant than that," or "this hurts me more than that." In any case, intellectual awareness and judgment inseparably involve affective awareness and evaluation; intellect and affective response are part of one complex of experience. Similarly, the will (or goal-directedness) belongs inextricably within this complex.[4] The organism is confronted with concrete choices: to live is to keep choosing. Even a response that follows from habit results from some basic purposiveness, which accounts for the habitual repetition of choice and the almost automatic dismissal of other choices. A habit may for a while act as an autonomous trait, but usually disappears when it is no longer needed. Thus will, or goal-directedness, is also an inseparable ingredient of response.

All these basic factors of cognition, affection, and conation—or thought, feeling, and will—are thus organically intertwined and interpenetrating in every response man makes. Each response, too, presupposes a reservoir of experience that preserves in the memory the result of the responses. Memory is what is retained from learning apart from growth and fatigue. As the person matures, his experience synthesizes the old and the new. For one part his judgments

[3] Alfred N. Whitehead, *Process and Reality*, Pt. III, "The Theory of Prehensions" (New York, Macmillan, 1930).

[4] Dean John Keith Benton has suggested the possible nontechnical terminology of idea, interest, and intention.

root far back in primitive experience, from a distant past of the race. They also become informed by his personal history, wherein thought, feeling, and will have become accumulatively and organically blended into a total pattern of experience. Thus the self comes to have a generalized understanding and attitudes toward the world that condition his will. These, to be sure, comprise also numerous concrete memories. General and particular memories form patterns for response to the world; they constitute the self's knowledge of the world in relation to dynamic drives, within which the inner springs of the will and the complexities of potential emotional satisfaction play an active and continuous part. Thus the will is "colored" and weighted, both intellectually and emotionally, by previous experience.

A brief summary of our analysis may be helpful. The world bears down on the self; to live the self must respond. Awareness of the world—of what bears down on the self—is the function of intellect. Through repeated experience, stored in the depths of the memory, the self learns to interpret and to evaluate the world; awareness of what is there takes on focus and feeling. Objects become distinguished more sharply from one another; and become colored with potential pain or pleasure, according to the accumulative verdict of the memory. The self is able to abstract this picture of what is there, and how it actually feels, by means of concepts that are not only intellectual but weighted with likes or dislikes. The will responds from within this reservoir of experience. The world to which the self responds is variable; sometimes the self can avoid pain or find more pleasure by refusing certain choices and waiting for others. With this analysis of basic experience as a background, we shall be able to show not only that the self has to respond as a whole in the inclusive sense, but also that the self can never know or correctly respond to the environment unless it responds as a whole in the sense of integration. The self may learn that a response, though immediately gratifying, may eventually entail distasteful consequences; the problem then becomes whether the immediate pleasure is worth the eventual pain.[5]

[5] Plato early called education the developing capacity to feel pleasure and pain at the right things. Cf. also Aristotle, *Ethics,* ii, 3.

Such a question, however, involves choice; the solution is no mere weighing of pain or pleasure. The difficulty for choice is not merely ambiguity as to the amount of actual present pleasure or eventual pain;[6] the self also has to decide whether to forego the present pleasure. If it lets itself be driven by its present wants, it will to some extent shut out intellectual attention to the eventual consequence.[7] It will allow its attention to focus on the present pleasure, and to hide from future pain. The decision is thus taken from within an inner struggle—at whatever depth and accompanied with whatever ambiguity. As the self yields to what is immediately desired, rather than its truest eventual good, it thereby obscures the nature of reality, and enters into a false relation to it. Disunity within the self leads to false seeing and wrong responding; and repeated wrong choices create a false view of the world, so that reality is neither correctly known nor received.

Or the self may learn that what is pleasant for it is not right. It may, for instance, want an object that belongs to someone else. It may learn, however, not only that the taking of such an object may lead to the infliction of pain on it by the other, but also that there is an appropriateness about the other's having his own thing even though the self wants it. For our purposes, we can say that the self learns that certain things are right and wrong, not only in terms of pain and pleasure for itself but also in terms of the welfare of others. Somehow it finds out that the world works in a certain way. In some general and confused manner the self learns that pain and pleasure are not the only considerations for choice; that within, too, there is some understanding and approval of right and wrong as necessary aspects of the world. At the point of this discovery, also, the self runs up against the problem of the whole response in the

[6] As a matter of fact, the pleasure-pain antithesis is inadequate unless it is interpreted within a moral context. The self is no automaton, responding to a quantitative pleasure-pain equation, where choice is needed solely because of ambiguity. We are using the equation not as a determinant, but as a pedagogical *suggestion* or prompting.

[7] Dean Benton questions this assertion. He points out that an alcoholic, for instance, will drink in full awareness of consequences. Nevertheless, it seems to me that an alcoholic is diseased, and therefore no longer fully responsible. Even so, does not even an alcoholic shut out much attention to consequences by focusing on the satisfaction of his desire?

sense of integration. It is now confronted with a choice not only as to what is immediately pleasant yet eventually painful, but also as to what it wants that is not right for it to have. If it decides in line with what is right, it makes an integrated response; there is integrity in the act.

If the self decides, instead, that it wants immediate gratification, it then no longer weighs the choices involved; on the contrary, it concentrates on the doing of what is pleasant: it focuses its attention on the pleasure to be had. But, since it must respond as a whole in the inclusive sense, it is faced with the report of the mind via the memory, which warns of coming pain and of wrong. (Feelings, of course, are connected both with the longing for immediate satisfaction and with the warning of a wrong choice.) The pain that follows wrongdoing threatens to spoil the enjoyment of the pleasant. Therefore the self refuses, as far as it can, to attend to the warning; and concentrates instead on the anticipated pleasure. The more it succeeds in so doing the less its present gratification is thwarted; but the more also the self has violated its own sense of what is true and right. The sharper the actual conflict—"suppression"—the more the integrity of the self is being preserved. The duller the struggle, the nearer is "repression"—the pushing of the conflict into the unconscious, where the self is hurt at the very depths of its being. Conscience is never dulled; it is only pushed into the unconscious, where its vengeance is more terrible.

Gradually the self may come to see mostly what it wants to see, because it has pushed out of focus what it wants not to see; thus it builds up a false world of what is "right and true." What is most important and most real is not what it could know—and would know if it had once cared and willed to know—but what is on the contrary a spurious world of its own invention. Yet this is the world as the self actually knows it. The world without and the world within both being false, the self forfeits its sense of what is real and important; deciding not to see, the self thereby spoils its own eyesight. By deciding to see its own kind of world, the self both impairs its focus and falsifies its world. If the intellect only were violated when the integrity of the self is lost! But the will and the feelings are also damaged. *Deep down*, even so, the will still knows that it is being forced to respond to falsehood. As the mind is made for truth, however, so is the will made for right. Therefore, drive is lost; convictions ebb; the self becomes either spiritless or defensively overzealous. Instead of the healthy feeling of integration that comes from integrity, the self suffers either from listlessness or from the fever of falsehood.

The feelings, too, when violated, either dry up or become poisoned. The inner self, having lost its reality feeling, becomes insecure; unable to hide its wrong from its deepest self, it becomes fearful. Therefore subconscious complexes accumulate; and penetrate and pollute the whole self. The body is inwardly drugged. Therefore it develops illnesses without valid external causes, and becomes easily susceptible to whatever predisposing factors of illness beset it from outside. Physical pain, mental problems, and social maladjustments accumulate in this anxious, confused, guilt-laden self. The feelings do not run full and free, to satisfy the self and to help it in its undertakings, but are wasting and poisoning it. They only partly sustain it, while it insists on living in a state of falsehood.[8]

Such a self not only avoids seeing, let alone seeking the truth, but comes increasingly to invent sights to justify and satisfy itself. Thus arise gradually a story world which takes the place of the real world. Pretense takes over to the point where clear grasp of the real and the right is lost. All the while the self meets other selves who similarly flee the real world and desire to believe in false worlds. From these it learns new "truths" to fortify its own position. This process of falsification, too, is as old as man and therefore the generations have succeeded in painting pictures of the world which are such a mixture of truth and falsehood that the new self really finds it comparatively easy to accept what it wants to believe. Some of these falsehoods are produced according to the patterns of simple people; others are as sophisticated as man's highest reaches of science,

---

[8] "Thus, also, when above eternity delights us, and the pleasures of temporal good holds us down below, it is the same soul which willeth not that or this with an entire will, and is therefore torn asunder with grievous perplexities, while out of truth it prefers that, but out of custom forbears not this." Augustine, *Confessions* VIII, X.

philosophy, and religion. Knowledge depends on the work of the ages; how hard for anyone, then, to find for himself what is true and real.

In the light of the preceding analysis we can see how necessary it is to interpret our definition of religion as man's response as a whole, not only in the sense of inclusiveness but in the sense of the integration of the main aspects of man's life. *Integrity is the price or condition of integration;*[9] *integration presupposes integrity*. Integration is necessary in order to have right relations with reality. Apart from a harmonious whole response the self cannot know reality aright, cannot have reality feeling, and cannot will to accept reality. In this sense of integration the self is organically related to reality. The world without as it truly is cannot be either known or reached apart from the integrity of whole response. What is actually most important and most real can be known and appropriated, therefore, only when the self responds as a whole in both senses of the word.

We may, nevertheless, have begged the basic question: is the real also the most important? Have we not taken for granted that an organic response to the world not only arrives at the real but also finds the most important? Is the real also good for the self? What if the self is organically related to a world that hurts not only immediately but characteristically? Perhaps the evasion of reality is best for the self; perhaps the distortion of reality will make life easier. Perhaps there is more reason than natural ignorance or lack of integrity for the invention of so many philosophies and religions that falsify reality. Could it be good for us to be hid from the truth of the real? These questions cannot be answered from man's side of his relation to reality; all that we can know from that side is that

[9] Lyman Bryson has championed intellectual integrity. We agree with him in his *intent*: "For this, we would have to trust finally to the moral values of our ideas to make their way, with the aid only of such symbols as stir men's hearts without confusing their minds. This would be a far harder task than to repeat ancient errors, or to trust ancient wisdom, and the creation of symbols of that kind would be a challenge to whatever greatness our generation can show." "The Quest for Symbols," in *Symbols and Values, an Initial Study*. Symposium XIII, Conference on Science, Philosophy and Religion (New York, Harper, 1954), p. 10.

(1) man cannot avoid responding as a whole in the sense of his total involvement, and (2) his response will falsify and miss reality unless he also responds as an integrated whole.

Perhaps before pursuing the analysis further we should summarize some aspects of the discussion so far. Religion is man's response as a whole to what is most important and most real. Naturally man actually responds to what he considers to be important and real. His response does not have to be right, either because of his natural ignorance or because he has gradually come to produce and accept a falsified view of the world.[10] Man can also refuse to accept the offering of the right, and accept instead a desired wrong—a refusal that makes something less real most important. Man accepts a mixture of truth and falsehood, or a distortion of what is real. Continued response to what is false so blinds man to the fact that his choices are not the most real that for him reality becomes distorted; and repeated responses form a pattern that then, as we have seen, constitutes man's actual religion. No one's individual religion, and *a fortiori*, no institutional religion can avoid being a broken or distorted pattern. Only a continuously perfect saint could respond continuously in a fully right manner. Some religions, however, are better; others, worse. Religions are therefore neither good nor bad in themselves, but rather depend on what men consider to be most important and most real.[11]

If such is the case, how can we know reliably what is a good pattern, what is real, and whether what is real is also best for man? The answer to these questions is surely the prerequisite of religion's being publicly taught. Though we have said that this question can be settled only from the side of reality, even from man's side there may be a bridge leading to what is most important and real. On this bridge we may be able to get at least an inkling of some objec-

[10] "The concept of adjustment as the goal, as used among religious thinkers in our society, is a bastard offspring, born of the union of the mechanical ideals of our culture with moralistic Protestantism, baptized at the altar of the lowest common denominator and dedicated to the achievement of mediocrity." Rollo May, "Psychotherapy, Religion, and the Achievement of Selfhood," in Wilder, *op. cit.*, p. 299.

[11] "Alienation is always *relative* to the social situation in which it arises." Talcott Parsons, "Sociology and Social Psychology," in Fairchild, *op. cit.*, p. 301.

tive realm that affords the basis for the great variety of judgments, individual and social, concerning what is most important and real. We may begin to grasp how even the relative and the negative responses may become clarified and explainable with relation to some ultimate and positive reality.

We can at least accept the suggestion that the self learns from experience that an honest and integrated response is best for the self in the long run. The self becomes convinced—if it is open to truth —by means of the accumulative verdict of experience, because it cannot escape suffering the penalty that follows the choosing of what is immediately desired rather than what is steadily needed. The eating of too many green apples, for instance, may teach a lesson; a child may eat candy instead of vegetables, to the point where it may get painful sores from vitamin deficiency. The self thus learns that there is an objectively right way of living. Wrong is punished by pain; right is rewarded by pleasure. As the self matures it also learns increasingly not only the utilitarian wisdom of right conduct but also a certain appropriateness about it. Right conduct becomes understood as right relation to the world. The importance of well-being comes to be understood and accepted in terms of *right* relation to what is real. The self may hide its lesson in the subconscious, or it may defy it; but no self can ever escape from its truth.

On the social level the self has the same kind of experience. Taking what belongs to someone else, for example, may lead to punishment. As the self matures it may also learn to understand and to accept a certain appropriateness about the fact that one should not take whatever one wants. Further maturation may guide the self into an appreciation of not only the rights but the feelings of others; it may learn imaginatively to enter into the lives of other particular people, and of the larger community group. It may begin to get some sense even of the common good. The self then pictures the general good as the standard for the inclusive group and accepts the wider good as its standard for conduct. The fact that in concrete instances of behavior it goes on seeking its own immediate or separate good does not altogether cover up its generalized picture of what is *right as the appropriate response to reality*. Whatever religion is accepted as standard by the self, it never lives up to the religious ideal, but yields to immediate pleasures or smaller loyalties, and rationalizes its action in an attempt to preserve a unified self. The self dreads conflict within. Both its wrong choice and its justification are usually due, to be sure, to a combination of ambiguity and what in plain theological language is called sin. Neither the truth of reality nor the falsehood of desire, of course, comes entirely clean or completely dirty; nevertheless there is a reality feeling to what is right, which can be both deepened and clarified by consistent integrity.

Thus religion is not merely what man *considers* to be most important and most real, in the relative or subjective sense, but something that refers through experience to reality. Confusion and lack of integrity within the self, magnified by a welter of confusion and lack of integrity in the world without, cause a breach between reality and its interpretation; and this breach is widened by ages of interpretation. Nevertheless religion *intends a right relation between what is important and what is real*. Experience at least indicates that they belong together. Beyond what any particular interpretation of religion may be, religion seeks reality as such. Thus what man considers to be most important and most real roots back through experience into what actually *is* most important and most real; and the two foci cannot be separated without loss of both integrity and integration.

Thus as we walk on the bridge from man's response toward what is most important and most real, we see before us an objective realm of religious reality. Only as we have been there, however, and walk back again to survey the territory we have left, can we see that there is a religious reality that unites the most important and the most real. From this direction we can also see that this reality is so inclusive and unifying as to give unity and creative harmony to education. We shall now go on to suggest such a line of thinking.

First, it is well to recall that man cannot escape responding to what is most important and most real. He must choose what for him is ultimate: the stance from which he responds, the presuppositions he cannot prove, the position that patterns his life. But what is ultimate cannot be deduced from, or defended by, anything more ultimate without a contradiction in terms. Therefore each man must live by faith. Faith in one's ultimate is the essence of religion—faith as whole response to reality. All must have such faith. But only a valid and adequate faith is rooted in a right response to reality. True faith is whole response, not only in the sense that man as a whole is involved, but in the sense that such faith requires the integration that can be had only at the price of integrity. Basic questions remain: Can such a faith be found in any universal sense and is it capable of public inspection?

We have ventured to suggest that the *right* response is to the most important as the most real. The *highest* religion, in that case, knows that value and existence belong inseparably together—at least in their ultimate status and in the long last. We have also admitted that the testing of such affirmations cannot take the form of proof, without our sinning against the truth that the ultimate is logically incapable of being proved by anything more ultimate. Nevertheless it must be required of any interpretation of the ultimate that claims —as it must—the right to universal acceptance, (1) that it be both self-consistent and consistent with all well-established facts; (2) that it be true not only in theory but in life; and (3) that it explain all that we know better than any other candidate for the ultimate. We finite beings have recourse to only partial proof; all we can ask— since choose we must—is that our faith be as true and as workable as possible. Our faith can avoid as far as possible being arbitrary.

Of fundamental importance is the fact that we live in a process. Cosmic reality, as best we know it, is not static; but more than that, it has changed and keeps changing its own nature in a radical manner. No interpretation of reality that disregards this basic fact can be adequate. Our knowledge of process goes back to an original creation.[12] Our material universe—we accept as fact—came to be suddenly, at a definite point in the past; since this abrupt beginning of our cosmic process, numerous new levels of process have ap-

[12] For a forceful and concise statement of the scientific validity of creation and of evolution from a supernaturalistic point of view cf. Edward McCrady, "Biology," in Fairchild, *op. cit.,* pp. 235-61. Our statement is of course controversial. For a careful scientific discussion cf. George Gamow, *The Creation of the Universe* (New York, Viking, 1952), where the relevant problems are raised.

peared within it. Creation is modified by new creatures; and these new levels are irreducible to the previous levels. At the same time they fulfill them. They are organically related to previous creation, not only in terms of the kind of being they exhibit and the kind of organization they involve, but also by the higher forms of expression that they release in the previous process. The new forms of being give further meaning to the previous levels of creation. The new "emergences" bring out properties from the old levels within hgher forms of organization. At the high point of the process man's creation and history arrive. History discloses man's use of reason and his need for community. At our present point in man's history, high religion knows that a certain kind of community more fully explains and fulfills process than any other candidate for the ultimate. Our next chapter will be devoted to the examination of this claim.

This sudden coming to be of our universe, plus later new creations that are organically related to it, cannot be explained in terms of themselves; these facts of creation must be accepted either on sheer faith as mere facts, or as more than mere facts within the most adequate explanation possible. Sheer faith, where a measure of explanation is possible, shirks the task of inquiry, and undermines the reliability of reason. To accept the sudden beginnings of this mighty process as caused by mere chance, and to believe further that the new creations that organically fulfill previous process have no previous and intrinsic connection with it, is to sin against reason.[13] Creation and continuous creation are literally supernatural in the sense that they are processes outside the laws of nature; they cause nature to be, and transform her.

Nature, if it is to be at all strictly defined in predictable terms, conforms to the law of entropy and to the principle of conservation. Thus the higher organization shall not come from the lower; by itself nature runs down, not up. It is characterized by a progressive

---

[13] "To believe that the universe and man's mind were caused by anything less than man's mind is simply to abandon science for magic, and is more preposterous and incredible than the belief that a watch or a gaseous diffusion plant has come into existence as a result of factors incapable of making a plan or having an intention." McCrady, *op. cit.,* p. 248.

disorganization of energy.[14] Empirical science operates with these laws as its presupposition. But creation and continuous creation bespeak a Creator. A process of increasing organization, including purposive and personal behavior, presupposes a Purpose; and Purpose, a Person. The conditions for creation are actually such, and the length of our cosmic time span is so relatively short, that to believe in the accidental coming together of the constituent parts of process—like a protein molecule—demands credulity. To consider the myriad organic combinations of our organic universe to have been a matter of chance amounts to nothing so much as unreasonable will not to believe in reason. Reason is overwhelmingly on the side of an organic purposive universe. Organic development presupposes an organism; purpose, a purposer; integration, an integrator; personal behavior, a person. Only a habit of reductivist thinking can make us blind to the implications of a purposive process for a personal Creator. Such not seeing comes from heeding the mood of validity or empirical verification at the expense of adequacy, or explanatory completeness.[15]

If the nature of cosmic process and its presuppositions can thus be known, it is sheer folly to ignore them. The real takes on depth of being. Within this depth are serious problems, both for thought and for life; like the problem of evil and seeming lack of purpose or dysteleology. Not to acknowledge these problems, nor to treat them with utter seriousness, is to forfeit personal and intellectual integrity as well as to misread reality.[16] To let these become the

[14] Cf. *ibid.;* also Edmund Whittaker, *Space and Spirit* (New York, Nelson, 1946).

[15] Many religious thinkers seem insecure and dependent on being correct according to current vogues. Robert MacLeod has hit the nail on the head precisely: "The very haste with which dubious psychological theories have been proclaimed as Christian truth from the pulpit, and allowed to dictate the procedures of religious education, is in itself an evidence of insecurity. A religion that is sure of itself would be less ready to adapt its doctrine to the psychological jargon of the moment." "Experimental Psychology," in Fairchild, *op. cit.,* p. 265.

[16] "If the student is to develop a respect for religion, he must have more than the friendly chaplain's assurance that there is no essential conflict between science and religion, or that 'obviously science is not enough.' He must have evidence, as tough and challenging as anything he meets in the laboratory, that in religion there is something to be discovered, and that its discovery is worth the effort." MacLeod, *ibid.,* p. 268.

excuse, moreover, for not explaining as much as we can is an even more serious matter: it is to flee from reality and to distort its nature. Especially is this evasion destructive, if a universal truth can be found that strengthens our hand in the practical grappling with life's problems, and that gives an over-all meaningfulness to human existence. The highest and most inclusive form of organization, of purpose, or of personal life, may afford exceptional suggestiveness for the understanding of the nature and function of the other levels of organization in their relation to the whole.

If this explanatory and practical adequacy inheres in the highest form of existence, and if the most real may not be explained except in terms of its highest manifestation, we can readily see the natural conclusion to be that the most high is the most real. If what is most important for persons in their organic and purposive interrelation with the world as a whole represents the truest clue to the nature of process—a Purpose that organically relates and fulfills all levels of process, and yet transcends the process itself as its origin and end—then we can accept as our least arbitrary faith the fact that the most High is also the most real.

One more basic observation as to the nature of our facts needs to be made. The world is a process. The cosmos is not stationary; it is like a moving vehicle. Process points ahead of itself; the world as we know it, in its long perspective, is goal-seeking. It is—at least in part—a self-adjusting process, but in organic relation to an end that caused its beginning. That which originated process works *within it* and *into it* from outside by successive creations to bring it toward the end that is indicated by the Purpose for which it was made. Cybernetics[17] gives us a suggestion that the world is being steered over a very long time to an unimaginably distant goal. Or our world may be *used* as a temporary means toward a goal that is realized long after the world has ceased to exist. That goal is indicated by the highest creation or level of ingression within the process.

If this cosmos is such a process, then no explanation can be ade-

[17] The study—with a view to the understanding of the working of the human mind—of complicated electronic machines that can adjust themselves in relation to a changing goal. For the strict, technical meaning of "cybernetics" cf. Norbert Wiener, *Cybernetics* (New York, Wiley, 1948).

quate that merely describes the facts as they are at any point of process—no matter how accurate and adequate the description may be; on the contrary, the most important aspect of all facts is the truth that the facts are changing and to be changed. Evidence must therefore be viewed dynamically with reference to the goal toward which the process is moving. No piling up of facts, and no quantitative weighing of facts, will do. Nor will a certain lack of facts invalidate what the positive evidence process now provides; no systematic arranging of facts as they now are will give truth. Truth, rather, is focused at the highest point of process, in accordance with which process it is steering itself and being steered. Recalcitrant facts are not contradictory of truth, but rather subject to eventual transformation. Both the negative and the potential—the "not" and the "not yet"—may have eventual functions within the process that can be determined with adequacy only in the light of the final Purpose.

To be sure, as we have seen, within finite process no stance can be proved ultimate. The category of finality must remain a matter of faith; choose our ultimate we must; and, in the last analysis, choose it by faith. Our freedom is forced on us; but only to make inescapable our practical choice concerning the nature of reality. To evade all possible explanation in our search for ultimates is the choice of darkness and irresponsibility. To choose naturalism, for instance, is to believe contrary to our best evidence; both agnosticism and naturalism are faith stances that reject reason and evade reality. When they inform education, directly or indirectly, there is serious lesion between reason and reality. Life loses meaningfulness; society loses chart and compass, as to the widest horizons and final destination.

Like agnosticism and naturalism, high religion is also a faith judgment. It affirms that what is most important for persons is most real. Such a faith stance cannot be proved in a world of contradictory evidence and of only preliminary attainment. This religion, however, fulfills reason as far as possible in the present, whereas every attainment of better understanding and living provides its increasing fulfillment. Reason faces reality with integrity. Reality itself aids such integrity, since the experience of the real requires integration. The whole man must respond to reality; not only as a forced participant in his entirety, but as a unified and willing person. And—we shall see in the next chapter—not only is the individual satisfied at the level of his deepest drives, but men also are satisfied at the level of their deepest togetherness.

If such is the nature of reality, education needs to be rooted in it to the bottom. If such is the nature of truth, education need fear only false religions. The ultimate can alone offer the kind of over-all understanding and the total context of human relations, which will make education most important and real. Religion centers in the truth of reality, and man's need for right response. Education that makes truth its aim is essentially religious.

The Harvard Report, *General Education in a Free Society,* declared that religion is too divisive to be taught in our "secular" colleges and universities; therefore, the Committee advocated a strong return to the "agreement on the good of man at the level of performance without the necessity of agreement on ultimates."[18] Such a course is possible only where some great interpretation of reality has made possible a general agreement on the good of man. Education now lives on inherited spiritual capital, which drains the original investment. Today, in any case, such an agreement is actually in dispute over increasing areas of the world, and even among ourselves. We need a renewed—or a new—unity of seeing what reality is, if we are to agree well and long on what is good for man. The recommendation of the Harvard Report would also split life from reality; it would isolate man from the cosmic process.[19] It would deny depth and power of meaning at the point of origin, end, and contemporary need. Persons would therefore be confused and thwarted in the relation of what they learn to the deepest response of their lives; their minds would be cut off from reference to the foundation of their very beings.

We shall go on, therefore, to show that there is an Ultimate which

[18] P. 46.

[19] In spite of its genuine and important contribution to education, Eliseo Vivas' *The Moral Life and the Ethical Life* (Chicago, University of Chicago Press, 1950), is inadequate precisely at this point. How very much greater would be its contribution if it were anchored in a fuller faith!

makes for co-operative agreement and for creative freedom. If this Ultimate gives reality, vitality, and creative unity to education, surely it is folly to neglect it. If reality as a whole reinforces separate truths and gives them a total unitive meaning, education sins by not making religion central to its task. If truth as the right interpretation of reality requires the correct response to reality, then education and religion should co-operate to the fullest.

Chapter III

What Is Christianity?

UNLESS the Christian faith is open to public scrutiny it should not be taught; whatever cannot be publicly investigated is unfit for public inquiry and advocacy. To be acceptable as education the Christian faith must be shown to be both cogent for reason and practical for life; it must be, not an esoteric theology, but a universal religion. Even though a religious view or posture is incapable of proof in an absolute sense, it yet needs to be vindicated by its capacity to explain and to direct experience. The Christian is under obligation to convince honest and willing seekers for truth that Christianity is the right response to reality, as universal as human need and as concrete as personal decision. If such truth cannot be found, to speak of education as Christian is inappropriate.

If the Christian faith is for the initiated only, requiring esoteric prerequisites, it has no place in any public institution. In that case, the question is closed as to its right to be heard within our generally secularized universities or colleges, whether public or private. The Christian faith could still be taught in Christian colleges, among its devotees; but the presupposition for such teaching would be either religious pluralism or a potential totalitarianism. Pluralism would involve religious relativism, with respect either to the nature of ultimate reality or to its manner of being known. The totalitarian claim to the only and all truth should entail aspiration for complete political control of education. The maintenance of Christian colleges in our land on these premises would be tantamount to a surrender of all hope for religious unity; at best there could be a democracy of truths, but no democracy of truth.

The Christian faith, on the contrary, expresses universal meaning, and requires free acceptance based on personal insight. Even though the heart of its faith is not meaning, but a Person and personal relations, the Christian faith can be both told and tested according to all the requirements of such telling and testing. Albeit Christian meaning derives from specific events, it can both explain and direct general experience. Though there are conditions for the right knowledge of the Christian faith, these conditions can be communicated and tried. The use of reason in religion reduces religion, no more than science, to rationalism; rationalism is the substitution of the tool of reason for the object investigated. The use of system in religion no more makes religion indicate entire continuity than a blueprint builds a bridge; in either case there is a gap between theory and actuality. Neither correct description nor prescription solves problems or eliminates gaps in experience. If freedom and sin be facts, reason is sinned against unless the stark arationality of both be given its proper place in theory. The Christian faith is an active candidate for man's ultimate faith because it gives universal meaning to experience, a meaning that has room for the subrational or arational. Those of us who believe that it should be taught, do so because we believe that the Christian claim to truth can be vindicated better than the claim of any other faith.

The clue to what Christianity means is concern, or Christ's kind of love. Christ gives meaning to the Christian faith. He is no unknown factor, no mysterious x, he is a person who exhibits a style of life. He lived and taught compassion for all men. He exemplified love; he had concern for each and all. Those who knew, accepted, and followed him found a new kind of community within which each self became fulfilled. The Christian claim is that the community of concern, when accepted as the absolute purpose for man and of history, is the highest meaning, which indicates the nature of the most real. Christ is then the answer to man's need to respond rightly to the real. Reality understood and accepted through Christ most fully explains creation, history, human nature, the reason for the natural world, time, freedom, and evil; but it also gives the power to change things as they are in process in line with the purpose for their fulfillment. Not that problems do not remain both in theory and practice! Nevertheless, reliable light is given for us to walk in; whereas no other interpretation of the ultimate can give so much meaning to existence and such power for life.

As we remember, the choice of ultimates is forced on us; all men live by faith. Faith in Christ is least arbitrary and most adequate, because it throws the most inclusive light on man's common experience, which also involves intensely the organic fulfillment of each individual. This point of view is consistent both within itself and with the changing nature of purposive process. The difficulty with the Christian faith, in fact, is that it provides horizons so far away that our customary landmarks lose meaning. We think in terms not so much of process as of human history. We even feel that things are real for the most part according to the proportions of our own life span. Within the Christian faith, however, both human history and cosmic process must be seen against the background of eternal Purpose. Our facts have not fitted together, because our pattern has been too small. Let us, then, look further at the meaning Christianity gives to life.

Through Christ, understood as love, we look two ways: toward the ultimate, and toward the world. In the direction of the ultimate we see God. His will is the eternal Purpose that explains and directs process. A person who is all love may best be understood in terms of an ideal parent; the Christian faith therefore calls God "Father." The violent beginning of our cosmic process in a sudden creation came through His power; creation and continued creation are activated and directed by His purpose; they come to be and are ordered from, and in relation to, the resources of His will. The manner of creation is secondary in importance to its Source. The material or lack of material of creation is less significant than the Person who creates. What matters most is the fact that creation is best explained in terms of purpose. Creative being is at the center of both creative event and creative process. Love prepares for life and calls it into being. God is thus seen through Christ as Creator.

God also steers process. Process is, to be sure, partly self-steering; yet history is the sum of men's responses to God. Though conditioned by nature, civilization is a work of freedom. Though the history of civilization sets limits to men's choices at any point in cosmic process, human beings have a measure of liberty. Man is responsible even for the way he uses or abuses natural resources. Where history goes is therefore partly a matter of self-steering. Process is neither blind chance nor mere determinism; God steers the process as a whole from beyond the process, but He steers it also from within by His collaboration with those who are open to hear and to do His will. Cybernetics[1] can teach us that God's goal can be reached more surely than a self-directed missile can reach its shifting target. God's direction of history and guidance of life are called His providence.

God also provides the means for man's transformation and fulfillment. Men are meant to grow into the community of the concerned; they are destined for fulfillment through creative freedom. Through ignorance men fail, and through ill will they refuse, to join the society of God's inclusive love. But God Himself comes into human lives, as they let Him, as light to drive out ignorance and as love to dissolve ill will. Through forgiveness He thaws out fear and melts down rebellion, and enables men to enter the community of the free. Set free from anxiety and from their slavery to self, they are changed into unified, genuine persons; they become transformed in line with their destiny and creative satisfaction. God's work as transformer and fulfiller is summarized by the life, work, and teaching of Christ. In him we see that the eternal Purpose is of this kind. God is thus seen through Christ as creative fulfiller.

Again, in Christ we see the determiner of our destiny. We understand that process can be read rightly only in the light of its ending; the nature of the ending fulfills the partial meanings of historic decisions. Truth can be had only be seeing things as they are in the light ahead. By so looking at life we can judge what is wrong with it. As we see the nature of the end we find hope for work. The presence of the ending, the Christian community, within the process *now*,

[1] Norbert Wiener, *op. cit.*

gives us ends for which to live. In Christ we know that future fulfillment is no endless chase; for there is an ending. In Christ we grasp the fact that the fulfillment promised for the future is presently possible as we accept the Purpose of the process. The world to come is the only hope large enough to solve our problems; but things which are to be at last have already come in Christ, and only await our acceptance.

The ultimate is near; the ultimate is here. God works to fulfill human lives, by having His own Holy Spirit come into human history. He keeps coming unto the ending. The eternal Purpose works and waits to fulfill cosmic process. With Christ came a new age, because God drew near within a new community. The fullness of time brought God's kind of community to light, but the qualitative fullness awaits its quantitative fulfillment. The very nature of God is seen in Christ to be the ultimate Concern who creates and perfects the community of His choice. The fact that He wills to do so shows Him to be Father; the fact that He can do so discloses Him as Lord. Such is the eternal Purpose that gives inclusive meaning to our cosmic process, while it also reaches by its very nature into the depths of every life.

In a kind of life, Christ, we see then the ultimate meaning of existence: God is concerned with creative fulfillment through community. He is the kind of absolute we need. His will is for the good of all. Man's organic needs for such community witness to the nature of His creation; they point through process to Purpose. Man's origin and end transcend process, even while God's Purpose for community offers fulfillment of organic need on ever higher levels of purpose and persons. Eternally God wills community. Historically God came in Christ to found the Church as the community of the new age; Christ and the Church, God in His Son and in His Spirit, are inseparable. God comes really both in the individual and in the community. In the individual He is manifested as the new being in Christ who is creatively fulfilled in the new community. In the community He comes as the new society of the Holy Spirit, wherein each person becomes most fully himself. The eternal Purpose of

God is to make freedom in fellowship real through the Church. In God the one and the many are creatively fulfilled.

God as the absolute encourages the relative; the relative finds meaning within the absolute. God as the ultimate directs finite purposes within a unity of purpose, and conditions for co-operation that give reality and zest to personal choices. The more we do God's will the more concerned we are for the community. The more we conform to reality the more we become the bearers of creative difference. The more genuine our intention to please God, the more we study the actual conditions under which we can best live with others and be of help to them; and the more we receive of His Spirit the more ready we are also to receive help from others. The more we are aware of our dependence on God, the more humble we are—while still retaining the confidence that our help is sure and our work counts. True Christians are equally gracious receivers and concerned givers.

The Church is the community of grace. It accepts reality with gratitude. It lives in the light of its knowledge that creation is a gift, life is a gift, growth is a gift, forgiveness is a gift, creative transformation is a gift, the integrity of satisfaction is a gift. The Church is a society of grace. Its community has been purchased by the suffering of the innocent for the guilty. God, the Innocent, suffers in human history to overcome the alienation of man; Christ and his Church bear the cross of concerned participation even for the rebellious. The fellowship of suffering is activated by love's seeing and bearing of the world's burdens. Within the acceptance of this community of the cross is also included *self-acceptance*, through which alone come both community concern and individual satisfaction. The acceptance of reality by the individual is a communal experience. It hurts but helps; suffering hurts the self, yet it alone can release the depths of joy, peace, and creative satisfaction. Christianity knows no community of God's grace apart from a cross of concern.

Christ and his Church, furthermore, show us the nature of man. Actual men become interpreted through their best representatives. The Church as a whole stands judged by the ideal community; not only by the Church as it should be, but as it exists among its best members. Potential man is proper man. Man fails; he sins; but neither failure nor sin is final—man can be both forgiven and taught. The will is ill, both through ignorance and through defect of love. The education of the whole man requires right personal relations. Right adjustment to God, the Absolute, must precede right adjustment to men, self, and nature. Self-acceptance requires the facing of reality and the living within its conditions. Nor can God's will be done unless the self knows itself as a *socius*, a member of a community. The Christian community is totally inclusive: it is *for* all men. Only through the concrete expression of the Christian society, however, can man know himself as the kind of *socius* his nature requires. When the Christian community and experience are right, no external barriers are allowed to induce the inner tensions that hide man from himself.

The study of man therefore becomes existential. Living and studying go hand in hand; without right living, study leads to false seeing; without right study, living gropes in the dark. Without adequate understanding of the nature of man there can be no effective education. Only by heeding the implications of a right interpretation of man can education become integrative. The purpose of teaching can be carried out only by the taking seriously the way sin affects seeing, on the one hand, and the way seeing what is wrong, on the other, can lead to forgiveness, new levels of adjustment, and creative personality. The so-called objective subjects may seem to have nothing to do with the nature of man. Such objectivity, however, has limited applications; nothing can be put in its proper place in life until the meaning of life itself is clarified. When men find their God and their community through Christ, God in man, they see themselves for what they are; and how they can become what they most deeply crave to be.

All history, too, is seen from the Christian perspective as man's striving for community. Such striving is not deliberate seeking; it is rather an acting out of human needs within a natural environment. At heart an individualist, man may be more gregarious than social —he covets community to enhance his own self-esteem and self-enjoyment. (Buddhism, knowing this truth, therefore falsely seeks salvation beyond both individuality and society, whereas Christianity fulfills both.) Yet whether he is gregarious or social by nature, man is at least a social creature. His knowledge is a social act; his conditions for life are social conditions; his need to perpetuate his kind is a social drive.

Man, caught in community, therefore craves the right kind of community. Most of his social experiences, of course, are not of his own choice; he is born into families, civil communities, and nations. Roughly, all these groups exist to satisfy situational needs: some in large part to meet man's need for food; others in large measure to provide the conditions for an orderly existence; another cluster of social experiences spring out of the need for self-perpetuation; others exist mostly to take care of his gregarious or social drives; still others minister to man's need to be right with reality. Participation in these groups is mixed with primitive drives, natural conditions, vague backgrounds, and some seeing, planning, and choosing; and no matter how much individual man may long to be free of such social participation, he cannot avoid it. Nor is he who he is, except in terms of the kind of community he needs. All human institutions more or less minister to man's social needs; they are to be understood in terms of his being made for community. Because the Christian faith offers the fulfilling community, it can explain history as man's organically necessary search for satisfactory community: the key to history is the Church as the right kind of community. Therefore beyond the explanation of history the Church, *in the sense of the true community*, is also the goal of history. In the light of this goal all inadequate communities, including institutional Christianity, can be appraised and corrected. The Church consequently interprets, judges, and offers to fulfill all human kinds of communities.

History, moreover, ought not to be viewed statically; history moves. History is the place for decision and transformation. It is the home of human development. It provides the scene for its own transformation. The nature of history is change; most human institutions have a changing partial purpose. They minister to a segment of human needs; and at a particular historic level and within a special historic context. The Church cannot therefore interpret, judge, or offer to fulfill the other human societies except at their own actual level of development. The Church is the universal community of fulfillment; it is man's standard community in God which interprets, judges, and offers proper fulfillment to all actual human institutions, including all actual churches—as the inner nature, original drive, and potential destiny of history.

History in its long sweep shows a widening of communities and a deepening of their foundations. The various religions, to be sure, have dug deep; but Christ is the bedrock on which the widening community must be reared. Or, to change the figure, Christ is the beginning and the end of cosmic process; "in him all things cohere." He is therefore also its true middle. The partial communities that minister to partial needs find their full meaning in God's purpose for the total man and for all of history. In the light of such meaning their relative falsity and their degree of destructive fragmentariness are also made clear. Opportunity is afforded furthermore by the standard community for creative variety on the part of the minor community. Although the universal community of concern cannot, of course, serve directly as the pattern for creative communities, nevertheless indirectly it is both a light and a lure for constructive concern. Freedom creates community; new creatures make new kinds of society. The general nature of right community, however, is given in the Church; the over-all conditions for all creative community are also given in God, in human nature, and in the natural world. In this way are organically combined the co-working of a sovereign Purpose for a free, creative community of concern—to be actualized through history—and the concrete decisions of men that affect this community. History is consequently both the stage and the means for the working out of God's deepest purpose and man's highest destiny.

With the community of creative concern to clarify the meaning of existence, nature also becomes understandable—at least in its relation to human history. For the sake of making man's freedom real, nature is purposefully put between God and man and between man and man. Nature makes freedom both possible and real, by giving men responsible power of choice. Freedom is more than inner approval or disapproval of experience as it comes to us: freedom consists of genuine options in the actual world; it involves power over physical chains of events. Purposes both initiate and redirect chains of causation. Freedom is the capacity in some real way to control our response to the world, not only within ourselves in attitude but also beyond ourselves in action. Responsible freedom entails the ability to direct the flow of events. In order to do so, streams of energy must often be redirected. Effective freedom causes consequences other than those that would occur apart from man's manipulation of physical forces. A creature who can learn has therefore the chance to mature by means of his experience of consequences; he can observe and appraise the results of his freedom. He may thus become more wisely responsible. Such learning is not only individual but also social. Man, furthermore, learns *from* others, while all men learn from the experience of the race. Thus freedom is the prerequisite for learning on the part of responsible selves.

Nature is put between God and men, and between men, in order that men may become responsible; they are allowed to come to see and to accept for themselves what is good; they are permitted to refuse what is bad on the basis of their own experience. God thus teaches by indirection. He not only permits but enforces the freedom to learn; it is such responsible freedom that makes man real. He needs to find and to accept for himself, together with his fellow men, what is real and right. For man's sake God will not do the finding for him; instead, God hides Himself behind nature. He is not only *hidden* within nature, but for the sake of our freedom and privacy He actually withdraws from it as a personal presence. He becomes impersonally passive, merely concurring with the processes of nature. But even when He is absent, the environment instructs man. Nature not only provides the conditions for life, but is also the constant challenge to life; by wrestling with it man develops responsibility and resourcefulness; he learns to predict and to provide. Nature gives incentive to physical and cultural progress, for it is pregnant with possibility. In its ever untapped possibilities it is like a cow yearning to be milked! Every new level of discovery or invention, furthermore, makes possible yet higher levels; nature acts as the spur to advance. The context of man's relation to God is therefore always conditioned by his relation to nature.

By means of nature man can become seemingly self-sufficient. Forgetting or not knowing that God keeps both nature and life going, man comes to think of himself as independent. He becomes concerned with physical power and possessions, and with the personal and social attainment that are possible within the conditions of this created world. Such alienation from God through ignorance or rebellion would be impossible, except for the provisions of nature and for man's sense of control over it. Man becomes confused as to his real purpose in life; "natural" life seems enough, and alone real. History speaks an ambiguous language; many voices call both to understanding and to action. Within this confusion of voices, and the difficulty of understanding even his own experiences, man must choose his faith. Desire for security mixes into the desire for satisfaction; conflicting calls as to what is right contend within.

The self that becomes real through responsibility in nature could therefore become falsely satisfied with what physical and social life could give it—if it were not for the precarious aspect of nature. Planning "for keeps" is impossible—things are taken away, and men die. Because what is pleasant is not certain, men seek what is right and real beyond such change; because life itself ends, men look for hopes that last. Thus nature provides the conditions not only for life on earth and for advancing civilization; but nature also provides the occasion for man's search for fuller life, beyond earth's danger and destruction. Planning must be done against a background of uncertainty. Nature helps develop life, but in so doing awakens drives it cannot satisfy. Nature exists to make responsible freedom real; but man's freedom seeks its fulfillment beyond nature. A sophisticated frustration may try to tame life to nature; but fundamentally man seeks beyond nature the lasting fulfillment of the community for which he is made.

Man's indirect relation to God makes it possible for man to have a genuine though measured freedom. His rebellion is never within a context of the clear seeing of all the consequences; it is always mixed with insecurity and ambiguity, both within and without.

His deepest self is made for God and the right kind of community, but he has to find and to accept both God and community through the long indirections of experience within nature and within imperfect society. Therefore his freedom can be both real according to its measure of power, and yet eventually within God's responsible, over-all control. Man is so made that when he comes to himself he realizes that his Father's home is best; so made that the farther he goes away from God the more he begins to be in want and to starve. Nature, again, is constructed in such a way that it cannot permanently satisfy the whole of life.

These facts together provide the clue to the solution of the problem of evil. The Christian faith has the power to throw light on this central question. Evil has four basic forms: ill will, or alienation from reality; precariousness; destruction; and death.

Ill will is due to rebellion or fear. Man rejects what he knows to be right in favor of what he wants. He sins; or he lets himself freeze fast to present satisfaction, because he fears the unknown or what he cannot control. Ill will may seem robustly aggressive; but central to the sinful life is fear's fever for satisfaction. The self is more driven than free. Or the self may cling to what it is and has in such a way as to be faithless to offered reaches of the real and the right. But whether the self seeks the false or refuses the real because of fear, its will is ill. It is separated from reality. It is sick. The first form of evil is the ill will. This kind of evil, however, can at least be understood. If the self were not free to reject the real, neither it nor its freedom would be real. Freedom presupposes more than the possibility of alienation; in order for the self to become real and to mature, alienation is necessary. Every self, to be human, must stand over against God, within the indirections of nature and history, in order to discover through the history of experience that God is real and that His way is best. Every self must experience a will that is ill, and learn willingly and understandingly to say, "Not my will but Thine be done."

The second form of evil is precariousness. Uncertainty, however, is the means whereby God keeps man from becoming falsely self-serious about his planning. Uncertainty thwarts a false self-sufficiency. Man cannot foresee the full future, nor can he prevent the upsetting of his best plans. Even acquiescence in the best he knows leaves man uncertain—both because the best he can know and do falls short of the full reality, and also because the best can never be obtained within our kind of world. Our world is a school where no final diploma is given. Uncertainty prevents a partial satisfaction from permanently capturing man's life; thus precariousness is a condition of life that God uses to guide, control, and fulfill one's freedom. Our lives are led, by means of the uncertainty of the things of this world, to seek for those realities that cannot fail.

Destruction, moreover, refers to physical things; death, to life: a city is destroyed; its people die. A social organization may be viewed from both points of view. A church may be destroyed, or may die; viewed as a function, it can be destroyed, like a machine; looked at as community, it is killed. If for our purposes we make this distinction, destruction is necessary if freedom is to be real. Without destruction, no painful consequences attend the ill-tempered or careless use of things. Without destruction, there would be no precariousness in nature; the hail would not harm and the flood would not drown. Nor could man rebuild and better his broken dreams. The facing of destruction gives ground for courage, resourcefulness, and depth. The fact that destruction comes both to the innocent and the guilty makes community responsibility and concern desirable; people who are in "the same boat" have need to pull together. Since reward and punishment—if we may use these terms—are not only in some manner consonant with personal ability and application, but also, in another way, are due to social situation and response, the achieving of community calls for both personal and communal effort. Destruction helps both to level life into a common human situation, and to heighten the chances for community. Free men, to be sure, can fail to make right responses; but this is at least the kind of world where both the individual and the group are most helped whenever there is mutual and maximum concern.

Death, too, helps man. By raising an uncrossable barrier against self-security and false satisfaction, death focuses man's attention on what is ultimately good and real. Death is more than an act; it is a state of being. Death is a decisive event, but it is also an inner drive. Death is the destruction of life, and in life this destruction works through anxiety as well as through physical breakdown. Without conscious awareness, man may seek death in order to escape the pain of living; or he may flee death in his search for satisfying and lasting life. Death in life therefore highlights what is important to life: it is a mainspring of motivation for the real and the right. Man, troubled in life by death, looks beyond the limits of life to find meaning beyond physical death. For some, this meaning grips them in devotion to values that last; they invest in oncoming life, and in the right conditions for future life.

For the Christian, physical death means the stripping from the self all that is false; the soul dies in order that the spirit may live better. The soul is the self as lived under earthly existence—it dies completely as a self. The spirit is the self as called by God to eternal life, called back to life by God's grace when He wills. Neither the soul nor the spirit has self-existence; both live by the co-operative grace of God. Death for the Christian is graduation from one school to another school. To the fearful, death is either a hoped-for escape, or the point of maximum dread. For the Christian, death is the highest peak he can see of God's creative riches. Both death in life and physical death point to God; they raise man's sight beyond earthly existence during life and beyond it.

Thus the Christian faith gives us reliable indications as to the meaning of evil, as well as the promise of power for its eventual destruction.[2] No narrower frame of reference will be large enough for truth; closer horizons cannot account for evil. If thoughts fly under a lower ceiling, they cannot lift the heavy facts of life into clarifying light. Only a great God can make goodness real. Kinder-

---

[2] Cf. John Oman, *Vision and Authority* (London, Hodder & Stoughton, 1928, rev. ed.), pp. 228 ff., where he speaks of the four veils that hide the mystery of life from us—ignorance, sin, weakness, evanescence. "Enshrouded by these four veils man stands before the mystery of God. By four great Christian doctrines they are taken away. The veil of our ignorance is removed by the Incarnation, the veil of our sin by the Atonement, the veil of our weakness by Grace, the veil of our evanescence by Immortality." But, he adds, as soon as we regard these great doctrines as metaphysical dogmas, "we enter upon the most debatable of all human enquiries."

garten or backwoods religions cannot cope with the growth of modern knowledge. As in science the few seers first behold the new truth that will solve old problems, so in religion we can find adequacy only by running close to its front-line thinking. Faith we must have—education cannot escape accepting some stance. The farthest reaches of the Christian faith, to be sure, lie beyond full seeing, and far beyond total proving; serious problems remain for reason.

But it is our conviction that no other faith can similarly account for the nature and facts of process and for the meaning of life. By their very nature these matters must point beyond both process and life to the eternal Purpose and its fulfillment. Because they so point ahead of facts they cannot be proved by them; but they can indicate that Purpose for life and process. By so doing they give a steady direction to the steering of life; more importantly, they give hope and creative zest to individuals, and increasing meaningfulness and satisfaction to the community. Education needs an absolute. The absolute must be a matter of faith; some stance, some ultimate, underlies what is taught. A false absolute thwarts and destroys; the true absolute releases creative life and builds community.

In closing this chapter on Christianity, we can at least suggest how the Christian absolute of God's inclusive concern can help education, as a total stance and as a concrete process. Modern education in general has shunned absolute categories—and with good reason. Education may well dread a theological absolute; it has taken it centuries to fight free of authoritarian dogmatism; men have had to suffer and to die for the right of free inquiry. The true Christian absolute, however, rejects dogmatism; it is an absolute that frees thought; the Christian absolute can never be confined to historic formulation. Even its personal appearance in history comes in finite form—in "the weaknesses of the flesh." The will of God is sovereign beyond all its human expressions; it is never possessed by any institution, and never absolutely expressed by any book or creed. Ultimate possession and expression transcend human capacities.

The will of God is for the total good of all at all times. That total good requires that men find it freely for themselves in every new situation. The absolute is sufficiently disclosed as the Christ—God's living personal concern for community—to form a reliable pattern for life and thought. But this general pattern is no detailed blueprint; eternal Purpose invites temporal inquiry. The eternal Purpose, too, is itself flexible, and varies with history's choices. God keeps reshaping His creative pattern for concerned community, according to the kind of choices human beings make. Those who understand the nature of the absolute know, therefore, that the kind of dogmatism that dictates to honest and competent inquiry in the name of some authoritarian revelation is neither Christian nor true.

Nor is the Christian absolute falsely other-worldly: God is concerned with man's creative best. Those who do His will must share His concern for this world. They must be freed of their self-centered concern, to center their lives in God's will for the world. Such sharing, too, is not only in attitude; the will is not good unless it be also as right as it can be. Concern for others involves the study of their concrete situation, and how they can best be actually helped. Inquiry into human nature, social conditions, the problems of effective communication—all such factors direct and correct good intention. The general pattern of complete concern, when it is accepted in attitude, has to turn into the concrete concern of appropriate action: the Word takes on flesh and dwells with us. He cannot dwell with us without working through us, with all practical wisdom and power; the Spirit moves us to social participation and physical effort.

Once more, the absolute becomes no rival of the relative, and no substitute for it. The nature of God's love is to create continually enriching variations.[3] Newness and difference are manifestations of the same Spirit; individual and social responsibility become sharpened. God counts on us. God never gives us truth outright, nor presents us with miraculous inventions; we have to search for truth with all diligence, and are made co-creators with God. The relative has its needed place; the finite person has his required task.[4] Within

---

[3] "The main problem of the report thus becomes: 'How can general education be so adapted to different ages and, above all, differing abilities and outlooks, that it can appeal deeply to each, yet remain in goal and essential teaching the same for all?' " Quoted from the Harvard Committee, *op. cit.*, p. 93, by Chalmers, *op. cit.*, p. 42.

[4] In this sense we can admit Leeson's assertion that "personality in itself cannot be an end, though doing something with it, making it better, is." *Op. cit.*, p. 9.

the Christian absolute such unqualified stress is put on the creative place and role of the relative, without the slightest chance of reducing truth to relativism. The absolute is concerned with the finite; there is therefore an infinite concern for it. But the finite itself loses its meaning and bearing apart from the infinite concern to which it is related.

A total unity of spirit and perspective makes for both co-operation and understanding. Truth has a factual basis beyond the merely natural; but truth, ultimate or proximate, to be Christian must be spoken in love. No teacher or student within this unity gets his satisfaction from the sense of superiority. Nor has he need to be defensive about his field of investigation; the greatest Spirit, and the eternal truth, pull men together in common endeavor. That Spirit and that truth also give personal meaning to each individual, and group significance to each community of inquiry, because persons and groups have irreplaceable tasks.[5] The absolute enforces and enriches the real need for relativism and pluralism. The more the absolute is stressed the more men must receive truth in integrity and humility. The more the absolute truth of God's concern for community is made emphatic, the more free those become who catch sight of it.[6] They become free in and for the truth; and from falsity and futility in life. The more they are indoctrinated in the Christian absolute, the more men must be fully for all and for each one, not only in attitude but in concrete wisdom. The more the absolute unites the self the more the self becomes freed from fear and enabled to open up to the actual problems of its own life and of those of other people.

Christian education is thus no God-centered education that makes for a false other-worldliness. It is no subject-centered education that removes teacher and student alike from the actual needs of life. It is

[5] J. V. L. Casserley has given us a fascinating task, namely to find "the role of the relative in Christianity, and the possibility of the absolute in sociology." *Morals and Man in the Social Sciences* (London, Longmans, 1951), p. 7.

[6] "What is the secret of the combination of authority and freedom? The answer in one word is Love. Love is the key to all true relationship between persons; in fact, persons can grow as persons only if they love and are loved. For that reason love is at the very heart of education." Jeffreys, *op. cit.*, p. 163.

no student-centered education that so focuses attention on him that he turns neurotic.[7] Education is ideally lifted by the Christian faith into an absolute perspective wherein truth becomes high and holy and the student of infinite importance, but teacher and student are both lifted beyond themselves. The eternal truth gives significance to the immediate subject: God's will gives meaning to the life that teaches and the life that studies. Within the will of God is freedom for the self: freedom for community, freedom for truth, and freedom for creative life. Education becomes a means to the better life, but a means penetrated and saturated with the eternal end of truth.

[7] Cf. "In brief, learning may be regarded either as a process of giving content to ideas through first-hand experience, or as a process of giving significance to individual impressions by means of ideas. The one is primarily the concern of the child, the other of the teacher; but ultimately they are phases of the same fact." William Boyd, *The History of Western Education* (London, A. & C. Black, Ltd., 1952, pp. 324–25.

Chapter IV

God as Educator

To SOME it may seem presumptuous to speak of God as Educator. How can man know God's way of educating? If he can find it out, moreover, has he a right to imitate God's way? We must respect this honest and humble questioning. All the same, whatever we do right we must do in line with reality. In the final analysis the physician does not invent new ways of life; he discovers how life operates, and uses his knowledge to assist nature. He does not heal, but provides the conditions for healing that are already at hand within the natural order.

Similarly a composer discovers musical harmonies, which he arranges creatively. While in one sense Tennyson had the right to call Milton a "mighty-mouthed inventor of harmonies," it would be even more true to call him *an arranger* of harmonies. A composer gives to the human ear through musical instruments a voice for God's great harmonies that wait to be arranged. The psychiatrist and minister who help heal people's minds and spirits can do so only by studying to understand the nature of mind and spirit. They help people to think or to choose in line with God's purpose for them in creation. As the physician, the composer, the psychiatrist, and the minister are not presumptuous but wise in learning to apply God's ways, so the educator is not presumptuous but wise in searching for God's method of education. He is, seen from the opposite point of view, both stubborn and foolish if he insists on going his own way without regard to the nature of reality.[1] The task in this chapter is to try to ascertain what general bearing God as Educator can have on education;[2] in the next chapter we must attempt some concrete applications of whatever insights may be had.

The first task then in trying to apply the meaning of the Christian faith to education is to see how God teaches. We have already seen that God's purpose with creation is to effect Christian community. The whole process of nature, history, and experience must therefore be studied as a means to this end. There are three ways, at least, of looking at process as pedagogical.

The first holds that the cosmic process exists for the sake of the completing of eternity. Augustine suggested that the reason for creation was to produce by means of earthly existence a community to take the place of the fallen angels. When the angels fell, eternity became unbalanced; God therefore redressed this state of unbalance by creation. Thus the whole cosmic process must be conceived of as needing patching even before its creation. Others have believed that God made man perfect on earth, that he fell from perfection, and that our present history is God's way of salvaging what He can from the fall. Both theories, however, lack basis in fact; neither a pre-temporal nor a temporal fall from grace can be known, nor need any "fall" be inferred. Neither theory will stand the test of validity, nor provide the most adequate heuristic device for explaining cosmic process. Creation is not best accounted for in terms of God's patchwork, either of eternity or of time; nor is history or experience.

A second approach to creative process as pedagogical is that God is experimenting. He is doing His best to effect His high goal, but

[1] One side of this truth is certainly that stressed by Boyd: "The starting-point was found in the familiar idea which all educators since Rousseau have accepted as fundamental: that the teacher can only do his work to good purpose on the basis of a sound knowledge of child nature, and must therefore study the child." *Op. cit.*, p. 390. Did not Comenius and Pestalozzi have a similar drive? An educator like Froebel, for instance, made God's way of teaching central to his *Education of Man*.

[2] "The relation to the Absolute will not come into consideration as an afterthought —as when a priest is sent to accompany a criminal on the way to the gallows—but as a forethought and a cothought that determines how everything is done that is done to him and for him." H. Richard Niebuhr, *Christ and Culture* (New York, Harper, 1951), p. 240.

is working with recalcitrant material. Or He is limited within His own self rather than by the conditions of the process. At the lowest levels of creation it took Him very long, relatively speaking, to get the process going. While He worked He made many false starts. Many revolutionary attempts were foiled. Many species failed. Recently, however, with the break-through of man's higher history, God has begun to see His way clear. There may be temporary setbacks due to man's false use of His freedom; the outcome, however, seems certain to be worthy of the Creator. The intention of this explanation, to be sure, is consistent with Christian love. It embraces the highest possible destination, and is honest about the crude and cruel facts of the prehistoric ages.

Why it should have taken God so long to get to this state of process is a real puzzle; faith and reason have to face it squarely. Depths of darkness underlie any light that issues from the meaning of process as it now appears—the darkness of long and low beginnings and the blackness of lost evolutions. Naturally this view of God as the cosmic Experimenter and eventual Fulfiller is better than any Hindu view that God plays with the world. As artist or playboy, God is irresponsibly lacking in love,[3] and such a theory cannot even be listed as Christian. This view of God as Experimenter breaks down, too, when it is seen that the explanation it gives is no more than a description of process! We might as well describe process as progress. God must explain both the coming of that new which is beyond explanation in terms of the process itself, and also how all new levels of being come to fit into the process and organically to fulfill it.

There is, however, a third way of looking at process. Without denying the problems this theory of God as Experimenter poses for Christian faith, we choose seriously to live and to think in the light of the highest purpose we do see. There is an amazing illumination, as we saw in the last chapter, of process itself when it is confronted with this Purpose. Our approach to the concept of God as Educator, this third way of looking at process, is that life as a whole is organically educative. The long background of process must pertain to

[3] Cf. Sankara's *lila* theory.

God's patient preparation for the teaching situation. No failures can be permanent for God, but all must be seen in the light of the fulfilling, ongoing evolution of life, body, mind, and spirit.[4] Our task, however, is not the interpretation of the low beginnings of mankind, but to see the work of God within our historic period, there to learn from Him His way, and by such learning to become His more able and willing co-workers in education.

God's main pedagogical method in creative process seems to be by indirect means and by vicariousness. God may give some knowledge directly to prophets and saints, but for the most part His truths must become learned indirectly. Experience is the school of life. We are not confronted with clear propositions to be accepted or rejected, but with complicated situations within which we must learn. Life's learning is mostly appropriation, almost through osmosis. Truth and wisdom practically seep into our lives. When mature insight is gained, it is not neatly intellectual; it is deeply personal. It cannot be shared in terms of mere syllogisms. It cannot even be communicated in depth and fullness in terms of books or long conversations. Life's deepest insights are living understandings that permeate our whole experience, and cannot be separated from that experience except as general suggestions to others. God teaches community by the rearing of children; each one is different within a common world and within general communities. Learning comes through countless rounds of imitation and of trying for oneself. As we face new situations we seek to solve our problems; and thinking becomes, as John Dewey maintains, problem solving. Sometimes we make attempts at solution, and from frustration look to see how others have found better ways of doing the same thing. Or we try to gather what insight and "know-how" we may before we make the plunge for ourselves.

Most of the learning process, however, is personal appropriation through general "feel" of situations. More and more we accumulate by means of such felt situations a stock of general experience that serves as the background for new appraisals and for decisions.

In the depths of our being we come to discover what we really

---

[4] Cf. the author's *Evil and the Christian Faith* (New York, Harper, 1947), chaps. X and XII, for several possible treatments of this problem.

believe to be right and good through the totality of our experience. All statements of these insights and beliefs seem superficial, because they are severed from their experimental base; all prescriptions or directions we give to others seem snatchy. Defensive persons become doctrinaire, peddling open and obvious solutions. The shallow become sure of some crusty surface of experience, and substitute this for truth. Those who are deeply mature have learned that wisdom and goodness can hardly be communicated, more than can "the feel" of the original experience in its intimate and total relation to the whole of their experience. They tend therefore to be less doctrinaire, and less sure of surface clarity or of authoritative rule. They point, rather, through depth and richness of experience, to certain aspects of concrete experience through which others might learn to interpret for themselves their own experience.

Having seen and felt the deeper intertwining of life and the patient riches of truth, the mature become humble. They become helpful instructors mostly by recognizing the need for people to learn indirectly. Seers of truth commend it by communicating whole vision. This they can do, where truth is at all personal, social, and complex, only by pointing to proportions in affirmations or negations, by stressing the meaning of aspects in terms of contexts, or by conveying through feeling, example of action, and symbol the center of their whole seeing. Such instruction avoids defensiveness and shallowness. It elicits most easily the creative whole-seeing of the learner. Instead of learning words, formulas, external knowledge alone, he assimilates into the indirect process of his personal appropriation of truth the more isolable aspects of it.

God does not teach by code and creed; He does, of course, make possible such summarizing pointers to truth as these are. God teaches rather by life, by chance for indirect learning, by making necessary nearly unconscious appropriation, by concrete confrontation with problems and the need to know the conditions for their solution. The more factual or formal the problem, the more it must be learned through an indirect approach. Perhaps the point to be learned from this analysis is that formal and factual knowledge can be communicated directly, but that the more the centers of life and civilization are involved the more the teaching, too, must be indirect. Perhaps this is the reason that Jesus used parables. This may be the reason for Socrates' dialectic, which forced the learner to face for himself the truth he was to see. The upshot of our reasoning may be that in all instances where strictly formal and factual knowledge is transcended the most appropriate and effective method is case study. Perhaps the profound use of life situation should become the center of all live study of personal and social truth in whatever department of education. The direct learning of social, moral, or spiritual wisdom is seldom applied by the learner, because it has not been personally appropriated. Education suffers from a chronic indigestion of unassimilated propositional truths.[5]

The indirect method is one aspect of God's way of teaching; vicariousness is a second. No one learns alone; he learns from the deep flood of knowledge from the past, within which he becomes necessarily immersed. Speech, language, and thought are the product of the long, social ages; apart from these ages man is merely an animal in knowledge. The content of knowledge, too, is through and through accumulative. All significant knowledge presupposes the nearly hidden indirect growth of the millennia as well as the centuries. Without social inheritance man's knowledge is thin and flimsy beyond imagination; or rather it would not exist. Even in the present, however, knowledge is a social product and a social experience. The individual has the chance and the responsibility to respond to society and nature, to feel his response consciously and in subconscious depths, to organize his material around his master motivation, and to initiate his own bit of discovery or insight. The overwhelming content of all that he knows, however, is learned from others not only from the past via books or records, but also in the present, because of the social overlapping of all experience. The more deeply experience is plumbed the more it becomes apparent that, except for the thinnest front edge of knowledge, public and private knowing are separable only by abstraction. Society thinks in the individual, and the individual thinks in society. How can such an affirmation be

---

[5] "Our error is that we have given them the food and do not trouble about the appetite without which they will not digest it." Livingstone, *op. cit.*, pp. 55–56.

true, however, if knowledge is mostly indirectly acquired, and cannot, except for formal and factual material, be communicated with any wealth of personal appropriation? If learning is the appropriation of knowledge and wisdom mostly through the indirection of experience on the part of the individual, how can knowledge at the same time be solidly social?

The answer is that man participates in a community of being that comprises a community of seeing, a community of feeling, and a community of doing.[6] Deep down man is one within the reality of God in history. He becomes individuated through a process of personal experience and decision. In spite of such individuation, nevertheless, to be man means to partake of the Spirit of God, which constitutes the core both of community and of personal being. Through the process of history man as community becomes differentiated from his mere being in God as a capacity for birth and growth; through the process of experience man as a person becomes differentiated from the community within whose womb he is conceived, brought into being, and given content. At the core of the being of community, however, is always divine Spirit; and at the core of personal being, in like manner, is community being. Differentiation is necessary for both communal and personal reality. The problem connected with differentiation is that it involves alienation and rationalization, and therefore, reorientation and restoration. For such return to integration on a higher level of differentiated reality, right reason is necessary.

The community of seeing depends on its use of reason. It is not vicarious in the sense that the group can ever substitute for the individual. In our discussion of knowledge indirectly acquired we insisted emphatically that no learning is real until it becomes incommunicably personal within a real and vital experience. In another sense, nevertheless, all adequate seeing means seeing through the glasses of social experience. No individual can be rich intellectually

[6] By "community" we mean a psychic, social, and spiritual reality rooted in God's activity in history. The word is used rightly when denoting this social reality, as for instance in the phrase "man's search for community." Such community becomes more or less concrete in history. Such concrete usage must be indicated by the context. Similar usages are "life is good," and "the life of Lincoln."

who does not accept with grateful appropriation what others have done to make his seeing possible. Only because countless others have seen meaning over the long ages can any individual now have a chance for vital understanding; and only because innumerable other people constantly share with individual persons what they see can he learn to see more truly the world and its meaning. Contexts and perspectives are almost entirely social creations that are given the individual. They do not substitute for his own seeing, to be sure; but unless society could act in the place of the person in the sense of the agelong and group-wide accumulation and integration of knowledge, personal seeing, in any developed sense of knowledge, would be impossible. In this sense learning is social, both inductively and deductively,[7] in a primary measure; it is vicarious. God uses vicarious seeing to afford personal seeing. Such vicariousness is heightened if all knowledge is organismic by means of a constant process of mutual immanence and overlapping selves, and even if differentiation in terms of personal response and experience, plus a bit of personal initiative, always presupposes a community of interactive contents of knowledge. Community of seeing is then not only based on a history of interpretation and common, external conditions for knowledge, but also on a process of internal relations within the community in the Spirit and within each person in the community.

The community of feeling is exhibited by the deep undertow of emotional responses to our world, which we inherit and which we share with the groups to which we belong. Rational or moral seeing may deviate from this. But like the waves lapping on alien shores, they are usually pulled back into the down surge of the undertow. Underneath our rational or moral judgments lie the oceanic depths of our arational or irrational and moral or immoral feelings. Rational or moral apprehension is usually pulled back into and submerged within this community of feeling. Take, for example, our response to the race issue, when it is not theoretical but deeply affecting a concrete group. Usually mere rational or moral argument fails to lead the group into a constructive decision; the community of seeing is

[7] For discussion of this topic see the author's *The Christian Fellowship* (New York, Harper, 1940), chap. I, "Religious Knowledge as a Social Act."

governed by the community of feeling. Or consider the case of nationalism, wherein liberal arguments for a world community or for putting all nations on an equal basis in one's affection and concern fade into ineffective shadows that have no power to move.

The community of doing operates in the same manner. The actual choices we make as a community have to be justified to ourselves and to others. Reason then becomes to a large extent a means to rationalize actions already taken. When a community has done things in a certain way for a long time, moreover, not only does purpose harden into habit, but institutional arrangements become so hard to change that they reinforce the actional rut. Rational or moral arguments for change, however logical and even expedient, have against them the mass of habit and the fixity of institutional patterns. Institutional inertia is a heavy force in history; all basic change is hard; new ways are costly in energy. Besides, thought has been so long focused on a certain way of doing things, and has for so long been used to justify this way, that practical reason itself becomes balky at the thought of change.[8] Therefore the community of doing seems fractious to the community of seeing. In so far as the new seeing wants to correct or improve the old ways of doing things, it chafes under the irksome inflexibility of the community of doing; it resents the reason used by the community of doing as its stooge.

All three communities, however, are organically part of the community of being. The community of being is effective only as the community "organism" is whole. The whole promotes *constructive tensions* among the three for the sake of growth, criticism of that growth in terms of actual decisions, and the satisfaction to which the community aspires. *Destructive tensions*, however, weaken the organism. The community of seeing easily becomes divorced from the community of feeling and from the community of doing. People need interpretation. Rational evaluation is good and useful, whether for government, society, or education. The academic sin, however,

---

[8] One aspect of the greatness of John Dewey was his insight into this stubbornness and his daring experimentation to overcome it. For a short summary of this emphasis see Boyd, *op. cit.,* pp. 394 ff.; also Dewey, *Democracy and Education* and *Experience and Nature.*

is to see the rational and the good apart from existential concern and participation; thought thus becomes divorced from actual life. Neither the true nor the good comes into history abstractly; and all attempts at starting from a pure vision are bound to fail. The intellectuals do not see why they are foiled and frustrated. Liberals cannot understand why they are considered brittle and not taken seriously by most people.

Education cannot deal with truth, ideals, or values apart from the concrete decisions of actual groups. Good education never becomes divorced from good government and good society—not so much theoretically as with regard to the actual choices that confront the various groups to which education ministers. The community of feeling and the community of doing are man's depth relations to reality. They may be false, but they go deeply into the heart of things. Ideas and ideals fail to move people, apart from deep rootage in actual feelings and accustomed patterns of behavior.

Education is often visionary, not because its truth is impossible but because it is impracticable. It is impracticable, moreover, because it is mostly a matter of ideas. Education has not sufficiently been aware that its chief task is to relate ideas to feeling and action within concrete communities.[9] This affirmation in no way amounts to saying that education should be preaching or prophetic injunction; these functions belong primarily to the church and to social and government leaders. The main function of education, we repeat, *is* to be a community of seeing; it needs to be the eyes of the busy world. The point of the affirmation is, rather, that seeing based mostly on abstract thought, though it is not without value in the long run of history, is nevertheless largely wasted seeing. Education constitutes a partial function of the community of being, and receives its

[9] Howard Lowry expresses a profound truth when he writes: "Fact-collecting, open-mindedness as an end of life, to be forever learning and never coming to a knowledge of the truth, is less arduous than reflective commitment. Reflection is easy and commitment is easy; but the two together—that is an educational task demanding the highest powers." *The Mind's Adventure: Religion and Higher Education* (Philadelphia, Westminster Press, 1950), p. 134. Two books that now stress this wholeness of life with regard to education are Henry P. Van Dusen, *God in Education* (New York, Scribner, 1951), and George A. Buttrick, *Faith and Education* (Nashville and New York, Abingdon, 1952).

mandate from the part its seeing plays within the community of being. Preaching and social prophecy are both handicapped *when the community of seeing fails to relate its seeing to the community of being.* It can do so only with depth and power by relating it to the community of feeling and the community of doing. The main question then remains: How can this be done?

The clue to good education is the fact that the content of knowledge is largely vicarious. The individual depends for his efficacy on the community, of which for the most part he is a passive part. The community depends for its efficacy on the Spirit, in whom it participates for the most part passively. The individual is part of a social organism; the community is part of a spiritual organism. The social organism does for the individual the bulk of learning and living without which he could never learn or live deeply; the spiritual organism, in whom the community is immanent and in whom the individual is also immanent, makes both transmission from the past and present communication possible.[10] In Him is the power both of participation and of appropriation. In Him is the capacity both for transmission through time and for communication through space or from heart to heart. The Spirit is the underlying reality of meaning. Meaning, however, is never merely abstract, but is itself organic. His will is purpose, and makes purposing possible. We might say with all directness that all profound education is in the Spirit. Without worship and work in the Spirit education, in its main purpose, is superficial and impotent; without the understanding and acceptance of the Spirit education fails of the deepest and most creative motivation. The Spirit is never wholly absent; therefore we can teach as we do. What we need, however, is a concentrated incarnation of the Spirit in the community of teaching and learning—a Pentecost in education.

Education is mostly a matter of being fed by God, and letting the community feed the individual. Feeding, moreover, is not mostly a matter of ideas but of motivation. The way to unite the community of seeing with the community of feeling and the community of

[10] For these concepts see the author's *The Christian Understanding of God* (New York, Harper, 1951), chaps. II and III.

doing is through the Spirit. Without right relation to God, the community of being and the individual within this community are alienated from reality. Alienation requires justification, and results in rationalization. Rationalization is distortion of truth; education can become isolated from truth and effectiveness through rationalization; it can court falsehood. The only way to reunite the communities of seeing, feeling, and doing within the community of being is through the Spirit.

The Spirit is common concern for the inclusive good. To be in the Spirit requires that man be broken as a self-concerned being, and find instead his inclusive self in God. The Cross stands for this fact, and for God's act to this end; the Church stands for this kind of community. Apart from worship and redemption education cannot be whole or be made whole. The college and the Church need to be reoriented under God, to be restored to integrity and integration within His grace, and to become revitalized within their common purpose to serve the whole community. Vicarious love, the gift of God, needs to express itself within communities of concern. Thereby we shall acquire motivation through forgiveness, freedom from guilt complexes, and the release of creative concern. If we are to educate the whole man and to make society whole we had better, in any case, understand the indirect and vicarious ways of God's pedagogy. Within this area of our depth relations in God and in community there are vast resources for educational theory and practice that are as yet largely unexplored as well as untapped. Knowledge is obtainable within the community of seeing; motivation, however, needs right religion. Right motivation comes only within a community of being that is itself within the community of the Spirit. Education, then, not only is religious in essence, but also in a deep and new sense needs to learn how to relate itself effectively to the Christian faith.

Another aspect of God's teaching is His use of permissiveness and punishment. He amazes us by the measure of freedom He gives us. God does not climb up the tree with the man who is about to commit suicide in order to cut the rope that will break his neck! Nor does He stop the most destructive aspects of war. He did not hinder the plane from flying to Hiroshima, even though it went to drop the atom bomb. Nor will He, it seems, stop us from committing suicide as a civilization. People after people as well as person after person have perished because of their own willfullness. He lets people harm one another and themselves to insane lengths and bestial depths. The price we pay for freedom, indeed, sometimes seems far too great; we feel, in fact, rebellious against God, not because He restricts us, but because He sets us free beyond our wisdom and strength. Have we, however, a right to imitate God in this respect? Should we be more liberal with our students in their chances to fail? Do we stunt their growth and stultify their thinking when we prescribe, regulate, and prohibit their actions? Can we afford to copy God at this point? Or does God give freedom in what seems to us a reckless manner and measure, in order for us to become a mature community, count-ing on the mature to direct the freedom of the young? Have we a right so to stir up our students that some "crack up" while others awaken to new levels of initiative, insight, and commitment? Must Jesus ever produce his Judas as a by-product? Is it better to have no Jesus and no Judas, or is it better to have Jesus with the Judas?

Along with God's permissiveness comes punishment. The Bible declares that those whom God loves He punishes. With our more advanced ideas we should perhaps say that God disciplines those whom He accepts, or better, those who let themselves be accepted by Him. The Bible, in any case, says "chastens." At least God is no sentimentalist, if we are to judge by the facts of history and life. Earthquakes and floods, idiocy and cancer are not exactly light scoldings. Life is desperately hard for both sinner and saint. Jesus is crucified; Judas hangs himself. What shall we say of his kind of pedagogy?

An artificially produced situation where "anything goes" is not life. Permissiveness is balanced by punishment. Fear and duty move men as much as, if not more than, love. The absence of love activates men as much as its presence. Death motivates men as well as life. This context is obviously not the right place to discuss the problem of evil.[11] What we need to do here is to remind ourselves that God's education is tough as well as gentle; it is severe and

[11] For a full discussion of this theme, see the author's *Evil and the Christian Faith*.

abrupt as well as patient and gradual. The mills of God grind both fast and fine, for they grind at different speeds. Nor does punishment fit the crime any more than permissiveness fits worthiness. Somehow both have to be seen in the light of the school of God as a social institution where the whole final result is what counts. Does Christian love have the right to be as austere as God's method seems to suggest? Do we have a right to put the general welfare first, and to believe that the individual is sentimentally treated unless his life is judged unequivocally with reference to the total fellowship? Are the Communists nearer God's method in their ruthless pursuit of the social good and in their boundless faith in the good of the end result? Does our sentimentalized education indicate that we are at the disintegrating part of Pareto's circulation of the elite? Is our educational pussyfootedness due to a common fear of life that makes us want to shelter us all within sentimental unreality? Does it indicate that we neither know God nor have genuine hope for eternal life? Has education agonized over the meaning of the Cross as the central means of God's pedagogical process? These are serious questions, which we only raise at this point, but which Christian education cannot afford to by-pass.

Another aspect of God's method is the way He uses decision and growth. To live is to decide; that is one side of the picture. To live is to grow; that is the other side. Life is neither jerky with decisions nor smooth with growth. In every life, consciously and subconsciously, both aspects are present and powerful. To know how they are interrelated, and how they can be made to cooperate for wholeness and soundness of life, is part of the secret of effective education. We shall later discuss the decisional aspect of life under the topics of the existential, the dialectical, and the eschatological; we need not here anticipate our discussion. We should stress, nevertheless, the crucial nature of decision. Particularly important is the fact that we have to choose ultimates without being able to get rid of ambiguity. Education has to confront the problem of the meaning of its existence and work. It must help students to face reality and to decide about it. God forces us to decide. We cannot escape the responsibility of facing or fleeing from reality and of how we are to face it or flee from it. Should education at its higher reaches deliberately produce situations where choice becomes necessary? Should all teaching have decision as an end view? Should alternate ultimates be presented? Should all possible both-ands of present knowledge be given, while we still subordinate these to the stark either-ors of ultimate choice? Does the educator have a right to choose an ultimate, and deliberately to indoctrinate his students in this point of view both directly and indirectly? Does Incarnation mean that God comes indirectly, making indoctrination impossible, even while choice must be made in the light that we do have? Or does Incarnation mean that a clear ultimate Light has come, which when chosen can be used to illuminate all subjects, and make further choices unnecessary? Does this light illumine directly in the realm of personal and social relations, allowing smooth growth in knowledge, or are we beset by the need for continual decisions, even in the circle of that light?

Growth also poses problems. Surely vegetative growth is no adequate analogy for intellectual or spiritual growth; mere growth is no standard at all. Cancer is growth run riot. Not even the development of one's nature will do. Raw human nature needs to be remade before it can grow right. If education could draw out or lead out what is most surgingly deep in human nature it might want to put back speedily into the unconscious what it found! Growth for growth's sake is educationally bad policy. Even maturity needs to be most searchingly defined, including the sources of motivation that will effect and sustain it.

Perhaps we had better, instead, consider the kind of growth that is needed and the conditions for such growth. If we do, shall we turn our back on God's method? God makes a jungle; man makes a park.[12] God makes fields bloom with weeds, sprinkling them with useful grain or decorative flowers; man helps in producing fine fields white with harvest. God lets varieties remain small and undeveloped. Natural cross-fertilization is slow. Man develops varieties

[12] Dr. Micklem is not happy with our illustration! He wants us to use Oman's, to the effect that man makes the canal, but God the river. Both illustrations are true. We need ours!

into ever higher levels of fertility or beauty; thus crossing grains and flowers into undreamed success. When we think of God as our Teacher, we might in our folly be disposed to think His methods slow, perhaps (if the phrase be permitted) sloppy in comparison with ours. What can we learn from this fact? To imitate God? The physician imitates God *by co-operating* with Him. He becomes God's hand in administering penicillin to a pneumonia patient, who left to nature's way would die. The same way the educator becomes God's mind at work to help grow the best possible plants in God's garden. He exists to prepare the soil, to sow the good seed, to weed, to water, and to harvest. *The purpose of creation is to develop community. The fact that the doctor, the gardener, the educator are needed makes them men and makes for community.* To learn of God is, then, to learn His best ways, which He counts on us to develop.

Growth in Christian terms—to consider this type first—is growth in Christian community. It is growth in creative concern. It is growth in creative satisfaction. It is growth in satisfactory human relationships. It is growth in our knowledge, service, and enjoyment of God. Christian education exists to further such growth. But such growth is not like the growth of a cabbage. Christian growth requires that men cog into reality at a new level that requires decision. Christian growth requires that men be born again from above. Christian growth demands that there be in man a true seed to grow. Such growth has to depend on a degree of decision on man's part to change from his own ego-centeredness into God-centeredness, from moralism to grace, from fearful striving to growing trust.

God's love in man grows he knows not how. Man matures as life trains him to be wise. No number of decisions or kinds of decisions can make men grow. No commitment by itself procures maturity. All we can do is to seed and to water; God alone can give the increase—the increase through growth. Wise education in Christian terms therefore involves at least the understanding of man's nature, seeing the goal of community, and learning the conditions of growth. Later we shall have to deal with growth in community directly, as well as with human nature and education. Here we had better observe that if the Christian educator is to help God grow man as the gardener grows flowers, if he is to help heal men as the physician heals bodies, he should be alert to the basic fact that human growth depends on decisions, but that decisions do not by themselves produce growth. Evangelism in the deepest terms needs solid education, while education needs emotional and conative supplementation. Apart from the right decisions, right growth is blocked and left without right direction. To observe God's method with men, which requires a constant combination of growth and decision and decisions and growth, should make possible our deeper probing into the relation of grace to effort. It should also make us responsibly wise as to what extent we must lead to decision or let grow. It should let us come to understand and use the rhythm of growth not only of growth in natural terms but of growth in grace. It should let us into the secret as to what part of growth is intellectual, and what part is emotional and spiritual. It should let us pace more ably the different kinds of growth in their total interdependence.

Decision is choice of direction; growth is development of the direction; decision is up to us; growth is given us. As a man driving a car only occasionally makes decisions as to the road, and most of the time merely follows the road he chooses, even so life demands few basic decisions. Most of the time we follow along the path we have chosen. Growth demands right decisions, the choosing of significant directions; it also demands decisions of keeping on, even as a driver must steer even when he is following a road. Such steering is not decision as to direction, but is the sustaining of direction. Without basic decisions, life is drifting; without sustaining decisions, life cannot attain maturing growth. Only by growing can we arrive at new destinations where the more significant decisions challenge. The question for education is how to interrelate growth and decision.

Particularly important is this in the case of Christian education. Core subjects demand a stance. Education is, in fact, ever choosing its core. Yet all too often not enough time or care is given to the study of the basic decisions. An education that does not make ultimate choices explicit can be neither Christian nor adequate; an education that does not provide a maximum chance for intelligent and honest choice is not responsibly Christian. No absolute comes with external authority, or without intellectual ambiguity. Choice of stance is a decision of faith. To obscure this fact is to go contrary to fact; it is to lack insight into religious truth. Nevertheless education should make plain that there *are* choices. Indoctrination cuts athwart God's way of teaching.[13] *Faith is dependent on freedom to see as well as freedom to choose.*[14] The compulsory teaching of only one absolute with no need of serious choice involves a totalitarianism which thwarts God's way of teaching. To prohibit all teaching of faith except the Christian is to act contrary to Christianity; it is as far as possible to undo God's pedagogy, which uses precisely the openness and indirection of a world like ours. Good Christian teaching involves the best possible advocacy of our faith as far as it is allowed by facts and by educational authority. But it includes also the honest facing of the problems of fact and reason with which the Christian faith must necessarily contend.

This wrestling with the truth must be done responsibly according to the levels of the learners' development, but always with a view to the fullest and earliest possible maturity; in this way basic decisions are made possible within the best possible context of life and teaching. Secondary decisions as to the implications of this stance for other subjects studied must also be made clear and important. Christian teaching must major in decisions of concern: to accept concern; to study with concern; to act out what one sees with concern in actual life. If such direction is given to life and to study, growth will be in the right direction, and will lead to new decisions along the way as well as the continual decisions of following the

[13] In general we agree with Jeffreys in the following assertion, yet not altogether; more stress should be placed in the need for faith as choice: "Indoctrination is not an educational crime; it is an educational necessity, in religion as in table manners. The crime is to indoctrinate in such a way as to destroy the freedom and responsibility of the pupil. It is by no means impossible—and the world's greatest teachers from Socrates onwards have proved it to be the very heart of teaching—to present a strongly held faith in such a way as to challenge the beholder to come to terms with it on his own personal responsibility. That there is no necessary opposition between doctrine and freedom is clear when personal freedom is at the very heart of the doctrine." *Op. cit.,* p. 56.

[14] "That is to say, freedom is not permission to flout the truth but to regulate your life in knowledge of it." Harvard Committee, *op. cit.,* p. 105.

chosen road. Decisions, however, cannot substitute for gradual growth; our choosing can never replace the gift of growth. Our concern must be floated within God's concern; our choosing of life must be enveloped by God's living in us and through us. What is done for us must ever be understood as more basic than what is done by us. Education must lead to decision, commitment, conversion, acceptance of responsibility, the entering into concern for the common good. But such education must be relaxed and rested within the gratitude and adoration of worship; decision and growth need to be nourished by worship and strengthened by work.

The last aspect of God as Pedagogue that we are to consider is the fact that He educates the many through the few. A very small percentage of people think for themselves; the masses mostly follow. Of the few who think for themselves very few think creatively; most of them are merely trying to keep abreast of what is being thought. Of the very few who think creatively only the exceptional spirits think great thoughts that actually help direct the world into fuller truth. Few live deeply enough into reality to bring back with their minds a truer and more helpful view of it. There are charismatic personalities; they are the rarest of the rare. Such an order seems natural to life the way God made it. What does this fact mean for education?

From a Christian perspective the first implication ought to be the acceptance of God's way; we ought, that is, to do everything we possibly can to give the very few their greatest chance. The Russian method has been to advance the crest of every class, until at the most mature level the scholars and research students are given almost limitless opportunity for creative discovery. We have done something of the same by means of scholarships and research positions. We ought, however, to make a far more deliberate choice at this point; those who are endowed with creative capacity ought to be set aside by society and sponsored by it with the maximum wisdom. How this should be done is a problem; that it should be done is a fact. In no way should the top thinker or scholar be held back by the masses or even by the select few; he ought to be given encouragement and opportunity to go at his own rate and to work in his own way.

Special attention and opportunity ought then to be given to the larger number of the select few who can think for themselves. The masses ought not to retard or discourage them. Education for the many ought to be according to their ability and initiative. It should not slow down those who want to run. The top-flight thinkers and seers should, of course, work mostly for and through the select few; the select few ought to work for and through the masses. This is not special privilege, aristocracy, or a failure in democracy; this is the acceptance of the way God made the world and the manner in which He teaches. But the whole structure and attitude of education ought to be for the whole of society. Christian concern does not arrogate privileges to itself for the sake of personal ease, glory, or reward; Christian concern lives by concerned service for the inclusive good. Without concern the few fail their Christian responsibility. The refusal to accept selection on the part of the many, however, is due to the kind of envy that hurts the whole body of society. Just as special ability for the Christian involves special responsibility, even so belonging to the larger group requires acceptance of, and gratitude for, the few who are given special opportunity and are rendering selective service. Education and civilization are both continually hampered by a rebellion against God's kind of creation, the demand that all be alike in ability and reward. Acceptance of fact is a prerequisite for social improvement.

Does this mean that the American experiment to educate as many as possible as far as possible is a mistake? No wholesale answer is possible. The ideal is good.[15] After all, God's way of working is to leave responsibility for the many to the few. The practice, however, is generally bad. The top-flight education of the rare few has not been sufficiently appreciated or furthered; the select few have all too often had to drag along with the many through all grades of education, and thereby education for the total good has been decidedly hampered. Instead, first provision ought to be made for the rare exceptions; then opportunity for the select few. Thereupon appropriate means ought to be taken for the education of the many as

[15] We agree in general with Ortega y Gasset in the following assertion, but more stress ought to be placed on the need of those of ordinary endowment for dedicated men of exceptional competence: "It is therefore necessary to consider any institution with reference to the man of ordinary endowment. For him it is made, and he must be its unit of measure." *Op. cit.*, p. 63.

widely and as far as possible. As a matter of fact adult education through life seems the only adequate answer for an enlightened general public. No solution to Christian responsibility for all can be had, it seems, apart from a total reorientation of education for all for life. Modern techniques, using such means as radio, television, reading programs, and round tables, can help revolutionize life and radically enrich it. This is peculiarly true when leisure becomes a common and ample possession.

The kinds and conditions of education, whether for the few or for the many, ought, however, to differ radically. Even so, the partitions between all groups should be constantly open both ways, and the best of discoveries on any level ought to be made available in an appropriate form to the other levels. Transfer ought to be open from group to group, whether for good or for temporary worth. As it is now we educate the masses neither in learning, nor in tastes that give incentive to keep reading or listening to what is worth while. Most people, after they get through their formal schooling, read stacks of inferior printed matter and listen to programs of little or no cultural value. Standards and tastes can be set by the leaders and developed wisely for the many. Our education fails now because we have tried to redo God's way. We have hampered the few and have handicapped the many by not giving the few their best chance, and by not centering the education of the few on the needs of the many. We have tried to make all leaders, whereas the task with the many is to make them wise and willing followers. The Christian faith teaches discipleship; but in education we have given the major emphasis of it short shrift. We need to make the many learn to see what they can for themselves, and both to feel and to choose for themselves within the measure of their competence and training; but if we are to accept facts as they are, they need to be able to appreciate a seer and to follow in the right direction. The many need basic training in right ways and right motivation. If the leaders are then trained in concern for the common good, they will be able to lead the many into the better promised land. We try to make everybody a Moses or a Joshua. There is great need for knowing "followership." By following and finding the lives of the many are fulfilled. Thus God works, and so must we.

Chapter V

Learning from God

As FAR as we can, then, we should learn from God. Nature's way may not be best by itself. We have already suggested that God leaves it to us to use nature's ways. We can intensify them, as in competent stockbreeding. We can redirect them, as in medicine. We can stimulate them, as in religion. Education can help us to understand them better, and to become more willing to use them aright. The following suggestions are intended as signposts in the direction of seeing the implications of our analysis of the idea of God as Educator. They can be no more; they dare be no less.

For our analysis of indirection and vicariousness we suggest the following practical counterpart. Instead of lectures as the backbone of the educational method, we propose, as far as is practicable, to center learning on the case method. The heart of this method is learning indirectly and vicariously.[1] By the case method we mean the presenting for solution of problems not artificially constructed, but as exemplified by actual cases from real life. They can be drawn from history or from contemporary situations. Generally the choices made in the case and their consequences ought to be known. In some instances the opportunities or threats that face the group that is studying, or some other modern groups, ought to be tackled; if

[1] Though we cannot fully acquiesce in Allport's startling statement, it no doubt leads a long way in a right direction: "What is taught turns out in the long run to be less important than the manner of teaching." *Op. cit.*, p. 31.

this is done both wisely and thoroughly, there is a real learning situation. The indirection of life ought, however, to be preserved and its vicariousness observed.

Perhaps some such method as the following would work. Before any studying is done on the case, each person ought to analyze it for himself. Thereupon he should withdraw into deep and prolonged contemplation of possible choices. His whole creative self ought thereby to be released. If the case is vital and significant for human living, no Christian can escape the necessity for the closed closet and the open heart. Faith and intellect, devotion and study ought here to be joined and help to make the thinker a whole man.

After this withdrawal, the student should have recourse to theoretical knowledge. The meaning and implications of the case ought to be studied with close, almost riveted, attention. All possible illustrative knowledge ought to be focused in the case, appropriated, and applied; there must be no slighting of real and thorough knowing. Knowledge as a social act here requires personal appropriation. The general lessons of history beg for concrete application. Each student ought to be thoroughly trained in how to gather source material for theory. He should know how knowledge is classified for the purpose in hand, or in how many ways it may have been classified. Yet time is wasted, of course, if each time each student must find the relevant material. The object is not skill in research, therefore, but organic learning. Special resource leaders should have made ready the fullest possible resources for theoretical analysis. Most of this material would no doubt be historical. The best contemporary thinking, moreover, should reflect as far as possible the special relevance of theory for the time of study.[2] Thus the realism of historical experience ought to enforce the freedom of each present time to learn for itself in its own setting.

After the personal preparation of each case, and after the finding and using of theoretical content to the maximum, past and present, the students should come together to hear an expert resource leader

[2] "The teacher's duty, apart from his share in the provision of these experiences by prescribed tasks, is to step in at critical moments and to perform a double act of interpretation: the first is the interpretation of the experience to the child, and the second is the interpretation of the child to himself." Jacks, *op. cit.*, p. 56.

analyze the case. Lecturing would then be not on some subject foreign to the students, with a good deal of time and effort lost for lack of communication; rather, lecturing would be part of a total learning situation, where all the participants as far as practicable would be acquainted with the maximum knowledge available. Naturally the student situation would preclude his having the thorough preparation of the professor, who has spent many years in reading and thinking about these cases. Nevertheless the best selective thinking would have been read by all, and some real thinking should have been done by each. Those who had truly meditated and used the wisdom of communion in the closed closet would also contribute an open mind and a concerned spirit.

The lectures should summarize the case, point out whatever historic theory bears on it, and then make a strongly Christian attack on the problem. In this way the Christian faith would be brought fullface to the situation. The lecturer would certainly have to guard against personal imperialism or aggression under the guise of Christian analysis. The purpose of the lecture should be not only to personalize the problems in terms of a human lecturer confronting the group, but also to lead the students to decisive thinking in the light of the Ultimate.[3] No lecturer would have done his duty who did not both confront his students with the necessity of making their own choices and exemplify before them how a choice can be made in the light of the Absolute. Humility and respect for others under God ought always to be part of the motivational context within which the choice is faced and made. Such confrontation of the case would acknowledge in education the decisional nature of all spiritual and social knowledge. Naturally we are not now dealing with mere information on the level of objectivity; such knowledge would either be acquired by the background reading for case study, or else would belong to departments where the present kind of analysis would not apply. Though some vocational techniques, mathematics, and science as mere physical fact would be exempted, the reach of this method would be amazingly inclusive. An intelligent use of the case method

[3] "For the proper object of school and college is moral maturity." Chalmers, *op. cit.*, p. 255.

would make strongly vibrant many areas that are often dully studied. How far the method could be extended we cannot now determine. In any case, the whole orientation would have to start slowly, painstakingly, and within small experimental areas.

When the students have studied the case itself, meditated and analyzed, read and digested whatever theoretical knowledge bears on the case, and listened to an expert open up the case in terms of his fuller knowledge and more mature wisdom, then, for the sake of personal decision as well as for a more focused learning situation, they ought to break up into several discussion groups. These ought to meet immediately after the resource leader has finished. The groups should be small; they ought to comprise no more than half a dozen or so students. Each group ought to have a leader. If education travels at two basic speeds, for instance, those who are the rare few with special privileges and opportunities ought to carry the burden of the more careful preparation—in analysis, in medita-tion, in preparatory readings, and possibly in intimate discussion with the professor before his lectures. The discussion leader should be trained in bringing out the best possible discussion. Group dynamics without personal and group preparation both in spirit and in content becomes drearily empty. Group dynamics under carefully prepared circumstances can release the creativity of group thinking. The community of inquiry, if it is real, open, and committed, can do amazing things. The most important aspect of the group is that it must neither be over against the speaker seeking a false inde-pendence, nor supinely yielding to the speaker's analysis. A far fuller Christian analysis and way of commitment than that of the speaker may come from some group.

The groups should not reassemble right away. The main result of each group should be recorded and exchanged with the other groups. Then the professor ought to be advised of the result. The students and he ought then to re-examine their own thinking and commit-ment in privacy. Thereupon they ought to reassemble, with the pro-fessor giving his response to the different reactions, and each group discussing for the final time, for these purposes, what had been learned in theory and practical commitment from the total study of the case. Perhaps some of this process could be integrated with social occasions, such as teas or meals or social evenings. In many instances the same case could be handled interdepartmentally and then subjected to cross-fertilization. These instances particularly could be geared into social occasions with a dead-earnest purpose. The social could precede, and be mixed in with the intensive purposive work as relaxation.

Certain cases, for instance, could be studied together in this way of separating and coming together by varied fields. A historic case, for instance, has been written up as literature. The same case has interesting psychological angles. As anthropology or sociology it offers a good case study. Certainly the philosophical aspects of the situation would be many and weighty. The fine arts could often light up a subject by their insights. Religion would not be worth its salt if it did not have its dimension of analysis. Could language departments supply illuminating material from other cultures? Undoubtedly many of the fields would have congruent interests. Ethics would have common areas with philosophy and religion, and many elements of social psychology would fit into many departments. The curriculum could become both unified and yet diversified by such studies. Interested groups could be formed by members of the university in mathematics, science, or administration. By so studying each department could function for itself, while yet learning and contributing to the other fields. The core courses, in particular, could be related in his way. Since some core courses would be required of all students, whether in science, mathematics, or professional courses like engineering, all students would benefit from the unifying yet variegated power of the case-method approach. No formal conclusions would be drawn, of course, by the total university, except in so far as professors and students alike, thus learning together, in concluding stages might want to let small groups of the most qualified in spirit and academic competence think through the case from "the wholist" point of view. These groups could then offer certain common observations and suggestions for commitment.

No action, however, should be considered the true way; the university is not an action group, nor should it prescribe final decisions.

Its work ought to provide the best possible road markers to truth and to individual and group commitment. All care ought to be taken, however, not to coerce minority opinion spiritually or intellectually, whether of groups or of individuals. Professional and vocational training should profit from participating, but have plenty of time for its own basic work. Similarly each department must study its own method, theory, and content from within its own presuppositions, up to the maximum limits of methodological efficacy. Nevertheless, having the case method as central to the university as far as possible would integrate education, would stimulate cross-fertilization, would combine organically the theoretical or content aspects of study with the decisional and the practical, would focus the study for each relevant field, and would make necessary the stringent application of the principle of economy in education. Transmission from the past would have to be focused in the significant. Creative discovery would result from the discriminate knowledge of the past combined with meditation. Best of all, the social and the personal development and appropriation would go hand in hand throughout the entire study.

Some would want to know what constitutes a case. This question would have to be determined by the resource professors, whom we are to describe a little later in this chapter. For what it is worth, a narrow case study might be illustrated in terms of an actual law case recounted by a lawyer in Minnesota. A farmer's widow rented her farm and some hogs to a thrifty worker with many children. He worked the land well, and paid his rent faithfully. The first year of the Depression not enough money came in for him to pay the rent. He felt that he had to feed his children. He thereupon mortgaged the pigs, paid the widow, and kept going. But when the Depression continued and became even more severe, he could not in spite of competence and thriftiness continue to pay her and meet his own necessary expenses. Nor could he find another job. He gave up all his personal possessions in the attempt to keep going. When the bank foreclosed the mortgage and took the pigs, the widow sued him for stealing the pigs, which were her own source of income. What are the social, psychological, legal, moral, and spiritual factors in this case? What are the economic aspects? What could have been done in the narrow sense? What needs to be done in the larger picture?

For larger cases we might possibly consider such live issues as whether the Civil or Revolutionary War was necessary or desirable, or the relation between the rise of Christianity and the fall of the Roman Empire. For modern cases we could take such wide topics as those of the Conference of Science, Philosophy, and Religion: Learning and World Peace, Freedom and Authority in our Time, Conflicts of Power in Modern Culture, or Symbolism and Communication provided the topic is centered naturally in concrete cases. The Prohibition Amendment, for another example, offers ample scope for co-operative study. Each case would have to be concentrated, focused, delimited, and directed before being presented to any group. The preliminary reading would have to be most carefully chosen in literature, history, social science, or theoretical knowledge. Each topic would become alive in some historic case that embodied the crux of the problem.

The topic of permissiveness and punishment is one with wide application; on this topic we shall suggest merely a few ideas. A Christian education should stop holding the student's hand and let him mature. A good deal of counseling, whether by professor, administrator, or committee, should be discouraged. Higher education is a period for maturation and for the serious development of responsibility; by this time each student ought to stand pretty much on his own feet, and need no one to lead him. Student-centered education to a considerable extent has been centered not so much in student welfare as in the neurotic anxiety of faculty members. Much of it has been well-meant, and where necessary, preventively or remedially, is still the right thing to do. We shall never develop mature interest in truth, work, and commitment, however, except as we let the students become sturdily independent. If we become *really student-centered* within God's truth, we shall come to see this fact ever more clearly. Students in higher education need to be left alone as far as possible and to be trusted, if they are ever to become real persons, ripe for mature community responsibility.

In the second place, course credit, and, as far as possible, course work ought to be eliminated. The student ought to be free to work for himself for a total goal, and at the end take total gain and total loss. Passing courses by cramming, only to forget what has been learned almost as quickly, is the chief academic sin of America. Credits pile up and earn graduation, even while we turn out mostly hollow men with a penchant for superficial ways of doing things. No lectures ought ever to be given, we believe, for mere information; that can be had from books. Students spend too much time sitting passive at lectures, and then reading about what they already have heard or are to hear. All knowledge that can be gained from books ought perhaps to be put into books, and given the students in as adequate form as possible. Books can be supplemented by records, motion pictures, or television. History in this way can become much more graphic and easy to grasp as well as to remember. Records and pictures can also be played and displayed over and over again. Besides, only the best thinkers and teachers in the field need then hand out information. How much time is wasted by droves of professors trying to say the same thing, seldom in an original way at that, and what time is spent by the professors on polishing lectures, or by the students on lectures given in a slipshod manner. Most importantly, the students need no longer be subjected to the hearing of only one man's view on the subject. Even the small college could have the top views expressed. Solid information, in any case, can be given far more efficiently by books and all kinds of audio-visual aids than by lectures. Most of the work for the different departments, whether in method or in content, can be presented in this way. History can be read as history. Eighteenth-century poetry, for instance, can be read and digested without professors, as far as knowledge goes. Lectures should be limited to the presentation of mature reflection on case studies, to the stimulation of decisive thinking, and to the rare front-line thinking of the creative edge of knowledge. Lectures should thus supply vitamins rather than be depended on for nutrition. When students are not put enough on their own, the result is an overwhelming neglect of education as soon as the diploma has been awarded.

As to punishment or discipline, we need mention only a couple of matters. Punishment should be social in nature—if we are to learn from God. The tower falls on the innocent as well as on the guilty. Bombs drop on saints as well as on sinners. Cancer strikes the noble as well as the base. The Chinese coolies, it is reported, have for years carried without theft unlocked cases loaded with valuables. The reason for such dependability is the fact that they know that if one breaks the code of honesty all are punished for the crime. No easy generalization can be made about this social truth, but from the perspective of the Christian faith it is easy to see that the Kingdom is a social, not an individualistic, conception. If we seek the Kingdom first *as individuals*, we may end up even as Jesus did. Even though he promised that "all other things" would be added to those who put God's things first, he himself met a criminal's death, poor and forsaken. Peter, who listened to Jesus' promises, died a martyr, we are told. It is everlastingly true, on the other hand, that if the statement about first seeking the Kingdom be universalized, history *as a whole* is in accord with our response to God. The seeking of the Kingdom is a social commandment, with social rewards and social punishment. In our unchristian individualism we have often acted as though the individual ought to have been punished for his own crime with no involvement of the community. Such severing of the individual from the community hurts both him and the community. As a matter of fact, the offender needs most of all to belong to a solid community, to have the sense that good and evil are social categories with social consequences. An academic group needs to feel that it is a solid community.

A wise college president said that when he first took office he tried to punish offending students with a view to their own rehabilitation; he made each one his focus and end. As he matured in office, however, he found out that both the individual and the community are helped the most by a nonsentimental discipline based on community responsibility. What is best for the community must be done. The individual should be shown how this alone is also his own best. Herein could be implications, too, for the grading of students! If marks were a matter not only of individual but of class rating, would the superior students be more likely to help the ones who struggled at the bottom? This whole problem needs mature rethinking throughout the whole length of the educational scale. The question is exceedingly complex. If we are to learn from God's way of doing things, in any case, it seems certain that all discipline should be unsentimentally social in nature and application, but by a society that was concerned with the good of each. Individual faults and failings affect the group. A Christian group responds with concern for each person if he will repent in deeds as well as in promise. Lack of response should mean rigorous exclusion from the educational society. In any case, respect for the educational enterprise should involve a resolute determination to expel whoever failed to measure up in responsibility to the privilege conferred on him.

Punishment should always have the whole academic community in mind. The forgiveness of the individual, as in the shepherd's seeking the hundredth sheep, is an expression of personal love, not of community discipline. God forgives the one expelled if he will repent. Individuals in the whole academic community, and especially administrative officers as far as practicable, should be personally concerned with excluded members. But the fruits of repentance should be allowed to ripen and be tested, before any individual is restored to the academic community; membership is a holy privilege, to be held in high respect. The Christian rule is theoretically simple: be concerned equally with the individual and the community. The practice, however, is hard. The simplest rule is perhaps to take the historic process as a general guide, and therefore to stress the social nature of punishment. No Christian community, however, can sacrifice the one for the many; totalitarian rule does that. Yet Christianity is certainly not individualism—no nominalistic Christ-centered therapy. Concern for the individual there must be; respect for his freedom and rights there must be. But in the long last, the solidarity of the community, if high and holy, alone provides even for the erring individual the genuine sense of belonging, of breaking fellowship, and of the repentance and restoration that can make life most deeply real.

Strictness should also match freedom in the final testing. In a sense the comprehensive examinations at the end of the student's educational career ought to constitute a kind of "last judgment"; the total life of the student ought here to be examined in a conclusive manner. Possibly the best method is an exhaustive list of examinations with no pressure of time to prevent thorough testing. How long these tests ought to be—certainly a matter of weeks—must be discovered by experimentation. Here if anywhere the case method ought to be used. Such testing would reveal thinking as well as information. For the most part they ought to be in writing. The examiners should not be members of the college or the university, but should come from a distance; by having outside examiners the educational institution as well as the students are tested. The examinations in the first place ought to be intensively a matter of actual knowledge. There is no substitute, for example, for the memorizing of data. Beyond that, however, they ought to test the student's personal insight and judgment. Besides, there ought to be developed—and we have already real beginnings—sociometric, psychometric, and spiritumetric examinations. If such examinations are sufficiently skillful and understanding, and based on democratic presuppositions, more than an academic profile of each student would result; there would be a picture of him as a whole. These final examinations ought generally to be the student's only chance. If he has had years of freedom and stands ready to be thus comprehensively examined, he should stand or fall with these protracted tests. Conceivably there could be the exceptional circumstance where mercy ought surely to glory against judgment, but the whole system would fall unless severity matched freedom.

In the previous chapter we discussed the relation between decision and growth. We said that decision is choice of direction, while growth is the pursuit of it. We saw how decision is basic to life; decision determines the kind of growth we are to have. Whether the decision is right and the growth that follows from it, depends on whether we are in line with reality. We are organically preconditioned for growth in grace, growth in concern, growth in community, growth within the will of God. Only decisions that choose this direction can be fully adequate. Only growth that carries through such a direction can be healthy. But how within the facilities of higher education can we implement concretely such decision and growth?

We have already suggested that the main function of lecturing should be not informational but decisional. We have to be careful at this point. Lecturing for decision should not be preaching; that is the task of the church. Lecturing for decision should not be indoctrination; so to lecture is to destroy vital education. Small colleges of liberal Protestant persuasion produce proportionately more scientists than do those identified with Roman Catholicism or Protestant fundamentalism. Both of these religious bodies know all the answers on authority; their general atmosphere of living and thinking reflects this fact. When a person from such an environment is plunged into an atmosphere of free thought his world is shaken; then he has to fight his way into creative, independent thinking. The feel for faith thereupon becomes supplemented by the feel for truth. *Lectures ought therefore to be neither hortatory nor confirmatory;* they ought, rather, to be existential, in the sense that they lay bare the necessity of choice and the conditions of choice. As we have seen, ambiguity is a purposed part of the Christian faith; any institution, book, or creed that promises ready-made certainty violates the Christian faith. It not only violates the faith but frustrates it at its center. Faith requires the struggles of seeing and the risks of choice. Faith and reason require each other organically at the center of their functions. Neither is possible, in any authentic sense, without the other; and such mutuality is a matter of a continued interfunctional relationship.

Such lecturing for decision ought to require existential participation on the part of the listeners, according to the nature of the subject. Not all teaching is theological. Theology requires faith explicitly. Philosophy is basically contextual, whereas science is factual. Literature combines the aesthetic with thought. All subjects, however, are attitudinal. No lecturer ought to neglect the relating of his subject and of his person to the total perspective of education.

The Christian faith has its bearing on all subjects. Mathematics, for instance, deeply affects philosophy, and who can read White-head's *Mathematics and the Good* without sensing the relation between formal order and the ways of God? Each subject taught, to be sure, has a field and principles of its own that are semi-autonomous. Its own truth is right for its own purposes; its own findings are appropriate for its own field. Even though reality cannot be reduced to wholeness as such, wholeness comprises genuineness of distinction. Nevertheless we live in a universe; there *is* a whole. Education consists of fact, thought, and faith. All need one another. The closer a subject comes to the field of faith, how-ever, the more that subject leads to the decisional approach: the demand that action be in accord with reality. The decisional ap-proach ought also to include the relational. Every subject ought to see its truth for what it is worth, but to see it also in relation to other fields and to truth as a whole. In general, of course, the more the field consists mostly of factual knowledge the more it can be learned from books or records; the less need therefore there is for lecturing. The more the subject, on the other hand, is part of an inquiry for better living in the light of life, the more the lectures will have decision as an end, i.e., the making clear the necessity for choice and making objective the pros and cons of any choice.

Another basic aid to decision is the chapel. What kind of chapel is possible depends, of course, on what kind of college or university we have to do with. In Christian education the chapel always stands central on the campus. It should do so geographically; it must do so educationally. By the chapel is meant more than a building; by the chapel is meant the basic attitude of the educational institution toward the ultimate. The campus worships whether it wants to or not. The more education is right the more it is Christian, and the more it is Christian the more the chapel stands at the dead center of higher education as the most vital Reality. Worship is more than meditation. Worship is more than forgiveness and restoration. Worship is even more than celebration. Worship at its center is a personal relation to Deity that cannot be had apart from decision. To worship aright is to decide aright about life as a whole, its meaning and conduct.

Naturally there should be group worship and personal devotions. Both smaller cells and private worship require basic decision. God never becomes real except to decision. But significant decision is never realized except relative to the patience of growth. God's decision for us is central. Worship is a gift of grace; it cannot be bid. Nevertheless, our secondary decision can accept God's basic decision for us. God has decided to make us for community. No one, therefore, can worship rightly alone who does not worship with other people. A Christian worship creates Christian community, whether that worship is a matter of group or individual experience. On the other hand, there is no group worship, in the deepest Christian sense, which does not consist of the worship by people who have learned to worship by themselves. Social experience is no substitute for personal decision. Community decision to be important presupposes depth of personal decision. Worship, both social and personal, magnifies the decisional aspect of life.

Possibly worship cells should be supplemented by study and action groups that would be decisional in nature. Study groups already exist within our proposed kind of case study; there would therefore be needed no new groups of this kind. Already these groups are directed to study from the point of view of existential participation. Indirection and vicariousness should both lead to more than the internalization of group education; they should both be conducive to serious decision on the part of the individual. Possibly, however, there could also be definite action groups. The Haystack group in Williams College decided concerning the future, and the American foreign missions movement was born. John Wesley and a small group in Oxford decided to live out the Christian life right then and there; they sacrificed time and money to visit those in prison and to help those in need. Out of such group actions came vital social impetus. In many parts of the world the students are now aglow with concern for the world. Even in America there are action groups in higher education that add to, rather than detract from, the seriousness of the academic life. On this point, to be sure, we need to be exceedingly careful. Education is the mind of the world at work. It should be allowed to be mostly mind rather than hands; otherwise its function in the economy of civilization is spoiled. Action groups, nevertheless, can have specific tasks that both are of help and give practical outlet to Christian concern. Such action delivers the believer from the feeling of make-believe and even from hypocrisy. For the most part action groups in higher education ought of course to be anticipatory; action groups are mostly preparatory for later life. A mock United Nations Assembly can be real preparation for serious political life. Political elections on the campus can become important educational activity.

As to growth—to turn to the other side of the same question—it is a gift from God. He alone gives the increase; yet we have both to sow and to water. We sow by providing educational content; we water by providing the conditions for creative appropriation. Most important of these conditions is prayer. No Christian faith is vital apart from communion with God. No communion with God is possible as a continued relationship, but prayer is its very life. Prayer, when it is Christian, reduces destructive tension and produces constructive tension. Prayer, when it is according to God's will, motivates the will with creative concern. Prayer, when it is through God for the common, inclusive good, provides the faith that releases the adventuresome reason that is yet within the control of Christian truth and responsibility. Prayer is partly decisional, partly a struggle. Most of the time, however, prayer is inspirational, the inbreathing of God's will and way. The first creative condition for growth is therefore Christian prayer. It is the Holy Spirit of God who gives the grace of growth. General growth is part of the created order; a tree and a child both grow without the use of prayer. But growth in Christian community needs prayer. Growth in constructive concern is helped by the right kind of prayer. Personal maturation is helped by prayer. Real prayer in Christ's spirit gives impetus—to use Allport's analysis—to self-expansion, to self-objectification, and to integration; or, in our own phrasing, prayer gives growth in existential urgency, in organismic harmony of being and seeing, in eschatological conviction, and in dialectic sensitivity, wisdom, and concern.

Besides prayer we need devotional reading. To live with the saints is to open our lives to their secret. Devotional reading should also comprise great biography. To live with outstanding lives in many walks of life is to let the contagion of the unfamiliar lure us into its good. Imagination is kindled; sympathy is born; compassion is generated; growth is stimulated. Indirection and vicariousness triumph in right biographical reading. Devotional experiences can also be mostly meditational. The meditation that the student should perform within the case method to prepare for existential understanding is an integral part of the preparation for growth; reflection is a straight avenue to valuable growth. As long as reflection runs heavy with responsible concern the car will stay on the main avenue of growth. Reflection is thus both a way and a means, an opportunity and a development of capacity. Prayer, devotional reading, and meditation can all be combined in carefully planned retreats by small numbers from the college. If retreats became an indispensable part of Christian education they could be improved year by year. Many smaller graduate schools have found retreats of genuine help in the deepening of the reflective attitude, as well as in enabling the faculty and students to know each other more deeply.

Still another way to encourage growth is to encourage group thinking, especially within an easy, informal setting. With real reason Whitehead writes that he became educated by participating in discussion night after night in the Senior Common Room at Trinity College, Cambridge. Anyone who has had the experience knows how very stimulating to growth such cross-fertilization can be. Very likely no mere imitation at this point on our part will work, yet the principle is entirely sound. Careful experimentation, however, could undoubtedly at this point accomplish educational marvels. The social and the educational would have to be mixed in the right proportion and under the proper leadership. The more decisively Christian the college or university, the more also the spiritual dimension could become a genuine part of the experience.

Thus, though growth cannot be commanded, the conditions for growth can be controlled and encouraged.

As to concrete suggestions for the handling of the few and the many, we speak with exceptional caution. When we say "the many," of course, we are not talking about the masses who cannot assimilate first-class higher education. Everything possible ought to be done for the masses along some way of continued part-time education. Vocational competence ought to be given first consideration, and after that the reception by the many of as much knowledge and wisdom as possible. Some system of adult education, perhaps even of special opportunity for occasional return to residential conditions, might prove very helpful for them, and therefore to the profit also of society as a whole. Denmark has pioneered well in this area of education. This problem, however, is not part of our assignment. When we speak of the few and the many we discuss the rare charismatic few, and the general run of students in higher education. Since the many are discussed in all we write about higher education, we confine our remarks here to the rare few.

Obviously all possible doors ought to be opened to the rare few. They ought to be put in personal touch with the leading thinkers in their field, regardless of educational barriers. Perhaps they could be released to travel to whatever parts of the country or the world could most fully satisfy their needs. Institutions should not be possessive about their careers; these students should not be limited by pride of institution. As long as they continue their creative advance they ought to be given all necessary financial help. It is good sense to spend many times the money on the few who can really develop into top-flight leaders than on the ordinary student, however worthy. Besides personal contact, the student of charismatic ability and character ought also to be given the chance to mix freely with the men who are already out in the profession for which he is preparing. By actual participation in the concrete problems he is to face later he is able to relate his brilliant theoretical knowledge to the world as it is, and thus become deepened and given a chance to mature.

Perhaps the deepest problem with regard both to the rare few and to exceptional students in general who alone would go on to higher education is the prevention of a closed caste. University education, if severely restricted, would foster a strong temptation to feelings of superiority; the growth of pride would then preclude the growth of creative concern. The whole stress in higher education ought therefore to be that privilege is measured by responsibility. Of him to whom much is given much is required. If a community lacks enough Christian motivation to give its exceptional students unusual opportunity, it will help to suffocate its best talent; by so doing it will seriously hamper its own living. If, on the other hand, Christian motivation is not strong enough to withstand the temptation of pride and power on the part of the highly educated over the rest, society as a whole will be handicapped. Concrete steps can be taken to make the many want to enable the few to become well prepared and to listen to their leading; on the other hand, other steps can be taken to make the few want to live humbly with their fellow men under God for the common good. The steps may be spiritual, social, and motivational and a matter of participation in specific social situations during and after training. If the philosophy of life is right on the part of both groups, social expectations can build up strong motivational directives. We profess no concrete wisdom as far as this problem goes, but it is one that calls for devoted and competent study.

A most important consideration for both these chapters is that educational wisdom requires educational transformation to be undertaken carefully, slowly, and with competent experimentation. Both the deciding on cases and the actual starting of this comprehensive process required mature patience. We have learned a good deal about human nature and about educational processes without requiring a basic re-evaluation to accord with what we have learned. Education has for the most part drifted down the stream of history, for deliberate change is hard and costly. No community of common seeing—even if such a community could be achieved—could successfully cope with the communities of feeling and of doing, unless such seeing was empowered and nourished within man's most essential community—that of the Spirit. The process of change that we envisage would be so basic that at every step there would have to be courage to go on and courage to learn from actual experience. Part of our seeing, of course, would be drastically improved and altered, as others would learn from actual experimentation along the lines of the educational possibilities that have been suggested. We have in mind not a few years only, but rather the work of a lifetime and of the generations. Confident beginnings can be made, and in many instances the way may be cleared for practical experimentation. Education, however, is as wide and as deep as life. Courage must combine with patience, and seeing with many failures, before there can be accomplished an experimentally verified educational process that shall deliver us from some of our present faults and usher us into better ways. At the same time it may be that the fullness of time is ripe with respect to education, and that a creative thrust forward in education may be synchronized with a whole new upsurge of creative civilization. Considerable appropriation of truth depends not so much on our being theoretically right as on our being educationally adequate *at the right time*.

Chapter VI

Community and Communication

THIS chapter concerns the availability for education of the Christian faith—not its general, but its specific relevance. In present-day higher education how can the Christian faith be most effectively communicated? We have already surveyed the Christian faith; the problem now is how to relate that faith to our actual colleges and universities. We take for granted that the Christian faith is more than doctrine, that it is, in fact, the promise and the power for a new kind of community within the will of God. We assume that to teach the Christian faith is to make actual not only Christian seeing but Christian living. Education of course is mostly a matter of the mind in relation to the whole person and the whole community. The intellectual aspect of it is thus primary. Nevertheless, no adequate view of the function of the intellect can be had apart from its organic relation to living decisions. Therefore this chapter has been entitled "Community and Communication." The question we are asking is how the Christian community can be actualized within different kinds of educational communities. What are the different kinds of communication that are required?

Analytically on the human level, the first fact to observe is that no community of seeing can become effective without right relation to the community of feeling and the community of doing. Thought without emotion and will is stillborn; thought driven by emotion and directed by the will has incalculable power. Analytically we must recall that only the community of being as a whole can generate creative changes. The more these changes are lighted and led by the Spirit the more satisfactory they are. How can vertical transcendence, God's will, most fully gear into our most relevant horizontal transcendence, the momentum of education? How can God's will for the fully inclusive and freely creative community, the symbol of which is the true Church, become genuinely effective within the thought patterns and modes of behavior that are historically available to education at any one time?

Truth at its deepest is a matter of personal and communal relations. Nature as impersonal exists to make these relations possible; nature must therefore be studied and used. Our real problem in education, however, is how community can be achieved. All knowledge is for the sake of personal and community decisions, growth, and relations. How then can knowledge as a whole rightly generate personal and communal well-being? In what kind of community are channels open, and of what kind? How can culture be internalized and personalized, and how can personalities transform culture? Perhaps the distinction between culture internalized and personalized is critical for the understanding of communication. In one sense man is a nodule of culture; in another, he is the personal origin of culture. The two processes interpenetrate and interact; the relation is at the same time deeply impersonal and personal. From one point of view a man is what he has been made, the totality of the influences that have shaped him. The thoughts create the thinker; experiences, the man. From another point of view the thinker creates the thought, and man is the subject of his experiences.[1] The rational and moral levels are important for effective communication; the vague compressiveness of life goes deeper, and affects life and culture on a more profound level. Communication between the two levels operates mostly by means of symbols that are emotionally and conatively loaded. In the wider sense the Word requires the Sacrament. The fact is that only by the under-

[1] An able biologist declares that man is not social by nature but gregarious: "At any level, human society is an association superimposed by human intelligence upon the primordial tendency to solitary life." Arthur W. Lindsey, "Biology," in *College Teaching and Christian Values,* Paul M. Limbert, ed. (New York, Association Press, 1951), p. 47.

standing of the kind of person and the kind of community with which we are dealing can we see how central to communication are the symbols of communication. Religion is attitudinal in nature; communication is also more attitudinal than we imagine. An adequate religion should therefore know how to communicate concretely with diverse communities of education.

In the American setting there are very roughly three types of colleges or universities. No scheme of analysis, of course, can more than serve as a basis for recommendations. The first is the openly and fervently Christian college. It is often fundamentalist or near-fundamentalist, and all too often educationally weak. There is also the generally "Christian" college. Sometimes it is church-supported. Such colleges vary in the degree both of Christian commitment and of academic attainment. Many struggle hard to be genuinely Christian; many are religiously slack. None is Christian, of course, in the full sense of a total community of converted and completely committed people—administration, faculty, and students.[2] At least no college known to the writer fulfills the description which he will give of a fully Christian college. Sometimes the college has cut itself off from the Church entirely or for the most part. Often it is educationally strong, but gives mostly lip service—if that—to the Christian faith. It may be strong in science, the humanities, languages, social science, and even in philosophy, while having no really first-rate department of religion! The tone of the college may also be outright secular, in imitation of the large secular universities. These generally secular universities, along with outright secular colleges, constitute the third group of American institutions of higher education. Often, however, there is more hospitability to the Christian faith, or at least to religion, in these secular institutions than in so-called Christian colleges. What are the factors in each case that make for a certain type of community *in some identifiable sense,* and how can the truth of the Christian faith be most effectively communicated?

In the avowedly Christian college of the conservative kind there

[2] For an excellent discussion cf. Kenneth I. Brown's *Not Minds Alone* (New York, Harper, 1954), chap. 2, "Can Education Be Meaningfully Christian?"

often tends to be a defensive attitude toward the progressive edge of higher education. There frequently tends also to be the rationalization of an in-group minority status. On the one hand, there is an aggressive parading and enforcing of Christian faith and standards; perhaps there are even public attestations of orthodoxy in faith and mores. All the same, there is usually an unhealthy desire for the approval of the more secular colleges and universities. This is evidenced not only by the drive for accreditation, but especially by a neurotic concern with any complimentary statements that out of context can be used to bolster up in-group morale. The community is united by a deep search for God's will, channeled very narrowly through a particular set of beliefs and practices. Prayer is wont to be made! The chapel services engender enthusiasm. Testimony meetings are at times a regular practice, officially or unofficially sponsored. The group, feeling insecure, is therefore both defensive and aggressive. The community has a narrow base and an enviable zeal, but not the zeal according to knowledge. Some of the deepest Christian motivations are nevertheless developed, which often launch out to wider contacts and become the driving power within many liberal movements in religion, or become constructive and transforming concerns in all the dimensions of human life and civilization. We have more reason to thank these small openly Christian colleges than we usually imagine.

At the same time, these near-fundamentalist or fundamentalist colleges are more often than not problems to themselves and to the world. They lack an *open* theology, and therefore fear to face fact. Their standard of authority is usually external and traditional, rather than truth as found through the community of competent inquiry. For an educational institution to hide behind an authoritarian standard is intellectual inhibition; the whole fiber of scholarship is weakened by such hiding. The sense of truth suffers; the integrity of inquiry is vitiated; with the loss of integrity comes loss of integration. Religion becomes falsely zealous, rather than truly possessed of a healthy motivation of concern for truth and community. We believe, on the other hand, that these conservative colleges may grow away from their narrow basis, learning that God's inclusive love will stand the strictest tests in any competition for an adequate ultimate to explain and direct man's experience. We recommend to these colleges the truth that if some other stance is more legitimate such a position ought to be accepted to direct education and civilization. The conservative colleges suffer from not having an open theology.

The fear of being found out by fact, usually hid behind an aggressive façade, gives a deep inner insecurity to these conservatively oriented Christian colleges. Usually they harbor too much special pleading to be open for stringent public inspection. This insecurity affects the relation of the college to the general community. By the keen leaders of thought and society these colleges are generally dismissed as anti-intellectual, or as guilty of intellectual dishonesty and distortion. Others tolerate them with an uneasy feeling that something is wrong. Their acceptance is mostly among conservative churches that protect their own position and prolong it by means of these pseudointellectual institutions. Usually these colleges tend to be socially and politically conservative, in line with the general mentality of their religion and constituency. They therefore often help to thwart progressive leadership in secular areas of life, whether by Christian or secular leaders, and often work at cross-purposes with the most dedicated seeing and leading of authentic Christian faith. What, then, can be done with these communities to communicate to and through them a genuine Gospel?

Bad theology should be corrected by a good one. The Gospel comes to fulfill, not to destroy. Many religious reactionaries are so for lack of adequate faith that will satisfy their whole self. They fear naturalism, humanism, effete liberalism, evasive neo-orthodoxy; and why not? Only if a wholesome and wholehearted Christian supernaturalism is introduced are they presented with a genuine option.[3] These colleges cannot accept a liberal theology

[3] An educator has furnished us one formula that is both broad and historic: "The Church college holds, essentially, that behind all life is a Creator, whose creation we and the world are. He has revealed Himself as a God of justice in a moral universe that makes man a responsible being, but also as a God of love, in Jesus Christ, His Son. In this stunning miracle of love, imperfect man, the mark of sin upon him, finds, beyond his own free choice of good and evil, the instrument of his true redemption and a compelling invitation to the renewal of himself and to immortal life. And there is a creative partnership with God possible for man in history, a share in practical goodness and a creative purpose." Howard Lowry, op. cit., p. 102.

without destroying themselves. *Community, thus far, regulates communication.* Only a deeply evangelical theology for the heart will do, which by its nature also sets the mind free for truth. The symbols of faith must be redefined, with the utmost concern for the kind of community that is involved in these conservative colleges. These colleges, in fact, hold on to something of inestimable value; but unfortunately they are also clinging to the old grave-clothes rather than to the risen truth. The first task therefore is to offer these colleges a freeing Christian faith deep enough to free them from fear of open, competent inquiry. Our theologians have failed us badly, and keep failing us, by rationalizing the status quo of church doctrine, rather than living into creative expression the heart of the Christian faith. To reformulate the faith, its implications, and involvements, will take generations of dedicated and gifted scholars, but even a few daring seers can make a satisfactory beginning.[4]

In line with such theology, education should be freed for creative inquiry. Integrity should rule the whole academic life.[5] The standards for finding, testing, and communicating truth should be tightened and enforced. The purpose of intellectual vitality and seriousness should replace religious imperialism. Intellectual habits should become disciplined and honored, as necessary to carry out the central function of the college. Professors should be hired for their intellectual competence and integrity, rather than mostly for personal piety and institutional loyalty. All aspects of the life of the institution should emphasize the high and holy nature of truth. A Christian college needs particularly to develop a strong climate of critical discrimination. The teaching of religion particularly should

[4] The task needs more than theologians! "Since professional theologians rarely view their task as that of furnishing a synoptic account of God, man and the universe, Christian scholars in the so-called secular subjects have a peculiar responsibility for the working out of this new Christian 'map of knowledge.'" Nash, *op. cit.*, p. 260.

[5] "The Church college seeks, or should seek, men with balanced interest in scholarship and teaching—and with something more. They must, of course, be authentic professionally, living off the fresh life of new fact and the imaginative synthesis of the facts they already know. As scholars, they should represent the critical spirit, the dispassionate mind, and the reflection that should precede and accompany commitment." Lowry, *op. cit.*, p. 107.

be subjected to the full view of all possible worthy criticism. Instead of the present usual prejudice that breathes through the publications of these colleges, especially on the subject of religion, there ought to be calm fairness and teachable objectivity.

In spite of the fact that there are a large number of these hamperingly conservative colleges, it would be a mistake to spend too much of our space on the analysis of their situation and its correction. Above all, they need the kind of theology that will allow them to grow into maturity, mellowness, and the co-operative spirit. Instead we want to direct our attention to the many colleges that mean to be Christian. There is a great company of dedicated educators who now see the need for a truly Christian college. Political considerations may make the church college of utmost importance. Certainly the church college and the Christian college in general ought to be fortresses for freedom; creative freedom to speak and act ought to be born, cradled, and reared to real strength in the church-related colleges. Anyone who invests his life to strengthen the nature of these colleges, in whatever capacity, renders valuable service to God, the Church, education, the community, and the nations. Let us then consider the improvement of these colleges.

Under no circumstances should there be less emphasis on religion here than in the fundamentalist colleges; we should rather learn from them in this respect. Christian theology itself, and Christian worship too, when rightly accepted enforce the maximum concern for truth. They are characterized by humble trust and by critical care. Theology ought to be avowedly the center of the curriculum. The curriculum should be anchored unashamedly on the absolute will of God; but precisely on this account it should be concerned to understand, accept, and actualize the multifold variety and relativity of expression that that will keeps creating.[6] Thus it would incorporate emphases that are both dependable and flexible. Theology would in this way center the curriculum in truth, provide cohesion at its directive center, make necessary the creative distinctiveness

[6] An attractive picture is drawn by Boyd of Vittorino's educational activity: "And interfused through all the work was the Christian spirit, represented by the daily devotions, and made real and living by the personality of the master." *Op. cit.*, p. 165.

and relative autonomy of all the academic disciplines, and offer guidance and incentive to the creative and co-operative Christian community.

Many have held that theology cannot be central to the curriculum of higher education. Dr. James B. Conant, former president of Harvard University, dismisses religion as divisive, and as therefore unable to give cohesion to education. Dr. Robert M. Hutchins, former Chancellor of the University of Chicago, declares metaphysics rather than theology to be the proper integrating factor. Sir Walter Moberly maintains that theology is too foreign to education as it actually is to be accepted as a unifying or rallying center. William Adams Brown, however, stoutly maintained that theology alone is universal and motivational enough to form the basis of higher education. A line of thinkers from Newman[7] to Temple have sensed the need to see all things in the light of God, realizing that if a good theology is not taught explicitly the likelihood is that a bad theology is advocated implicitly. Our own view is that some theology is always being taught, unless several theologies contend for mastery—perhaps in the manner of a masquerade. In answer to President Conant it can be said that he himself in a famous baccalaureate address advocated truth and a universe that is benevolently inclined to the needs of man as a desirable climate for democratic education.

Truth and concern, however, are the identical twin pillars of the Christian absolute! No harm can come from either. The more absolutely they become central the more truth will share with co-operative good will the reign of teaching, research, learning, and living. To Chancellor Hutchins it can be replied that no entirely objective metaphysics is possible; every metaphysics involves a posture of faith. Certainly no dogmatic, institution-bound theology has any place in university life. An adequate metaphysics must be

[7] "John Henry Newman saw long ago that when theology is not taught, 'its province will not simply be neglected but will be actually usurped by other sciences, which will teach, without warrant, conclusions of their own in a subject-matter which needs its own proper principles for its due formation and disposition.' " As quoted by Lowry, *op. cit.*, p. 81, from John H. Newman, *On the Scope and Nature of University Education*.

the result of a free faith and an open decision with regard to all possible information. Perhaps he has in mind as "metaphysics" what we call theology—the open and informed mind dealing responsibly with ultimate truth. We trust, too, that nothing in our view of theology as central to higher education would appear to Sir Walter Moberly as harmful or impractical. Indeed, this book was written because several people felt the need for a theological orientation that Sir Walter's book lacked; he wrote avowedly more as an educator than as a theologian. We surmise, however, that he would want to insist that Christian theology is less general than we have made it. He seems to think of theology in more dogmatic terms than we do.

Our reply is that the Christian faith, however particular in historic fact or focus, is nevertheless also as universal at least as we have shown it to be. Our concern here, too, is with the confessedly Christian college, whereas Sir Walter dealt with the secular universities. If the Christian faith is understood in its deepest and widest nature, nothing hinders its becoming central to higher education. False theologies, ignorance, and fear are the real deterrents that debar the Christian faith from its natural place at the center of both the thought and life of higher education. If rightly understood, the heart of the Christian faith—truth and love—in ultimate personal terms can also become more and more acceptable to the higher education that today feels cut adrift, and not a little longs for a dependable anchor, or—to change the figure—is weary of dead ends and detours, and seeks for the open highway.

The academic life, moreover, should itself center in the total life of the Christian community.[8] This means concretely that the worship of God should be primary; the vocation of the college is to find for the world, and to help the world to do, the will of God.

[8] Cf., "In analyzing the objectives of common education the committee considers the criticism heard for two decades: that there is no guiding principle to unify a student's studies, and that in consequence the university in modern times has become a multiversity. It rejects the four major proposals for reform: to abandon the elective system in favor of the traditional curriculum; to organize studies according to medieval rationalism; to make the solution of contemporary problems the unifying aim; and to find in scientific method the presiding principle." Chalmers, op. cit., p. 41.

God becomes real and regnant only through worship. Chapel services should be held daily, and be so integral to the whole purpose and "feel" of the academic community that no compulsion should be necessary. At the same time all must attend as part of the integrity of the college. Such an ideal seems impracticable; but it is not if compulsion is eradicated by community conviction. Attendance can be as necessary as in the case of the most popular lecture classes in some college where the students feel no compulsion.

Great objective worship can mold a college into a creative community. Perhaps there should be "morning prayers," with all that can be involved under this expression.

These should be as corporate in nature as the worship of a Christian family or of a truly worshiping church. They should be as necessary as eating; we eat while attending college not because we are required to do so but because otherwise we die. In the same way spiritual feeding is part of Christian education. Other chapel services and convocations also have their place. Real imagination can develop concretely this general stress for a Christian college on the centrality of Christian worship. Besides these formal worship services there of course should be voluntary group worship to meet different needs; devotional reading and living should also make the individual members of the college rich before God and rich for Christian community. Certainly the Christian college should make its members well acquainted with the Bible.[9] Worship when real is the secret to our great need for rich Christian motivation. Christian concern comes only from God through the grace of worship. Grace of creation is strengthened and replenished through such continued worship.

[9] We cannot go all the way with Gaebelein, but he has pointed out a basic lack in Christian education: "It is therefore plain that no institution which fails to give the study of the Bible priority by placing it at the heart of its curriculum and providing for its competent and inspiring instruction can reach full Christian stature. The greatest need of our American Protestantism is for Christians who know the Word of God. Independent Christian education must shoulder its responsibility for the supply of that need." *Op, cit.,* p. 121. The Bible cannot be a textbook for education, but interpreted in the light of God's love in Christ as the criterion of faith and truth, it can be of immense practical importance in both Christian education and devotion.

Christian ethics ought also everywhere to govern the relations within the community as a whole; Christian community stands or falls with the reliability of Christian character. Beyond Christian ethics, however, though never below it, should be a spirit of mutual understanding and concern. The administration ought to be chosen for its Christian vision, and its practical wisdom and executive competence to actualize this vision in the concrete college community. The administrator should first of all be Christian, motivated by high religion and a holy zeal for truth. He ought in the second place to be a first-class student. His opportunity for study will of course be curtailed. He needs therefore, to begin with, to be a man of intellectual curiosity as well as hungering and thirsting for righteousness, a scholar as well as a man of faith. No less, however, must he be a practically competent administrator. Trustful he must be to get other people to join in and help make the college a Christian community of common responsibility. He will take constant and genuine advice from faculty, students, staff, and alumni, a practicer as well as a believer in democracy. The gift to take advice and to let other people join authentically in responsibility is, however, one thing; failure to take personal initiative and to keep the finger on the pulse to see that all is well is quite another matter.

An administrator should be a wise but efficient and nonsentimental executive. He must do all he can to consult the group, and try his best to satisfy the genuine needs and insights of the community as a whole. But in the end he must make the decisions, firmly as well as considerately and humbly. He should be a man of self-discipline based on inner strength and freedom, as well as a man of strict respect for personality and group standards to keep resolute discipline. He will know persons as well as jobs, and tasks as well as men. He will be part of all aspects of the college, yet always as more of a father than an ordinary member of the college family.

He will represent not only staff, students, and the teaching members, but will also represent to and for these the trustees and the community at large. He will be both a listener to and a leader of the trustees. He will be practical in the way he knows the complexities of human motives and social and political affairs. Therefore he will not be visionary as he represents the Christian college family to the trustees, but neither will he be afraid to guide the trustees into a Christian appraisal of all aspects of legal and monetary responsibility. He will lead by high inner honor and integrity, and elicit the noblest qualities in men of practical affairs.

To the general community he will be a symbol of the Christian college. He should understand sympathetically the nature of the community and of the relation of the college to it. The college should lead in the Christian intepretation and demonstration of social issues and solutions, but must do so in love. Superiority of moral or spiritual tone should be a *fact* of the Christian college, but never its *feeling* toward the community.

With the alumni the administrator should be a fair interpreter of the college and of the changes in its life. He should be concerned with them as well as concerned to use them for the institution. Possibly extension work and general education could be carried out as a service of the college through the alumni, so as to educate both the graduates and the community. All these aspects of manhood and leadership belong to the Christian administrator. Greatest of all, however, is spiritual genuineness, depth, and vision, and the kind of inner acceptance of scholarship that makes the Christian college always major in its two central functions: spiritual reality and intellectual leadership.

The faculty will know Christian teaching to be a holy calling; neither the administration nor the faculty is a mere profession. A profession it must be and worthily; but the Christian college knows a divine calling beyond the standards of the profession. Its personnel do all things first unto God in gratitude and commitment. The Christian professor is ordained to his work in the truest sense of holy orders. This fact ought indeed to be properly symbolized. As keeper of the intellectual conscience of the Church, the Christian professor is part of the Church's very life and work. The faculty of a Christian college is united by the purpose of Christian teaching; it is dedicated to combine with God's grace full spiritual commitment with full intellectual integrity. The result when reached is the integration of life and of the college community. With respect to God the faculty knows reflective dedication; with respect to intellectual inquiry the faculty knows integrity. Its members work to combine adequacy of insight, motivation, and direction with sterling validity of thought and fact.

With respect to the administration the faculty is open, willing, respectful, but at the same time imbued with a sense of dedication not to prostitute its truth in spite of pressures from administration, alumni, community, or from secular colleges in different institutions of higher learning. The faculty is appreciative and co-operative with regard to the administration, but minds its own business; which is competent instruction, and the conditions for such instruction. With regard to its own life, it knows that all members are both professional colleagues and brothers in Christ. Dignity joins with community of concern. The professors are joined into community by their purpose to serve God and men in the truth.

Democracy characterizes the life of the faculty. Democracy means delegated authority, maximum trust, and Christian concern for all members. As far as the Christian faith actually reigns there can be no defensive attitude among departments, no imperialism or jealousy, no grasping of power; to whatever extent such conditions exist the Christian faith is victimized. If this fact is once honestly seen and accepted, the standard at least is set; the power for increasing realization is always present with genuine Christian faith. The Christian faculty will be concerned with the students as people, but its concern must be with students as people in college to learn. Absorption in one's subject is a prerequisite for good teaching. To be the best for the students the Christian professors must be competent in their tasks, and know that integrity and mastery of knowledge are for the sake of effective communication.

The dignity of truth should set faculty apart from students in the sense that students should not make falsely free with their teachers. The teachers are no longer students, and should be willing to recognize that fact, just as wise parents realize that they are not children; for when respect is lost for the sake of some assumed democracy the child is inwardly hurt. At the same time there ought to be open channels of communication through personal dealings and through faculty student committees. Teachers who "stand on their dignity" had better adopt a more Christian posture! The community of worship should also erase artificial barriers, and foster genuine understanding and partnership in a Christian undertaking. With regard to the maintenance staff the faculty should be aware that the Christian college as a whole is a family, and therefore should naturally respect and include its every member, though the staff cannot be included as part of the academic community. Functionally such hobnobbing is a lie; the staff belongs as working members of a common labor in the Christian college and as human beings as well as brothers in Christ. Spiritually and socially the Christian college should know no difference. Functional dignity is part of life, and when genuine never raises barriers, but creates respect for difference in competence, albeit with a common commitment under God.

We believe, furthermore, that the teaching staff ought to be divided into three parts: research men, resource leaders, and creative thinkers. Those in research ought to be mainly the preservers of the past. They ought to know books and how to use them. Perhaps all who enter the profession should spend the first five or ten years in getting thoroughly acquainted with man's rich resources of knowledge. This would give opportunity for all in the profession to have their feet firmly planted in knowledge. Some ought no doubt to spend their whole life in this kind of work; they could then become expert consultants to the students. Possibly some real tutorial work ought to individualize education. If these men had the functions both of knowing in detail, comprehensively, accurately, and increasingly, and also of steering the students in their individual need to know, they could contribute essentially to the educational process. They could also act as consultants to resource leaders and creative thinkers. By all means they ought to comprise the examiners.

Resource leaders ought to be disciplined within the case method. They ought also particularly to study where modern knowledge is going and ought to go. They should have competent *functional* knowledge. Besides, they ought to be so deepened in faith and spiritual commitment that they could lecture for decision without arbitrarily imposing their own points of view or that of some inflexible understanding of faith.

The creative thinkers should have access to the resource men both for material and for constant checking. They ought also to relate themselves intimately to the lives of the lecturers in a kind of two-way traffic, learning from them what are their practical problems for steering knowledge and giving them the result of their own latest seeing. Some opportunity ought to be given creative teachers to lecture at the edge of their knowledge. This would stimulate the community and help them to articulate and to feel their insights through the processes of communication. However complicated this subject may seem, one thing is certain: we can gain functional efficiency when as a Christian community we are willing to recognize diversities of gifts and interests within the unity of the Spirit. The practicality of the division depends on how realistically it works out in different circumstances. The small college could not do even haltingly what the large university can do very well. Our suggestion is *an emphasis* on the diversity of gifts and function which should be recognized and promoted as far as practicable. Every working safeguard must be employed to keep the division of labor from becoming *an isolating rather than an integrating function*. At the first sign of sterility, for instance, the creative thinkers should be immersed in life's activities, or the resource leader made to do increased research. The point is to let each group develop its own ways and wisdom, only again to combine and strengthen the life and the seeing of the Christian college community as a whole. Effective specialization is ever against the background of total competence and concern for actual life.

The maintenance staff should be selected with a view to Christian character and efficiency; work should be done well and in a Christian spirit. The staff in Christ should be able to feel itself at one with the whole college enterprise. It should think of itself neither as inferior nor as having to show its importance. As a matter of fact there is an actual Christian institution of higher learning where the staff is now and then specially included in the chapel services, and where the entire staff participates in Christian "family days" that are celebrated by the school as a whole one evening a month. Some of the men working on the grounds appear at some prayer meetings, and others encourage both faculty and students by their lives of prayer for the college. The superintendent of buildings and grounds is a deeply committed Christian of superior ability to whom the students look up, and who serves them willingly in many ways. He is a close friend of the faculty families, takes a real burden of the administration by his wise and courteous treatment of visitors and strangers, helps the rating of the school by his dealings in the community in trading and caring for the property, is admired in his church, inspires his co-workers to work well and hard, and sets with them a tone of Christian courtesy and service for the whole college. The right selection of staff members and the right relations with the staff are of high Christian importance. Perhaps opportunities ought to be given to the staff for some extension of their education, or for some acquaintance with what is being done in general and with what they can do to make the Christian faith become more real. Christian vocation is meaningless if the staff experiences its calling any less than the students, professors, or administration. Christian calling is for all legitimate work, and of absolute importance if done for God in humble trust, thanksgiving, and service.

Naturally the Christian college exists for the Christian student. The college is not a hospital for the student's healing, but a training ground for his mind and spirit; the mind comes first, because the function of the college is education; the college must never become a church. If it becomes primarily religious it loses its distinctive stress; its primary function suffers. The trouble with some Christian colleges is that they exist as promotional or maintenance institutions of the Church, and are not, in a high and holy sense, educational. There must never be a question in the student's mind but that the college exists for study. The whole atmosphere of the Christian college ought to be colored sacred by respect for truth; the very air of the campus should breathe the sanctity of intellectual inquiry. The demand for validity, or competently established truth, should be insistent. Without playing to low motives of invidious comparison, intellectual achievement should set the standard for student leadership. The rewards of the Christian college ought to be for devotion to truth. Singleness of heart should produce singleness of mind, in the sense that the intellectual life should be the pride and joy of the Christian college.

The Christian student body, naturally, should be motivated by Christian gratitude and by concern fired by Christian worship. Individual worship should feed the heart's fire; corporate worship should engender Christian drive and direction. Some of this worship might be in the several dormitories; possibly the morning and evening prayers should be said there, while the fuller services should be held in the college chapel. Close contact ought to be held with the churches in the communities, and with the church life from which the students come. In some instances the worship could be supplemented by religious projects. Why should not a college sacrifice to become solidly Christian through the meeting of some definite need in a world like this? Why, for instance, could not a college community adopt college babies among orphans in war countries? Or why could not the college as a whole support missionaries on the intellectual levels? Could they not send out young men of competence and a real calling to secular universities? Could not Christian colleges foster Christian teachers and care for them in pagan lands? Could they not visit prisons, mental institutions, and hospitals, under competent supervision and with careful planning? Could not some speak in the communities for the fuller Christian faith? Could not some go out to lonely communities not too far away, with a full evangelical, ecumenical gospel? Christian commitment starves without Christian action; a Christian college community should find many ways to implement its faith.

Neither should the social life be minimized. Some of this would be intellectual in setting. As we have seen, many of the discussions connected with the core curriculum of case studies would involve not only group dynamics in a formal setting, but actual evenings of a social nature around vital intellectual topics of discussion. Some of this social life should be spiritual in nature. Those who have never known how much fun there can be in going out to work or witness as a Christian group have missed a good part of life's best time; both the intellectual and the spiritual life suffer and men grow inflexible when there is lack of humor and fun. The social life comes naturally to college students, and should not only relieve but relax and nourish the whole life. Social life, however, can never be merely an adjunct to intellectual or spiritual life; it craves its own free and distinctive expression. There is no conflict between Christian fervor and play. A false holiness has taken happiness out of life, and reduced its creative drive and its essential joy. Some of the social life can be aesthetic creativity. What satisfaction there can be had through participation in strong Christian drama! To find drama that is both good art and also Christian, to be sure is hard; it can be done, however—at least in the sense that life is celebrated on a high and holy plane.

Piety must never take art out of aesthetics. Although we are to discuss art in a later context, let it be said in this connection too that life is not all piety, but should be also integrally beautiful. Beauty must never be substituted for prayer, but neither must piety be made to take the place of art. The Christian college should be the patron of high art; beauty should naturally blossom from the Christian college. The students should be encouraged and trusted to write Christian drama, to act Christian drama, to write poetry, and to cultivate the arts. All should be done with a Christian background and attitude, but the word "Christian" must then cover without any apology or diminution all legitimate forms of beauty. We worship a God who creates. Christian formal worship is good, provided that it does not become a policeman, making such forms sacrosanct. Better let creativity flourish and find control within the love of God which abhors the ugly, the low, and the mean. In other words let Christian liberty be real. Let no watch and ward society exist on the Christian campus; let not prudery prevent artistic production and appreciation. Let life be celebrated for life's sake, and God is sure not to be displeased with His creative children!

Another form of social life is athletics. Not only should this be clean without being prudish, but it should give opportunity for the creative competition that is part of creation. Intramural sports should be for all normal students. We have too many spectators; the fun of the game is for all. Ample equipment and time for play ought to be part of the official college program. If such play really satisfies, much unclean social life can be prevented. Sex is too much with us because life has not demanded enough of our young at a critical time of need. Both boys and girls ought to have a rounded program of athletic activity every day. Exercise is necessary to a strong and vigorous life. Ingenuity can yet find new kinds of group competition to satisfy college needs.

Athletics should also develop teams for intercollegiate competition; students need to identify themselves with a great group in hard competition. Let hard play become the emotional outlet for the feelings that in part generate war. Sports need not be feared if worship and study are really central to the college community; naturally the Christian spirit will keep games within bounds and control. They serve, however, a great function of dramatic outlet. Heaven will be the poorer if God cuts out great games! Pity the sophisticated nature that can find no enjoyment in honest and hard contests of skill. Running around hitting a ball may not be bad training for chasing a word or catching a spirit! But sports should be for all, and integrated into the total social life—not only for the few who symbolize the combative spirit of the college. Sports take the upper hand only where there is no great intellectual integrity and vitality, and where the life of the spirit is too weak to satisfy.

It may be well to summarize our understanding of the Christian college. A college is Christian only if it is a fellowship of inquiry under God. The college exists for the students; somehow this fact should be central. If possible, we should have written this book more from the point of view of learning than of teaching. A college exists to pass on to learners knowledge from the past and to find for them new truth. But the students must themselves face out into the world. A college that does not accept as a primary function to be the mind of the world and the intellectual conscience of the church is not Christian. Integrity and competence should characterize its whole intellectual life.

Within the Christian faith, however, the intellect is only a part of God's creation. It is a servant of life; life directs it, whether in a person or in a community. Therefore if the mind is to be set free for the truth, life itself must be dedicated to truth. Truth for the whole life comes only through worship of the true God. The Christian college celebrates life through wholehearted worship; through worship it accepts its task gratefully and carries it out faithfully.

To do so the Christian college should center its curriculum in the will of God for Christian community. Theology becomes the unifying intellectual pursuit of the college campus by its humble commitment to discover, to accept, and to make regnant in life and thought the unity of the universe, which alone gives universality to the life of the intellect. Christian theology is never more important than any other subject, and can therefore neither lord it over the others as superior nor imperialistically infringe on their legitimate independence. Rather, Christian theology makes central in attitude as well as in thought the love of God, which makes Him sovereign, with all subjects serving Him and human need. Christian theology—when it expresses truth and love as ultimate for life because they characterize the nature of God—gives education an absolute that is as deep and wide as the heart of God and as flexible as truth. It sets men free to find and to do the truth for themselves. It therefore bestows dignity on all subjects and the spirit of co-operation on all teachers and students.

The Christian college is furthermore a Christian family in the sense that all parts of it—administration, faculty, students, and staff —work within a common loyalty to God, an intensive community of Christian purpose, and an outgoing concern for the community around it and for the world as a whole. Its total life, whether intellectual, religious, aesthetic, social, or athletic, is within both the liberty and the control of the love of Christ. The intellectual life is characterized by integrity; the spiritual life, by genuineness; its life of art, by creative satisfaction; the social life, by naturalness; and its play, by invigorating release.

The Christian college can be Christian in reality as well as in name only when its standard is Christian concern, its motivation, the Holy Spirit of truth; its goal, Christian community; its task, growth in knowledge and in human service; and its deepest loyalty, the eternal will of God for universal freedom and faithfulness in fellowship, in this life and in the world to come.

If this is at least a correct suggestion toward the ideal of the Christian college, how can this ideal be realized? A writer who has not been an administrator dare hardly prescribe with confidence; nevertheless he may offer a few general suggestions for the realization of this aim. We might begin anywhere within the Christian college community, because all parts interpenetrate; let us, however, begin with the trustees. Often they are Christian ministers, educators, and professional or business people. Their common loyalty is Christ. Anyone truly concerned with the Christian college should make an effort to keep close to these men, to share with them their own view of the Christian college and to offer them, if need be, the fuller Christian pattern. The trustees can always become more concerned with the administration and with the faculty. Such concern may, of course, invite trouble, unless the spirit of the trustees and the pattern of their minds are truly Christian. Such concern may also find many things on the college scene that ought to be changed. In any case the trustees should be selected carefully. After all they do appoint both administration and faculty. Suppose theoretically we begin with this fact. Let them find the most qualified man for president, from the perspective of the needs of the Christian college. How much the administration can do if it truly knows how to lead! How can it lead, however, unless it genuinely sees and feels the Christian claim on the college? Therefore the administration ought to be made thoroughly aware of its Christian responsibility and opportunity. It may be in a concrete situation that the administrator can best take the original lead in transforming the college according to the Christian pattern.

Let us next give consideration to the faculty. Perhaps the first thing to say is that Christian faculty members ought to be given every opportunity for leadership on the campus. The most important strategy to make a college Christian is to win the real intellectual leaders of the faculty for the Christian witness. Much can be done to this end through the faculty Christian fellowship. The Christian college could also be the topic of discussion groups. Such books as Sir Walter Moberly's *The Crisis in the University,* or *Religious Perspectives in College Teaching,* edited by Hoxie N. Fairchild for the Edward W. Hazen Foundation, may be used with real profit. New appointments must be watched with the greatest care. A young generation of Christian scholars must be raised up for a coming day; the Danforth Foundation is sponsoring a strong program to this end; the Hazen Foundation is contributing literature, and makes discussion groups possible. Large foundations should be brought to see the importance of the Christian college and university for constructive social motivation in a world like this. We know more what to do than we do. Even though only a few faculty members are men of peerless integrity and the highest possible competence academically, they can win many others for the Christian cause, particularly if they are humbly positive and equally open to learn from others who do not share their full commitment. Those who create unwholesome tensions or who actually obstruct the Christian pattern in life or teaching should not be retained. The place of tenure ought to be reformulated in the light of responsible freedom according to Christian standards. There can be no question of witch-hunting in a Christian college. There is no question of freedom in the truth. The Christian faith is open, humble, and flexible; it has no brittle, external standard. But it is committed. A committed college has no right to be sentimental about its insistent witness to the truth which claims it and for which it exists. In the specialized subjects there are certainly fine lines that must be drawn with patience. Often the attitude of openness is more important than intellectual position. Any subject, however, that is slanted to deny God and the truth of God's love in Christ with its insistent and trustworthy implications is made to sin against the truth that governs the Christian college. Great care must be taken, however, not to cause instructors to be dishonest for the sake of their bread and butter. Other ultimates than the Christian faith also have a right and a need to be presented with rigorous honesty and fair-mindedness. Christian implications, for that matter, must be tested in all fields against the validity of the field itself; Christian faith must accept and live by fact validly established. It is quite another thing, however, to accept the distortions of truth based on secular presuppositions and on phenomenologies that in fact have falsely assumed contexts.

Inspired by love for God and man and with devotion to freedom and truth both trustees and administration will be given the necessary wisdom to deal with this complicated problem of building a faculty of men and women who are great teachers and also devoted Christians. Above all, the attitude of the college must be positive and not negative; it must be creative not defensive. It must help raise up university leaders sufficiently competent to set the standards of what is intellectually acceptable in both the sciences and the humanities. Professors who are both scholars and Christians will find freedom in truth and thus be enabled to shape the civilization of the future.

We now come to the students. Students are important to the development of the Christian college, first through their selection, and second through their cultivation. Selection begins before college age. The Church, the home and the college must combine to hand-pick potential Christian leaders while the child is laying the foundations for his life. It is not enough to say that the Christian college will be certain to admit convinced Christians, at least for a good part of its enrollment; it is necessary also to plan positively for the rearing of Christian youth who come predisposed to Christian commitment in the large realm of college life and truth. Beyond such selection there must be selection of the leaders who set the tone of campus life. Then cultivation should set in with all possible vigor.[10] A Christian administration and the Christian portion of the faculty—be it larger and larger—should study the student body with the

[10] "A student who is a Christian, as W. A. Visser 't Hooft has repeatedly urged, is not the same as a Christian student." Nash, *op. cit.*, p. 283.

best student counsel for the sake of developing a creative Christian leadership. The rest will be taken care of through all the channels we have mentioned, such as worship and religious group activities. Full use of church organizations such as the Student Christian Association, the Student Christian Movement, and other religious movements like the Y.M.C.A. or the Y.W.C.A., ought also to be integrated into the total Christian activity of the campus. Particularly important is the organizing of study groups, as we have seen, which are continually applying the Christian perspective to the subjects studied not only theoretically but also by means of at least prospective existential participation. All activity, however, is reduced to consecrated individuals. A little leaven does the trick if it is strong enough; any few on fire for Christ can change a campus —provided, of course, that the fire gives light as well as heat. The world—to change the figure—needs steering as well as drive. Often the Christian college has drive without the clear seeing of Christian direction.

Selection and cultivation also apply to the maintenance staff. Next to selection in importance is the genuine inclusion of the staff within the Christian life of the campus. The staff can find new meaning in life if it becomes an integral part, through prayer, faith, and devoted work, of the total reason for the being of the college. The administration naturally holds the key to this relationship to the staff. Faculty and student members, however, make or break the Christian community in its wholeness by their natural relation to staff members. If there has to be conscious effort, beyond a certain point that is true of all life, the community needs much perfecting in love. The test of the inclusive Christian reality is the ease with which it transcends functional and social barriers within its own positive experience of Christian community. Christians know people as people, and all life as sacred under God.

What, however, of the nominally Christian college and the secular university?[11] Both can be treated together under our last

[11] "Secularism consists of a preoccupation with the interests and values of the world of the senses, with the here and now, with time to the exclusion of eternity. Though it may not be based upon a formal rejection of religious beliefs, it relegates religion to a peripheral place in life." George F. Thomas, "Problems and Principles," in Fairchild, *op. cit.,* p. 6.

point. As to the first of these two, it is Christian at least in declaration; it is so either by heritage only, or also by connection with the Christian Church. In the former instance the college may in fact be as secular as any university, with a sense of shame, perhaps, or at least of embarrassment as to its Christian origins; if such be the case, it must be classified with and treated as a secular university. No mere moral or spiritual appeal will be effective. Pride in academic record and other attitudes of many colleges that are named "Christian" prevent desirable communication with Christian advocates. They feel themselves beyond such special pleading! Wherever there is actual church connection or any active concern about the Christian name, however, there appeal can be made to this fact, particularly by those solidly within the college community itself. This appeal cannot be one of loyalty alone; very likely it must be an approach through the world's need for adequacy of spiritual and moral guidance. The integrity of the college purpose must not be tampered with. Only intellectual competence will open the needed doors. The Christian connection may not be accepted with any understanding of the Christian claim, but may be actually repudiated by the college community. The Christian faith will therefore be accepted only as it proves to be true.

Christian truth is sensitive enough to human nature and human needs to win its way in any day only if it is competently interpreted. Therefore the selection of administration, and of faculty, and the right use of the most competent and yet dedicated Christians on the campus, become of paramount importance. There are at least in the case of these nominally Christian colleges no legal barriers, whereas on the contrary there are actual opportunities for faith to speak its austere and needed truth. If at the beginning the student body is taken in hand rightly much can be done to transform the campus on the basis of the Christian faith. Possibly there can be increasing emphasis on Christian character and openness to faith, even in the selection of students. Christian community must be *demonstrated* in scholarship and life by its open advocates.

If the Church knows enough to keep out as a power and to stay in as a helper, it can also open doors to understanding and appreciation of the Christian way of life and seeing. The point is that the

Christian faith is professed by charter; this profession can be either a barrier or a door. Let therefore the few committed Christians who are in power, or who are at least of strong influence, be wise in their concern to transform the campus according to a Christian pattern; let them be as patient as the truth; but let them be urgent with love and confident with faith. This type of college changes only when the Christian faith is *exemplified* as not only respectable but superior in both life and thought.

The secular university presents a not too different problem to be discussed with that of the nominal Christian college. On many state university campuses there is a good deal of concern for religion. In both instances, however, the general atmosphere is certainly secular. The power of the few holds equally true in both institutions, if these few are genuine enough to carry influence both in life and in academic attainment. One or several competent Christians in any department of the university can make a vital difference; they can make a difference in what is taught, in the running of the department, and in those lonesome Christian students who tend to be lost, confused, tentative, and wistful within the secular atmosphere. With both professor and student the fact stands firm that if either is to accomplish his Christian end he must be a person of integrity, competence, openness to all truth, humble, and co-operative. A Christian is never defensive or inflexible; he has a deep sense of cosmic humor and patience. He is rooted and grounded in the love of God and in the reality of eternity. The burden of proof as to his faith's validity rests on him as a Christian. Let him join with others to form a genuine Christian minority, a creative minority for Christ. Let them win others by the kind of people they are, in order that they may point to the kind of life that is the summit of truth.

A few more practical points may perhaps be made. The first is the importance of mastering the indirect method of communication. Open assault on error is useless if the community of feeling is basically set against the fuller truth that requires change of life and commitment. The relation between community and communication must be kept resolutely in mind. Without compromise of position, therefore, the Christian witness must know exactly how to puncture rationalization, how to set doubt at work in the case of distortion, how to make concrete suggestions by indirection that will bear fruit as God gives the increase. Nor must this witness be constant; there are times of the spirit and times of the mind. Only those sensitized to human response can know when to keep silent and when to speak up. As matter of fact the Christian witness had better be held back than become a sore point at the wrong time. The holy privilege of silence should be exercised a good deal by an effective Christian advocate. The incidental word addressed with integrity and with adroitness is the most fruitful seed on the secular campus. Truth is not correctly spoken unless it awakens proper response. Care for truth is far more than concern for theory; concern for truth is above all concern for God's will to be done and concern for actual people. As a matter of fact a really important course to be developed by the Christian college is the relation between community and communication. We need to know what to say, to be sure, but even more we need to know how to say it.

On the level of administration or public relations, much can be done to reinterpret hampering legal restrictions or interpretations. Many universities have found a practical way around our separation of church and state, which really should be a barrier to sectarianism rather than to the teaching of truth and reality. Often divisive religion, however, gets in the way. Let such religion cease troubling the university waters! Only high religion can win an effective place within the secular college. If the religious forces will really co-operate the problem is immensely simplified. Even the most unbending religious bodies stand to lose if they shut religion out of the universities, and thereby surrender to secularism much of our trained leadership. When the several denominations or churches seek God's common good on the highest possible plane and on the fullest possible level, legal barriers and secular distrust will begin to crumble. We believe that the kind of theology we here advocate is open to all churches and religions in the United States. Dogmatic difference or varied theological stress can then be added to this basic Christian faith by the churches themselves. If the churches agree, we shall have more and more opportunity for vital religious instruction on the highest graduate levels within our universities. There are many ways to do the same thing! If some form of evolutionary development is demanded by geology or biology, truth will be taught even if forbidden by state law. If religion is man's main truth and need, effective ways can be found for its proper teaching.

Other concrete suggestions are rather obvious. Work within all given channels. These vary from place to place. If there is a week set aside for religious emphasis, secure if possible a real scholar who is both a committed Christian and a good speaker. Let a group of highly competent men accompany him for group work and for class teaching. A week's seminar with faculty members has proved significant in different kinds of secular universities. Let no one come onto the campus as a representative of Christianity who cannot handle himself with ease in a company of scholars. Such at least is the ideal that must be filled as soon as possible if the right communication is to take place. Develop Christian faculty fellowships, furthermore, in the secular universities that have the aid of the parent body. Hold interdepartmental discussions that break down barriers and open channels for communication. Let religion have its careful and weighty say. Introduce substantial Christian literature into every aspect of university life. Discuss most carefully the bearing of religion on each field with the leaders in that field, with professors and students.

If religious teaching is allowed, let the department be filled with top-flight scholars who are not ashamed of their commitment to the Christian faith. Support them rather than criticize them when they try their best to communicate with their colleagues. Do not expect them to act and talk like preachers on the loose. Staff the denominational foundations on or around the campus with deep thinkers and men of high human concern, rather than with denominational promoters and protectors of sheep, or with organizers of social functions and church affairs. No more effective investment can be made than in the higher training of committed men to work with students. This is true a fortiori of any chaplain or religious executive. Work to have the chapel services, if any, manned by men of God and deep thinkers, rather than by popular speakers and fluent entertainers. The harvest will be slow, but it will bear fruit many times greater than that we are now reaping. Lend the best men in religion to the college campus, to live without obligation in dormitories or fraternities. Let the seminaries send the top thinkers among their students to visit the secular colleges. These suggestions could go on through every level of university life, but Christian ingenuity itself will find ever more ways to accomplish its worthy end.

This chapter will close with two more suggestions. First we must remember that the Christian faith is not host on the secular campus; may its sponsors remember this enough to be humble and courteous! It is allowed to be present by the courtesy of large-minded men who may not themselves be certain of ultimates but who grope for them vaguely. If Christian advocates would display obvious integrity and fair-mindedness, their presentation of the faith would be more welcome. If the Christian witnesses would themselves listen with open minds to other points of view and dare to learn to the limit of truth, they would themselves be more listened to by serious students. All special pleading, all appeal to emotional needs apart from the criticism of the mind, all harping on childhood loyalties to win professors and students who come from committed Christian homes—all approaches to the human heart, in fact, that by-pass the highroad of hard truth will fail to lead the secular community to religious insight and commitment. The university at least intends to live on the level of truth. Let the Christian professor and student meet the secular community without equivocation on that level.

This insistence on intellectual integrity as the door to the secular university should not obscure the fact that the divergence between the secular and the Christian community of feeling and doing is often the basic cause for the lack of communication. We fail more often than we think because God's universal love for the world as enacted by Christ is actually not wanted. The offense and foolishness of the Gospel are real, not all offenses in the presentation of the Gospel are the foolishness of its messengers! How shall we overcome this basic problem of communication? The fact is clear: the Christian and the secularist belong to different communities of feeling and doing. Their worlds are different and therefore they think differently; they live in different ages, and therefore they fail to understand each other.

The most effective answer to this obstacle is prayer in the closed closet.[12] The Spirit is every man's deepest reality. He constitutes the living image of God in man; He is the unresting reflection in man of God's reality. When we dare to live and to speak in Him we shall find a way to live and to speak beyond mere experience and reason, let alone beyond mere expedience. When we shall have learned to speak through prayer and faith within the grace of the Spirit's communication, then we shall also speak in the tongue of the secular student and teacher. The deepest community of being is community in the Spirit. All men are united by their relation to God. Wonders can be wrought beyond our highest expectation if we learn the secret of Jesus and of St. Francis. Laubach teaches millions of illiterates to read their own language; he lives his love of the masses into a practical way to help them. The spiritual illiterates, too, long deep in their lives for life's final meaning and satisfaction. When we demonstrate in our lives the spirit of God's universal concern, and when we exemplify with our minds the integrity of truth, we shall find the way, no matter how few we are, to transform by the grace of God and the power of the Spirit, even the stony ground of the secular university. We may be too sophisticated to practice Christian prayer; but only prayer helps us to be instruments of the Spirit unto whom all hearts are open. Backed with secret prayer, the Word comes with open power.

[12] We are pleased to note the stress on prayer in John Coleman's *The Task of the Christian Student in the University* (New York, Association Press, 1947).

Chapter VII

Human Nature and Education

"The proper object of school and college is moral maturity."[1] "The nurture of personal growth is found to be the essential meaning of education."[2] If educators generally agree on statements like these, it is obvious that human nature dictates the possibilities of education. The task of Christian education is to have God's will taught in such a way that thereby it obtains its maximum effectiveness. God's will, the educator, and the learner are naturally essential factors in education. No discussion of either the method or the content of education accordingly becomes significant except in relation to human nature.

Some social scientists have talked as though education ought to be human engineering. Professor Ulich, for example, has unapprovingly told us how young social scientists at Harvard have affirmed that since social values are only the results of conditioning, modern knowledge makes it necessary and increasingly possible to carry on scientific human engineering in the sense of predictable conditioning.[3] Well and good, if the problem is that simple; cybernetics could indeed be adapted to a method of social regulation that, under properly controlled circumstances, could steer society with astonishing power. We witness constantly how masses of men think amazingly alike. Is man, then, a self-adjusting mechanism

[1] Chalmers, *op. cit.*, p. 255.
[2] Jeffreys, *op. cit.*, p. vii.
[3] Ulich, *op. cit.*, pp. 425-31.

that can be controlled by the setting of goals plus the manipulation of psychological conditioning? One thing is certain: there is much truth in this contention, and those who care for mankind should be open and alert to the fullest possible use of social conditioning or human engineering.[4] The engineering of human beings as an exclusive practice, however, is consistent neither with the need for freedom nor with the dignity of responsible choice; it is in fact contrary both to man's nature and the purpose of creation.

A political scientist has asked therefore the deeper question: "What is his [man's] essential nature and ultimate destiny? And in seeking answers to these questions we may very well be led to ask an additional question, namely, who is man? It is not indeed the function of political science to answer these questions, but political science cannot adequately fulfill the tasks peculiar to it until it has sought answers to those questions and sought them from the disciplines most competent to answer them. The political scientist cannot know whether the means he prescribes are appropriate, adequate, and possible unless he knows the nature of man and the end for which he is destined."[5] Certainly education drifts unless it has taken these questions seriously and found for them the truest possible answers.

Particularly is this demand necessary since our basic problem in education and civilization is motivation. Again, we know more what to do than we do. Yet we cannot know why this is so until we understand the nature of man. Of course understanding is not enough; we need also both prescription and execution. Correct motivation also is a critical need. The Christian faith has not only a perspective in terms of which to analyze the nature of man in relation to education. Such analysis, to be sure, must be undertaken. But the Christian faith has also the power in terms of which to make men willing and able to commit themselves to the ideal they see by means of constructive action.

The Christian faith is wind and weather, unless it can cope with

[4] Helvetius saw rather clearly how very much man can decide his own destiny through educational conditioning of the rising generation. Cf. Boyd, *op. cit.*, p. 291.

[5] John H. Hallowell, "Political Science," in Fairchild, *op. cit.*, p. 394.

human nature in relation to its actual transformation, its moral maturing and personal growth. Nor is individual growth enough. Our age has become sharply aware of the social nature of knowledge, of growth, of satisfaction. Persons are not such apart from community. Education must therefore know how to further personal growth, while at the same time effecting genuine community with reality and importance all its own; the personal and the communal belong inseparably together. Christian education should understand human nature, personal and social—along with all the problems that are connected with each mode of being; but beyond understanding, it must have the power to motivate men to enact their vision. Let us explore these lines of thought.

One thing is certain: the Christian faith knows that man is the creation of the love of God. If man knows that fact, he also can accept himself as such. If he does, he feels that he is known, understood, and has ever available God's faithful love. Nothing can give man a more ultimate sense of belonging than such acceptance of the love of God. Nothing can give him deeper security. Nothing can help to release in him more creativity and courage. Life as a whole finds meaning at its center. Human nature is ennobled in origin and destiny. Man is no longer a confused alien in a hostile world; he is not lost in a universe of change and decay. He is not overcome by ambiguity. Among all his problems and struggles man then finds by means of the Christian faith a purpose both in and for life.

The fact that man is God's creature gives dignity to every individual. No one who really accepts the Christian faith can ever look upon a fellow man without respect—respect for his status as a creature of God's love. There is awe and celebration in the presence of any creature of God for anyone who has His Spirit. Such dignity is rooted in reality. It can neither be conferred by man nor taken away by man. Man walks with a new gait when he knows himself to belong to God. No education that is aware of man's true status can ever talk of human engineering in any sense that would remove man's freedom to find the truth for himself, that would reduce man's satisfactions to material and social conditions, that would manipulate men without giving them the permissiveness that is God's own gift. No education that treats man or his destiny on a level lower than God's nature in him and purpose for him can succeed in the fullest sense, because it goes contrary to the nature of the universe. There is a divine dignity in man that Christian education can most fully recognize and help realize.

Not only does the Christian view of man disclose man's meaning and dignity, but it also insists that man is free to find and accept the will of God. Man is a creature of God's love. Love fosters children by setting them free to the maximum of their development. Love never forces community; it cannot compel like-mindedness. It rather allows and encourages different mind-sets in order to make men truly free. Only when men are free, as real selves, does love fulfill the freedom and the selfhood by making for an open and creative like-mindedness that is attitudinal rather than positional. Such freedom is part and parcel of man's practical experience. Only because of it can we hold anyone responsible for what he is doing. Therefore we make no apologies for our use of it. People who teach those subjects that for the sake of exact manipulation of aspects of man's experience work with a behavioristic hypothesis must be careful, on the contrary, not to *generalize their purposed reduction of scope*. Even though freedom is a fuzzy term, with various meanings according to its context, there is reality in freedom. Freedom is a fact; however complicated its context, freedom is real.

For our purposes we are dealing with moral and spiritual freedom. We believe, also as we have said, that there is freedom in fact; that the brain is not only a switchboard, but that, as Gardner Murphy puts it, there are "centrally initiated motive patterns."[6] Motivation on the psychological level is a most complex problem. Those who have long dealt with motivation in relation to organismic deficiencies, chemical regulators, controlled conditions of reward and punishment, growth and fatigue, and other problems of learning, know how careful the investigator must be to allow high positive correlation between controllable factors of motivation and the prediction of human behavior. On the phenomenological

[6] *Op. cit.*, p. 109.

level this question must be studied with integrity and competence. On the other hand, these investigators must be equally careful not to arrive at some assumed behaviorism, merely because of such positive correlation.

Arguments from complexity, ignorance, or lack of controllable conditions to freedom are of course invalid. But argument from a partial identification of controllable aspects of human behavior to behaviorism is an equally unscholarly procedure. Freedom on the level of fact is organization of selves and the direction of selves within a framework of inner drives that in some respects are stable and within an outer setting of relations that in some respects are predictable, freedom being and effecting a constant interaction among inner drives and outer conditions. Freedom never exists apart from motivation or cause, but always with reference to both. Some careful field theories approximate a description of the intimate interrelation of predictable conditions and choice.

Our concern for our present purpose, however, is with moral and spiritual freedom as the acceptance or rejection of the will of God. Man is free in spirit only in so far as he accepts the will of God in his spirit and then carries it out in fact as far as his freedom avails. Man's nature and God's purpose for him are both fulfilled by such acceptance and enactment. Man becomes free by being real within and right with reality. All education that neglects or disregards the absolute nature—but not the scope!—of man's freedom as rooted in the will of God thereby impairs man and distorts truth. Man's freedom requires a corresponding permissiveness in education. It demands respect for selfhood and for group rights. It makes responsibility necessary. It makes common concern the precondition for satisfactory community.

At all times and under all conditions education should make recognition of freedom one of its cardinal aims; freedom is at the heart both of the universe and of man. For this very reason freedom must not become the occasion for propaganda. Freedom springs neither from the causes and conditions that constitute its context—such as physical causation and social control—nor is it made possible merely by the correction of these external causes and conditions. For human beings, however, both inner and outer freedom are always limited. Christian education cannot afford to become Utopian in either direction—we are not God and we live in no Paradise!

For man is not only a creature of God's love, and as such endowed with meaning and dignity, a free, responsible being; he is also a creature who abuses his freedom, debases his dignity, and makes a lie of his meaning. Man is a sinner. If education forgets this fact, it is no longer realistic; education deals far more with sinners than with saints. Most of man's education should therefore be gauged to this track. The business of education is to release man's dignity and to make his freedom effective. Modern theology has become increasingly willing to accept the fact of sin. What, however, does it mean for Christian education? It does not mean that man in spite of sin lacks meaning, dignity, and freedom. It does not mean that God is not man's Creator and Father. These facts are ultimate; these perspectives are central for education. God's purpose and not man's sin is our primary viewpoint. Man's essential nature is therefore good by origin, by destiny, and by his present ultimate relationship. What God is making of him is essentially more important than what for the present man is making of himself. The eventual outcome of man's freedom is more real than man's present abuse of it. If sovereign love is ultimate, such a view of man is necessary. Therefore education should glory in man's freedom, dignity, and possibility.

On the other hand, the fact that man's essential nature is sound does not preclude the fact that he is now very ill. The truth that God's purpose for man's freedom cannot be frustrated in God's long run, does not contradict the observation that man abuses his freedom by putting himself in the center of things. Man is a sinner both in faithlessness and rebellion; education becomes unrealistic if it fails to take this fact into account. Even such a stark fact, however, in order to be dealt with effectively, must itself be seen in correct perspective. Man lives in a precarious universe, where physical and social insecurity and ambiguity are constant tempters to spiritual insecurity and lack of trust. His faithlessness and rebellion are therefore in large part occasioned by his creaturehood. Man needs to become real through willing.

Such willing, however, becomes serious only within the ambiguities of self and society, of nature within and of nature without. Man needs by his choices to learn what is truly from God and what is falsely claimed to be ultimate or most important. Sin is indirect faithlessness or rebellion, and is enveloped in both intellectual and emotional obscurity. Life also shifts scenes with most bewildering rapidity. Man is a sinner *as a creature, and as a very frail creature at that;* he sins within a heavy drag of weakness of flesh, mind, and spirit. Those who know how utterly hard life can be and most likely is for most people should not speak glibly about man's being a sinner. The surprising thing is that man is as good as he is, and that he dares to keep on suffering and caring. If education in false simplicity treats men as sinners, and not also as sinners who are pitiable creatures, it will lack depth of pathos; it will therefore fail to be effective.

To understand all, to be sure, is not to forgive all; but it is to understand how very much of man's failures and sins are occasioned and conditioned by circumstance. It must also be remembered, however, that part of man's load that drags him down toward the pit of sin is itself the result of previous sin on the part of the individual or of society. Much of man's ambiguity is of his own making. The world is hard on life; often it seems relentless. To what extent such ambiguity and hardship are God-given to educate man, and to what extent they are due to the needless burden of man's guilt, is beyond our competence to determine. Somehow, therefore, education must become wise enough both to pity man and to lift his burden where such action is needed, while also leading him to repentance and to transformation of life wherever such a course is open. No education in any case can be adequate that does not wrestle long and hard with the relation between man's sin and his circumstance.

The fact that man is sinner, furthermore, means that he is alienated from reality and has rationalized his separation from God. He therefore lives and thinks with his own self, or with some selfish group at the center of his life. Neither he nor any group is, of course, totally selfish. Men do much genuine good. Usually they have camouflaged their selfishness with idealistic slogans. Their zeal is for partial loyalties, which give them a chance to feel righteous about being over against other people or groups. They do not see themselves as sinners. Looking from a biased point of view, they see in a distorted light all issues that involve them. Often a guilt feeling will make them impute to others their own kind of sins; actually therefore they often see things turned inside out. The context is perverted—even converted! Whenever education deals with live personal or social issues, therefore, in whatever subject, from the social sciences to religion, unless its focus is corrected it usually acts as the justifier of the status quo. Education thereby abets social conflict.

Sometimes, to be sure, educators go far beyond the usual point of view of society as a whole. When the educator's own drives are involved in a subject, there usually is little objectivity available; in such a case the educational perspective, because of sin, is seldom conclusive to radical correction. The more largely the educator is identified with society, the more the community of feeling and the community of doing prevent corrective education. A genuinely Christian motivation, however, restores integrity and integration, and thereby affords a chance for objective analysis. Love's deep, existential participation in the pain of sin alone can both judge radically and still stand solidly with the group that is under judgment. Such love can "become sin" for the group. It can unite the community of being within the deepest community of the Spirit. It can tie men together, beyond their needed differences, within their common boundness before God. By unmasking the camouflage of sin such teaching, however, awakens fear and hate unless it leads to genuine repentance and redirection of life.

The problem of motivation in education is the question of integrity and integration. Motivation is basically a matter of freeing the self and society from destructive anxiety and guilt, in order to release within both of them creative concern and constructive adventure. To by-pass the fact of sin is to evade man's basic frustration. Motivation for the good life is inhibited by a guilt-tentacled attachment to the bad life. Understanding can aid in seeing the hampering condition; but most understanding follows rather than precedes man's becoming freed from the frustrations of sin. Such freedom, plus the understanding that results, are also mighty means to change the external conditions that thwart and hamper man's freedom. To what extent, however, can education ever hope to enter this main avenue of hope? Can education as such deal, legitimately and effectively, with sin as well as circumstance? The rest of the chapter will be devoted to this question.

An organism lives by adjustment to the environment; it must maintain a fairly stable relation with the environment of give and take if it is to survive. Health depends on right relation to reality. Metabolism and catabolism are processes essential to life. So also a person lives by adjustment. Motivation is not something dragged into life; it is part of life. There is no separate compartment for motivation; there are only degrees of motivation throughout the whole life. Possibly anything that needs to be artificially motivated is unnatural. If human nature, therefore, must be lured to religious living it is perhaps the wrong kind of living. If religion is, rather, man's right relation to what is most important and most real, no motivation is necessary except for clarification and maturation. If a person needs medicine, his desire for health motivates him to take even the most unpleasant ingredients, provided of course that he is mature enough to understand the need for the medicine. If a person requires a difficult operation that alone can restore him to life and normalcy, a mature and well-adjusted person needs no motivation except his desire for health. Religious motivation similarly should require nothing but the need for right adjustment to the will of God.

Socrates saw the close relation between knowledge and virtue. To equate them outright and immediately is obviously to forget both freedom and maturity. To separate them is to forget the organic nature of motivation for fullness of life. An old educational dictum holds that teaching is most effective if pleasant; attractive teaching is part of good teaching. Yet moral, social, and religious teaching is far from pleasant, in that it reveals the sinner to himself. For the maturing person, however, to see whatever hampers him basically and how the handicap can be removed is good, in spite of the fact that he must undergo an intellectual and emotional operation. Men live by meaning, by truth, by reality, by integrity. Deepest in their nature men want genuineness. The only motivation that is natural enough to release healthy desire and action is man's need for reality; no drive is more native to man than this. Religion is motivational whenever it is right. Real religion is right adjustment to reality, the way to man's perfect health—in the deepest and most lasting sense of his being. Religion alone can provide the full drive for creative living. High religion is the heart pump of right motivation.

The trouble with adjustment as an educational ideal is not with the idea itself, but with its content. Adjustment to the environment in its actual behavior leaves us exactly where we are—in trouble and in need of help! We need adjustment to reality—or right religion. To what then are we rightly adjusted? There can be adjustment to an ideal or some nonworldly reality that inculcates complete detachment from this world. Such, for instance, is the Buddhist ideal. We believe, however, that this kind of adjustment wrongs the nature of man in its organic need to belong to human community, and in its drive to live creatively in this world. Detachment results in a thin integration. The ideal of detachment is not generally relevant to our Western world, however rapidly it is now making its way in our direction. The most prevalent ideal for us, rather, is social adjustment. Psychological integration itself is usually defined in terms of social adjustment. Functional psychology makes adjustment to environment a key concept. Since society is itself alienated from reality, such adjustment is of course no solution; it lacks integrity. It involves complicity in a lie. Society is, to be sure, never wholly turned from reality; if it were, it could not go on. It is rather turned only partly in proportion to its own assumed need to distort the world in line with its own self-will. Part of this distortion, too, is due to immaturity and divided responsibility; part of it is due to a social inheritance that is difficult to transcend.

The more integrity and right relation to reality an individual person has, however, the more he will see through the camouflage of both inheritance and contemporary creation—and reject it. When he does so he reveals to other men their hidden wounds, the illness that society has repressed into its subconscious. He therefore becomes hated. Neither Jesus nor Socrates was loved generally, nor were they even understood! Social adjustment as such is at best a partial cure for the seeking self, for to be socially adjusted is obviously to be religiously maladjusted. It is to partake of society's alienation from reality. *When education accepts social adjustment as an ideal it rejects therefore integrity in favor of false integration.* President Chalmers rightly writes that "our greatest schools have been founded precisely in order that the young would not be content to adjust themselves to society, but would set about with vigor and courage to adjust society where they saw it in need of change."[7] If adjustment either as detachment or as integration in terms of society is the educational ideal, motivation can only be partial—and distorted at that. In the former case the need to be right with this world is repressed, while in the latter case integration as religious integrity is neglected. In either case truth is the victim; and the business of education is to find, to communicate, and to implement truth.

There is another kind of adjustment advocated by a false Christian theology, wherein man adjusts himself to God's will solely in terms of penitent decision. God, however, is a judge so holy and different from man that the more man hears God's word the more the net result is that he understands himself to be sinful. The nearer he comes to God, consequently, the more tense he becomes, the more he fears and trembles and cries for God to go away, for he is a sinful man. This ideal is neither true to the Christian faith nor educationally practicable. Not God's holiness is ultimate, but His love. Tension is produced and maintained, whereas repentance should lead to forgiveness, and to restoration to reality. This view of God as Judge is, therefore, partial, and cannot provide the kind of motivation that is necessary for right relation to reality. To this sense of judgment and of tension with the world some theologies add that man by his repentance becomes humble, and besides that he can live in a new dimension of eschatological grace. Knowing his sinfulness, no man is in position to judge others; and though he cannot arrive at any transformed experience, he can experience an *inner* transcendence

[7] Chalmers, *op. cit.,* p. 30.

over evil. Such analysis is more true than the kind that leaves man in increasing tension the nearer to God he gets; but it still leaves man without full restoration to reality, whether to God or to the real world.

The Christian faith requires, as its educational ideal, adjustment to the will of God, who is holy love. Without full judgment there can be no grasping of the depth of sin or the width of alienation. No sentimental evasion such as "leave things as they are" is ever Christian; the Christian faith is unsentimentally austere. Therefore personal or social integration is impossible apart from integrity unto death—even the death of the Cross. Nevertheless, this faith also teaches that God is more willing to forgive and to restore integrity than we are willing to ask. Why then do not men avail themselves of the Christian faith? The answer, for one part, is clear. Right asking demands man's full self-acceptance, and the remaking of his life by grace in line with God's will. To sinful fear such surgery is dreadful.

To those who do accept God's will, however, restoration to reality releases the more basic motivation, removes basic inhibitions and frustrations, and gives life new peace and drive. Those who accept God's will and way know His strength in and beyond life's conflicts. The new drive is not the old zeal, but is rather the natural living in the truth, which to the fearful often seems slackness. The adjustment also involves right relation to the world. The light judges, however kind it may mean to be, and therefore it hurts. As a rule, too, men hate what hurts them. The Christian faith, even so, is more than light; it is love's light, and therefore practical concern. Such concern sets out to remake the world in terms of God's will. Love's witness and work may meet hate and hurt, but they are inwardly satisfying and outwardly helpful; they provide both vision and fulfillment.

To be Christian, education must have such adjustment as its goal. When man reaches reality, motivation will be released. To reach reality, education, as we have seen, needs to use both knowledge and decision; it needs both to clarify and to attract. Education never can be effective without an understanding of human nature in its relation to reality. Men need integrity. How, then, can such integrity be had? Can education learn from human nature to become effective, even at its motivational task?

Alienation from reality requires restoration. The theological word for this operation has been "conversion"; men have to turn, or *be* turned, full face to reality. "Conversion" is preceded by the preaching and the teaching of the Word of God, with its light on sin and its judgment of it. Repentance as the surrender to the will of God and what that requires has been the traditional description of man's part of conversion; God's part is regeneration. Man's part is the turning that he cannot accomplish except by God's grace—his *being* turned. Is this kind of thinking real and right for education? We generally associate such thinking with evangelism; does evangelism form a necessary part of full Christian education?

Man is alienated from reality, and needs restoration to integrity. Jesus was realistic when he told Nicodemus that we must all be born again, or be born from above, if we are even to see the Kingdom of God, let alone enter it. If the goal of life is Christian community, and if Christian education is either for, or in, Christian community, such an experience is a prerequisite for Christian education. All education in this sense is preparation for conversion[8] and the development of its implications.[9] To claim anything less is to sell the Gospel short.

Nevertheless the term has been so much abused by institutional and traditional Christianity that it may now be a hindrance rather than a help. Reality is God's will for community, wherein the self is both fully lost and completely fulfilled. No self ever turns itself fully away from God; man can never turn his back completely on God; because he lives only by means of some positive relation to God. But the self needs to be delivered from the distortions of self-will

---

[8] Conversion is both an act and a process, a reorientation of life and the subsequent progress along new lines of advance.

[9] "Education is . . . the art of converting the Reason." Quoted from Arthur T. Vanderbilt, "A report on Pre-Legal Education," by Chalmers, *op. cit.*, p. 118. Also, "Our dispute with the Kremlin underlines the fact that American education should choose: condition the attitude or convert the reason." Chalmers, *op. cit.*, p. 252.

and of group-will, and to be caught up in God's inclusive will for community. Such in any case is an ideal statement of restoration to integrity; actually of course the feeble and partial self accepts God's will in intention and direction, more than in reality and attainment. Such acceptance is at best both a partial willing and a fragmentary seeing. What happens in conversion is the registering of the intent to integrity. What takes place in conversion is at best the acceptance of integration as a vague feeling-thought—the self's basic, beginning decision for integrity of life. However this act takes place, whether gradually or suddenly, and to whatever extent it is genuine beyond mere social conformity, such restoration is necessary to Christian life and community. In this profound sense education must deal with sin and conversion. To be adequate, education cannot by-pass the realism of Jesus, who knew that man is sinful and must be born again. Education fails if it does not succeed in the restoration of self and society to the will of God, which is its origin as well as its destiny.

Institutionally conversion usually means being "saved" and joining the church. Both acts are usually a matter mostly of social conformity; they are not so much sham as shallow. The self, in fact, accepts the verbalization of a status quo compromise with the Gospel that keeps him from being either hurt or helped by it; he merely becomes used to it. To a very large extent becoming saved is an institutional device for spiritual safety; it is an insurance policy. It is a sanction by the church of spiritual conformity, and consequent respectability and assurance of acceptance. By such devices and institutionalisms much morality and respectability are perpetuated for the good of the community, as well as for the spiritual integration of the church members. Actually, however, much if not most of the experience is the subconscious acceptance of the world as it is, by means of which to lessen or to hide real guilt feelings of alienation. Salvation can be and usually is, even openly, a most selfish quest. Thus evangelism is a problem as well as a power. Education, as the conscience of the Church, must unmask such subterfuge, and help unscramble what is good and bad in it.

Actually some churches have abused the term "conversion" to the point where one act of public conformity guarantees eternal salvation; "Once saved, always saved" is the slogan of this particular distortion of the Christian faith. The Christian faith, however, teaches that "by their fruits ye shall know them." The fruit of such conversionism is mostly in-group zeal, smugness, and narrowness. Education may not support any false kind of evangelism. Instead of thinking of salvation in such life-preventing terms, let us consider restoration to reality in terms of Kierkegaard's idea of repetition. Restoration is finding the purity of the single eye by the acceptance of the present will and reality of God in such a way that the past becomes lived forward. The future too becomes accepted—not as an unreal dream, but as having hope. The past is no old dowager, nor the future some dreamed-of maiden, but both past and future are enjoyed in the loveliness of a young wife who is really there both to have and to hold. The glory of the past and the hope of the future are, then, both incarnate in the present.

Such is Christian restoration to reality. Conversion is therefore both more than an act and less than an act; it is a lifelong process in dynamic interrelation to decision. It is a state of being or a stance toward God. It is the acceptance of grace in order to live by it. It is the decision for grace for the sake of growth in it. The state is preceded by a process of preparation, within which are many minor acts of preparation; and it is also dependent on an act of acceptance which is itself within a process of God's grace for the converted, while requiring at the same time a process that cannot continue apart from man's decisions for continuation. We must be born again by the grace of God from above, but restoration is no simple act, process, or state; into it enter God and man's fullest collaboration of grace, faith, and obedience.

We may think of this act as "cogging in" our lives into the life of God. From birth and before, we are dynamically and dependently related to God; we are "cogged in," whether we want to be or not. The decisive question is how we are "cogged into" reality. The more we understand God, and the more we want to accept His will, the more we can "cog" our lives into God's plan and purpose. Only as we come to know and to understand who He is and what He wants, of course, can we fit fully into His love and become members of the Christian community. Even such coupling of our lives into God's is mostly with our conscious lives—and not wholly even with them. The depths of the subconscious remain to be educated and to be converted. Such "cogging in" and staying in is possible only as we commit ourselves to the grace of God, and determine to live by the power of the Holy Spirit according to God's requirements for Christian community.

The higher we "cog in," and the more fully our lives know the power of God's life, the more we are delivered from the burden of self. We stop fearing others or physical pains and problems. We become free of circumstance, not by detachment from it nor by the rejection of it, but by an inner God-given freedom. This freedom sets the self free to help others, and to overcome in spirit—and as far as possible in fact—all outward circumstance. Christian freedom turns limitation into opportunity, and hardship into a chance for witness to God's reality. As our conscious and subconscious lives are both motivated together by God's Spirit, there is new power for creative transformation of life and society. There is also reality, to enable us to live deeply and with profound satisfaction. Such power and reality education needs.

What has this analysis of conversion to do with education? First of all, no college can be Christian that does not make Christian community its aim. Christian community, moreover, cannot be had apart from right relation to reality. Right religion means the overcoming in intention, and as far as possible in fact, of alienation from reality. It means the organic integration of life and reality by means of the restoration of integrity. This state of life is one essential purpose for Christian education. Nor can any teacher claim a Christian vocation who is not conscious of this larger framework of life. Man is a sinner who needs adjustment to God by acceptance of His will. Such acceptance is conversion, as restoration to reality. Every Christian teacher must aim at this above all else, even though his specific commitment is to the teaching, with integrity and competence, of a special area of truth. He who teaches merely chemistry is not a Christian teacher; the chemistry professor, by his very being and total stance, makes people conscious of the deeper reverence and the holier reality. Beyond the scientific reason he shares his inner sense of religious reality.

Perhaps no college can be Christian in any vital sense until a good portion of its administration and teaching staff is Christian, in this deepest sense of concern for God and His will for community. Christian teaching exemplifies and commends Christian commitment. Possibly home, church, and previous schools can prepare students for commitment before they enter; thus a few may enroll as committed Christians. We are not now referring to church conversion in the merely conventional sense; conventional piety may indeed be the greatest obstacle to Christian scholarship and community. But we do believe that home, church, and community can somehow begin to have a theology and experience of living integrity—God's concern for the inclusive community—which shall prepare many for becoming authentic members of the Christian college.

Certainly after matriculation deep concern for this experience must permeate all of college life: its worship, its study, its social life. We have previously tried to point to the decisional nature of education; decision for this kind of community is the context of Christian higher education. In the nominally Christian, or in the secular college or university, the stress Christians make must be the same. It can be expressed openly, however, only within Christian cells, whether of senior or junior members of higher education. Most of the time the community must communicate its faith and life indirectly. No Christian cells can exist, however, apart from such commitment to God and to the Christian community. If the word is given solid—not sentimental or institutionalized meaning—what is required of Christian education is *commitment to Christ.*

This converted nature or committed life will not remain such, however, apart from active nourishment. Human nature, to remain Christian, must keep growing in grace; not to grow is to starve spiritually; continued starvation entails death. A life once "cogged into" God at the level of Christian community easily slips out of the high place—slipping instead into a lower cog, where the Gospel is neither full nor real. Usually such a slip is not consciously known;

all that the person feels is that life lacks the depth of active conviction, and that the Gospel loses its sharp edge. To the outward view
such a life does not look very much different from the life of the
committed. But the difference grows; the paths diverge. In order to
prevent such slipping from active commitment, Christian education
needs to know how to nourish growth in grace.

Christian education, to be realistic, needs to acknowledge that man
is a sinner and must grow in grace, consequent to his being born
again. Christian education, however, has in its own hands the key
to such growth. Prayer is one answer to the need for Christian motivation.[10] Those who are born again, who have committed their lives
to Christ, need to be nourished by steady communion with God.
They must learn by prayer to live in the Spirit and to walk in the
Spirit. To do so, however, is never easy. Prayer is man's greatest
problem, because it is his mightiest potential power. Prayer has been
one of man's most pervasive experiences throughout his long and
varied history. Not all prayer, however, helps. How can Christian
education deal with prayer realistically and unsentimentally? If
prayer is one real answer to the need for Christian motivation, how
can prayer fit into a high and dignified academic program?

The difficulty with prayer is that it usually is not on the Christian
level or in the spirit of Christ; we usually pray to get our own ends,
either by magic manipulation or by sham acquiescence. Whether we
are importunate or yielding, we still want what we want. Out words
of prayer may hide this truth even from ourselves. Our feelings, too,
may be made to accept God's will. Deep down in our lives, however, is our own drive, the self-same and self-assumed. Somehow
Christian education must give Christian criticism of prayer; it must
do this by making clear and urgent both the content and the attitude
of true prayer. But how can this be done? Private prayer is sacred in
solitude; no one can reach it except the person who prays. If there
are on the campus great spirits of prayer, however—authentic, natural,
outgoing—their example and instruction have contagious influence.

[10] It is interesting to note, as Spencer Leeson observes, that Plato would recognize no
power in prayer; see *op. cit.*, p. 51. But where would Socrates have been unless he
could have consulted his demon? Prayer gives power for *creative and concerned
seeing and doing.*

Perhaps the simplest answer to the need for prayer as Christian motivation is Christian education in the presence and power of the Christian campus of Christian men and women who know in their own lives the beauty, joy, and power of prayer.

Public prayer is more and more difficult. Psychology and prayer mix with great difficulty. Prayer is public self-revelation; and what selves we reveal! We often can hear the hypocrisy in the prayer of others, of course, while still not recognizing our own. College should help us to pray. To say wise and beautiful prayers is not enough; prayer should become a personal help to enlighten our conscience and to make us want the common good. Psychology should be applied to our own lives. Prayer should be purified through psychology and through the social sciences. Thus study and spirit help each other according to God's plan of creation. If we really commit our will to God's inclusive will, the morning and evening prayers of the college may have to be radically rewritten. If we really live the life of God for all, our inner praying also may have to change drastically.

When such change takes place, at first the reality of prayer and the need for it will both seem gone. Life itself seems starved. Our old drives are inhibited; our ambitions are frustrated. We no longer have hearts that beat faster or a blood system that warms up at public prayer or in private supplication. Instead, however, as time goes on, quiet reality steals into public togetherness; simplicity fulfills sincerity; genuineness replaces the anxious pretense of experience. It is altogether likely that faculties, students, staffs, and administrations can learn to worship together in a transformed manner if religion becomes genuine, and if modest concern and humble service under God become real incentives, rather than appropriate words with which to entertain and placate deity. Christian colleges certainly cannot exist apart from prayer; prayer in some genuine form is as necessary to the Christian college as air and food. The creative source of significant social relations is prayer. The larger results may come in future generations; others may harvest what we sow. God is in any case the Source who alone gives the increase, especially by blessing the children of those who pray through many generations. Perhaps the Christian college must learn by humble and modest prayers how the motivation of prayer can best be integrated with the understanding of a study.

Here we can only remind ourselves of Christian living as motivation. Without it prayer can be but sham. If space permitted we should also have discussed the way Christian meaning lifts and directs life and thought; without such meaning Christian prayer and Christian life both suffer disastrously. The kind of God we worship also matters decisively. In some instances we have enough prayer, but not enough of the right kind. Nor may we in this connection more than indicate the fact that Christian faith in God's possibilities for history, in this life and for our lives and values beyond this life, is an educational essential. Man lives not by knowledge alone, but also by every word of truth, beyond knowledge, that God speaks for the renewing and re-creation of his people. Motivation is a most complicated affair; it should not be falsified by being simplified. Nevertheless we choose deliberately to stress prayer of the right kind as the most effective answer to motivation. Christian educators may have to wrestle long and fervently, in their own closed closets, before they can begin to become effective teachers of Christian motivation. The answer to moral and spiritual power is mostly not techniques or programs, but reality in our "inward parts."

Most important, however, is an understanding and acceptance of the Holy Spirit. Faith and prayer are human responses to reality; the Spirit Himself is ultimate reality. All worship must be in Him and in truth. All right motivation comes from Him. He comes disguised in forms compatible with those with whom He wants to work. As an alien in us He works His preparatory work of individuation and group consciousness. He is also the power of communication on any level of social intercourse. He is the *logos* by whom the Christ is born in history. The *logos* makes possible communication among various kinds of communities. The *logos* is meaning for all on their own level of being and understanding. We may not be aware of His presence, but, apart from Him, we cannot exist, work, or have community. On His own highest level of complete and all-inclusive love He speaks His true language. Paul asserted that "the Lord is the Spirit." He is in such a case the Spirit of Truth whom the world cannot see or receive, for it knows Him not; but to all who understand and receive Him, He gives the grace of motivation, and the gift of the community that truly fulfills life.

In each of those who understand and receive Him as the Christ, He becomes final as person; and in them together as the Spirit, He becomes final as people. In Him individuality becomes cherished without individualism; and community fulfills life without collectivism. The Spirit is thus the power we need to effect man's dignity and freedom. The Christian college, when all is said and done, is due to the creation and continual presence of the Spirit. Only as He becomes real and regnant can there be the judgment which shows man to be sinner in need of being born again; only He creates anew; only He gives growth in grace. When education becomes a matter of prayer and love at its center, as Moody advocated, then God Himself will be present to open every needed door of faith; then the Spirit Himself will be present to give community in truth.

Chapter VIII

Natural Science
and the Social Sciences

In a broad sense, science means public knowledge; in a narrow sense, it means a method for investigating the physical world. In classical times theology was the queen of the sciences; today some natural science, like physics, becomes the best exemplification of the scientific method. The general problem of education is the fact that the natural and the social sciences have not been as organically inter-related in education as they are in actual life. The wholeness of science in the totality of life has consequently been frustrated by education. Our task in the next three chapters is to study the two kinds of science, both in their natural distinctness and in their natural togetherness.

Roughly speaking, science serves to control knowledge. It stands guard against the arbitrary and the false; science sponsors tested truth. Science is not shared experience based on mutual testimony, but common experience objectively confirmed; even what we see or feel together, that is, has to be validated by objective means as being what it purports to be. Science, however, is not only checking, but also creation; it hunts new knowledge and it invents new things. Many think of science mostly in terms of verification, and thus lose its glory of adventure. Who nevertheless is more free and more in the mood for creative experimentation than the scientist? The modern world has been remade by science more than by any other fact. Therefore we honor the modern era in truth by calling it the age of science. This creative transformation includes man's knowledge in every realm of study as well as his physical mastery of the world.

Science in one sense can hardly be viewed moreover even in terms of control or creativity as much as in terms of growth. Science has shot up like a giant youth; the growth in its physical knowledge has been most obvious. Yet its growth in mind and spirit has not been inconsiderable. Science certainly has exemplified growth in mental maturity. The giant youth of science has stopped heeding tales and attended to facts. In its infancy science took magic seriously. In intent, at least, science has now shed superstition, and sought only such knowledge as can square with tested truth. This immense, over-all growth of science has been so impressive as to obscure and call in question all other methods of truth. Sometimes suspicion is near to the effect that the giant youth is unable to cope with personal and social relations. Suddenly, in fact, the youth himself, as well as others, wonders whether he is mature enough to play with matches. Science has evinced phenomenal growth, and is possibly even now about to display a new spirit beyond belief. Admiration has begun to become anxiously mixed, however, with a sense of great risk; destruction and self-destruction threaten as the possible gamble of further growth, along with the hope of undreamed advances in every area of life.

Science is both a censor and a creator; it is needed in both instances. As it has grown by its own creative thrust, seemingly pushing every obstacle out of its way, it has also shown others—or helped them to see for themselves—what false growth is. Our real problem now, however, is whether the growth of science must itself be scrutinized, and whether in order for this to be done there must not be compensatory growth outside the realm of science. The following questions should consequently be asked with critical care: What is science in itself, and how is it related to the whole field of knowledge? What is its legitimate function as a censor, and how can its censorship become damaging? Never has the need been greater for these questions to be answered with open honesty, and never has the mood to receive the right answer been so generally open as now, among both scientists themselves and all intellectually responsible thinkers. No book on education today can avoid addressing itself to this need and to this mood.

The kind of science with which we are to deal in this chapter is modern experimental science, which centers in the physical realm. It is precise knowledge publicly tested; this is the ideal of such science. To be sure, scientists are not in general naïve about their actual findings; on the contrary, they are sophisticated. They are themselves aware of the different kinds of obstacles in the way of precision in any sense of finality. One of its own great historians and systematizers, Alfred North Whitehead, went so far as to say that science is the "confident expectation that relevant thoughts will occasionally occur."[1] He knew that science in one sense is after all in the minds of men. Eddington in his *Philosophy of Physical Science* has almost rivaled Kierkegaard in his stress on subjectivity as truth. As a matter of fact, there is often a negative mood among scientists as to the possibility of real knowledge.[2] Statistical averages, the relation of signs to symbols, the inaccuracy of tools for testing—such indications of the lack of precision are commonplaces of scientific discussion. The bearings of context on fact, of perspective on perception, of presupposition on selection in seeing—no, modern science is by no manner or means naïve!

The bearing of limits of control on conclusion, for instance, of human fallibility on physical relativity, or of ignorance on incomplete predictability in the quantum theory, are commonplaces of scientific controversy. Who can read Schrodinger, Heisenberg, or Einstein without being aware of the sensitivity to philosophic presuppositions

[1] "No, science is in the minds of men. But men sleep and forget, and at their best in any one moment of insight entertain but scanty thoughts. Science therefore is nothing but a confident expectation that relevant thoughts will occasionally occur." Whitehead, *An Enquiry Concerning The Principles of Natural Knowledge* (Cambridge, England, The University Press, 1925), p. 10.

[2] "The more we pursue scientific investigation the more we discover that it does not lead to knowledge of the *intrinsic nature* of things. The knowledge it attains is *symbolic* knowledge rather than *intimate* knowledge; behind the symbolism there is a reality which escapes the measuring techniques." Hugh S. Taylor, "Physical Sciences," in Fairchild, *op. cit.*, p. 226.

and implications that permeate their thinking?[3] Scientists themselves are both perplexed by and proud of the almost incredible pace of change in scientific theory. The first thing to say, then, is that science itself is keenly aware of its problems of limitations, and of the dangers of premature judgments. Precision as a final over-all result is simply not the sum and substance of the scientific method, especially in its most modern drive. Scientists have their eyes open to the deeper questions of the inquiry for truth.

At the same time the main drive of science as a method has been for accurate, testable knowledge. Such knowledge can best be found in the physical realm; physical fact lends itself most readily to objective verification. In the physical realm the description of phenomena can be most fully controlled; there precise analysis lends itself to invariant prediction more than in any other field of inquiry. The prediction of an eclipse in the starry world seems nearly miraculous. In the world of minute matter the construction of explosives that threaten the very atmosphere stuns people. Whether such knowledge of microscopic physics is only a matter of statistical averages and of theoretic formulation, the predictability of the result gives external credibility to the claim of knowledge. Such prediction is essential to the control of knowledge.

Predictability seems also to constitute one aspect of personal and social security; what is uncertain threatens us. Science in its concern for maximum predictability has accordingly had both an objective and a subjective appeal to mankind. Prediction itself, moreover, depends largely on mathematics. Mathematics is a symbol both of what can be publicly verified and of what can satisfy man's inner craving for certainty. Men have honored science not only for its material benefits but for its inner order.

Mathematics has been the scientific ideal. Therefore a science like classical mechanics has been peculiarly a model for experimental knowledge. In it even the dynamic can be translated into equations. In analytical mechanics physical process itself becomes an exemplification of applied mathematics. Time can be treated like intervals or

[3] Or compare the observations of such thinkers as Karl Heim, *Christian Faith and Natural Science,* and Charles Raven, *Science and Religion* (Cambridge, England, The University Press, 1953).

slices of process, which, after that, can be analyzed at will without injury to the total process. The quality of a physical event can thus be analyzed entirely in terms of quantity. Process is thus an operation that can be converted into structural terms without damage to truth. To be sure, motion must be added to time and mass, in order for mechanics to be studied as such. Nevertheless the motion picture can be stopped, and every picture can be examined for itself. The motion in time gives the subjective effect, but mechanics itself can be rethought in operational terms. Structure is a slice of physical process. The most elaborate problem in classical mechanics calls for complicated equations, but apart from being difficult these problems are not one whit different in essence from the more simple exemplification of mechanics. Modern probers into mechanics, in the light of new presuppositions about nature, may be humble about the depths of mystery that beset them, but classical mechanics operated with notions of Cartesian clarity.

This emphasis on accurate testing gave its greatest yield in the field of physical fact. Mathematics was the ideal; classical mechanics was the model. Under this impact the world of physical nature yielded up to its investigators those aspects that made it appear to be a vast mechanism. The selected parts were considered to be the whole of nature. Purpose, value, and goal directedness had no place in this scheme; and, as Laplace so well told Napoleon, there certainly was no need for the hypothesis of God. This thought we shall develop shortly. Our interest now is in the fact that science made essential—even all-important—the physical basis of things. It did not even slow down to acknowledge a modest "for our purposes only." Newton climaxed this process for cosmology; Darwin, for biology; Freud, for psychology. This stress beyond a doubt was a healthy relief, and needed escape from an institutionalized theology that relied on the Bible and on the edicts of the Church in all realms of truth. The revolt of science against an oppressive and false theology was necessary and good.[4]

[4] Kenneth Boulding points out a real problem: "The highways that could handle the traffic from Ptolemy and Aristotle with comfort have hardly adjusted themselves to Copernicus and Darwin, and are hopelessly congested by Freud, Keynes, and Einstein! Consequently, the true center is by-passed, rival centers of nationalism, Fascism, Communism, and so on are set up, and the whole vast city threatens to disintegrate." "Economics," in Fairchild, *op. cit.*, p. 381.

We are also more rooted and conditioned by physical causations than we imagine. These aspects of life and nature are not to be denied. When Marx furthermore showed how history and sociology are basically controlled by power over the physical means of production, he re-emphasized the same truth in new realms. The effect of this stress on the physical on people in general, however, was to center both their knowledge and their hopes for a better life in the physical nature of things. Not only did trade flourish as a result of scientific progress, but also fortunes made by trade were plowed back into scientific endowments. Business spent millions on science indirectly by its support of institutions of higher learning. Businessmen became leaders in education; money became the gateway to social leadership; prestige shifted more and more to technical-professional vocations. In general, John Dewey's philosophy exemplified much of modern man's hope as it centered in science and in common sense.

The upshot of this concern with science as experimental knowledge was a steady magnifying of the regularities of nature, and a raising to primary importance the knowledge and manipulation of physical fact. Thus by means of science, both as inner order and as the power over the physical realm, education and culture both became captives of science. Other subjects had their place and devotees, but science occupied indisputably the dominating center of the stage of modern history. To stay there, however, became more and more difficult and embarrassing, because the two main supports on which science rested tended themselves to split apart and move away from the center of life into opposite extremes of abstraction. Let us now look at this curious but understandable fact.

What happened was a basic split of knowledge into two opposite camps: on one side was the pole of physical fact; on the other, the pole of logical coherence. Scientific experiment headed one way, and mathematics the other. No wonder that there was a rise of nominalism, the theory that only the individual fact is true. No wonder that realism became moribund: faith in thought as intrinsically indicating also factual truth. Realism meant that fact and thought are organically connected, and logically involve each other. Nominalism is the assertion that there is no necessary relation between thought and fact. There is obviously some truth in nominalism, since thought is partly the product of fallible human beings. Science, on the other hand, in one sense seems to support realism, since it deals with regularities and with universal operations rather than with individual things as such. This fact has fooled many into thinking that there is enmity between nominalism and science, that science is an order of abstraction incapable of handling that which is individual. But mathematics alone is uniformity without physical substance; it is such an order of abstraction. Actually the working model of science was classical mechanics, where the equations even of dynamics could be converted into physical things. For all intents and purposes the goal of science came to be to establish and to explain physical fact.[5]

Aristotelian substance theory as a matter of fact came to triumph in science, but minus its original final causations. Science in substance became akin to the natural philosophy of St. Thomas, minus his dimension of purpose—let alone his level of revelation and spiritual reality. Realism affirms at its basis that the realm of physical fact experienced through the body and the realm of total experience registered in the mind are the same, except as man distorts thought in relating one realm to the other. Such is the meaning of the adequation of intellect and thing. Except for its abuse therefore thought not only intends, but conveys truth. Reason is innately reliable, not as having any esoteric or isolated content of its own, but as the native interpreter of reality. Thought does not contribute to reality, except for creative activity, but is rather its faithful reporter, interpreter, and evaluator.

Nominalism denied this truth of realism at the one end of experience, claiming that empirical fact alone controlled theory; at the other end, positivism made the same kind of claim, namely, the independent verifiability of the realms of fact and thought. Science and mathematics in the disguise of philosophy thus joined from both

[5] "Science derives its validity from the accessibility of its accumulated findings to the check of any scientist without limitations of chronology or (in a free world) of geography." Taylor, *op. cit.,* p. 217.

extreme ends of knowledge to demolish the middle. Reason became shorn of content, except for its own laws of self-consistency on the one end, and for the power to describe the physical realm at the other. Science and philosophy became tendencies in education that bifurcated experience and helped to cave in the middle; knowledge and life in their actual togetherness. Science and philosophy in the name of reason joined forces to destroy its efficacy where it was most needed.

The irrationalism of the modern era has been engendered, more than we perhaps think, by means of the undermining of reason by two disciplines that, strange as it may seem, boasted of exalting it. To be sure forgiveness is easy, since they knew not what they did; but they did it. Philosophy itself, however, registered this split in knowledge, inasmuch as it was enamored by the certainty of the mathematical ideal on the one hand, and by the exactness of science, with its technical mastery and world-realistic power on the other; besides being glad to be delivered from the yoke of an oppressive theology that was bound by institutionally vested interest. Philosophy wanted to be free for the truth—and who can blame it? Whereas, however, as we shall soon see, it should have been the censor of science and of religion alike, it floated nearly rudderless with the prevailing intellectual tide.

The craving for certainty and the lure of prestige combined to increase the emphasis placed on the poles of scientific experiment and on mathematical consistency. The scientific ideal, humble, demanding integrity, cautioning patience, and critical care, climbed higher and higher in the educational sky. In the meantime the middle realm of knowledge became both less cared for and lost in prestige. Sometimes the realm of experience as lived was simply ignored as inaccessible to exact knowledge; sometimes it was cut into educational pieces and studied, part by part, with the tools of scientific inquiry. Man's body became treated as a mechanism; man's mind became a matter of determined physical behavior; man's social experiences became a subject of attempted sociological statistics and of human engineering. Purpose as such, however, freedom, significance, social decision, or spiritual steering—all this vast fullness of the middle region of experience could not be handled by exact experimentation, and consequently became a lesser kind of knowledge—*if knowledge at all*. Many competent thinkers limited the word "knowledge" to science, and refused to call anything knowledge that could not qualify at its bar. The teachers of these broader subjects often suffered from a feeling of inferiority, and tried their best, in some way or other, to become certified by science. The mischief was already done, however, because Antaeus had been lifted off the ground and had no strength.

Reason depends on its reliability as correspondence with reality; it lives or dies by being the bearer of truth, when correctly used, and of falsehood, when abused. Reason, however, was rendered impotent in the rough and ready matters of real life. It became "kicked upstairs" to the realm of pure abstraction, or to the realm of exact physical prediction. The very original sin of the intellectual life, however, is the "all or none" fallacy: man's attempt to be as absolute as God is, to know absolutely and to refuse the creature-hood of partial knowledge and of veiled choices. Actual life is not a matter of crystal-clear seeing, but rather of walking by such sight as is needed for moral and social choices. Not wanting to live humbly as a creature, but coveting instead the absolute power of knowledge, man chose as of primary importance the thin abstractions wherever exact prediction was at least a relevant ideal, and thereby forfeited the hard task of finding the fuller light for his more practical tasks of living.

This original sin of the intellect led to the wages of sin—moral, spiritual, and social blindness. Knowledge came to be declared impotent in these primary realms. Thus where man needed the light the most, he sought and believed in it the least!

During our own century of wars and threatened destruction, however, the understanding of man's deeper needs began to turn. Technically the tide had begun to turn in the middle of the previous century. The Kant-Laplace method was called into serious question by the finding of a planet by deduction as early as 1844. Nominalism quavered under such impact of universalism in science. In the realm of thought, Kierkegaard at the same time raised basic questions of method that, though growing out of his own seemingly extreme nominalism, yet called into play many factors of subjectivity and decision that challenge to death the reign of objectivity. Not until a generation or so ago, however, did the full tide of a new era set in. Enough to say here that science came to accept theory as part of truth, even where many operational factors were definitely theoretical constructs. Science had to accept concepts not only by inspection but also by postulation.

When natural science once could accept and utilize this extension as natural to scientific theory it had become educationally mature. Science itself could then begin to appreciate similar methodological approaches in other fields. These other fields thereupon began to breathe a new creative freedom. They have by now begun to develop methods strongly native to their own fields, and to converse creatively with other fields. Science has been subjected to a large-scaled barrage of criticism: some friendly and understanding; some, unfortunately, protective of methods and beliefs that cannot endure the test of truth. Many scientists have asked for such co-operation. Science by its own efforts and by the help of others is thus gradually coming to see what is its legitimate field and claims to truth, and what is presumption or ignorant imperialism. The result is that we are on the verge most likely of a new era both of science and of competent and daring leadership in the fields of the previously excluded middle. What then does this mean for scientific method in relation to truth as a whole?

For some time now science has been seen as the servant of life. Science is a method for the careful checking of truth—not all truth, but such truth or as much of truth as science can handle. Science is also a controlled way of finding new truth;[6] the creative aspect of science must never be underestimated. Science besides is a growing system that builds itself up in truth. The greatness of science is its historic depth of historic accumulation that is utilized almost entirely for present needs, whether to know or to do. Yet science is today also seen as a major risk apart from intellectual,

[6] An interesting approach to science is James B. Conant's *On Understanding Science* (New Haven, Yale University Press, 1947).

moral, and spiritual control; catastrophic destruction by means of science is spectacular. The hidden destruction in the fields of personal decision and of social steering, where man's understanding of science has actually served to discourage investigation or to throw hampering doubt on the results that could not measure up in exactness to its own canons of precision—these, however, are not equally noticeable, but they are indeed the basic occasion for threatening disaster by scientific invention.

Such turning of science into scientism is now more and more a publicly recognized fact. Scientists themselves have long been aware of it. Some of them now call science "positivistic," i.e., being only a matter of method, and not of metaphysics. Such men now openly disavow the connection between scientific method and philosophic naturalism. But many are also aware that scientists have a moral obligation to be concerned about the meaning and the end of science; they know that they as scientists are not automata, but men. They therefore must also be educated as to the meaning of life, and how whatever is done in any significant part of life should be interpreted and integrated in the light of all the rest. There is consequently a coming together of men of science with other scholars in such gatherings as the Conference on Science, Philosophy and Religion, The Institute for Religious and Social Studies, and similar undertakings.

A new synthesis is also being worked out, of science, philosophy, and religion. Knowledge is understood as scientific, philosophic, and decisional; the categories of being, seeing, and doing are becoming more and more organically related. There is no disposition among the more thoughtful scholars to minimize the obviousness of the objective. A recent revolt against the "cult of objectivity" may at times go too far, but the real aim of their revolt should become to show that the objective aspect of knowledge is good as far as it goes, and when it is used where it belongs; but that it is deadly dangerous when it is made into an "all or none" affair, or when it is used out of place. Perhaps the simplest way to summarize the tendency that prevents and disrupts knowing is that people crave certain knowledge and therefore tend to identify publicly verified knowledge with truth. That is only fair. Certain knowledge can be tested and shown to others most easily; that is clear. Men feel secure about knowledge without, and about their own knowing within, when they can rely on objective tests; that is obvious. Hence the main tendencies in logic and psychology have been overwhelmingly to emphasize the certain aspects of knowledge. Consequently science has been more than a revolt against theology, and more than a materialistic concern of men. It has been more than a craving for security.

Science has been, and is, the acme of man's knowledge; his pride and joy in being able to find and do the truth, with the least bias and with the most objective helpfulness. All these stresses on objective certainty and exactness, however, have undermined the use of reason to illumine man's living decisions. Science is good, and very good, in its place. Only when it prevents and disrupts intellectual, moral, and spiritual knowledge—in so far as these can be had—is the use of science an enemy of human welfare and of truth. This fact is now becoming a matter of general understanding.

The synthesis that is taking place stresses that knowledge is best known at the poles of physical fact and of logical consistency. This kind of demonstrable knowledge is called "validity." Validity is good, and ought to be sought with all critical care. There are realms of knowledge of the highest significance, however, where validity is not high, but where knowledge is better than ignorance and where seeing is better than groping. There is present in these areas personal and social wisdom grown out of deep experience and long history that cannot be logically or scientifically demonstrated in the sense of having high validity, but that has high practical relevance for personal and social choices. The reaching out to see things together and in relation to concrete needs of life and of society is called "adequacy."

Adequacy means first of all an attitude. It means that we have no right for the sake of the purity of knowledge to stop short of whatever interpretations bear on life. Adequacy insists that knowledge is not for its own sake, but for the service of life. Truth is truth, to be sure, regardless of whether or not it serves life. Nevertheless we are under obligation to find all the truth that we can to direct life. Therefore adequacy aids attitudinally the prevention of the abuse of science, and serves as the creative spur to its use in the service of life. Adequacy is also contextual. It insists that any bit of proved knowledge is not what it is except in relation to its total context. Myriad other facts which can never be tested all at once, and are in fact assumed in experimentation, go into its being what it is. Explanation that stops short of context stops short of factual truth. As far as possible adequacy tries to introduce the truer and fuller picture of what is fact in terms of the interactions of the fuller reality. When this is done, validity is sacrificed to adequacy, in the sense that the larger context is incapable of exact testing, but even so truth is filled in and corrected.

Adequacy prevents satisfaction with piecemeal knowledge, and strives for the synoptic vision. As a matter of fact, in actuality there is no such thing as a totally isolated fact. The pole of fact obviously is understood only in terms of a long history of theory. The separation of fact and theory is only apparent, not real. At best, it is a device for logical analysis; at worst, it is a psychological blindness —whether ignorant or willful. Truth of every kind is always a synthesis of fact and theory, consciously developed or experientially implicit. Adequacy debars the way to the idolatrous "worship at the holy altar of fact." Adequacy delivers science from being abused as scientism.

Adequacy also strives for significance, not only in terms of life, but also in terms of functional value. Often questions of purpose and significance are ruled out of experimental knowledge in order the better to control the situation; such a procedure is legitimate, and necessary for its purposes. Adequacy insists that when such an operation is performed, however, the result must be submitted to the light of the further question of its meaning or its end. Adequacy is thus a call for the fuller picture of truth. It is an attitude; it is a striving for context; it is a demand for the seeing of any isolated experiment, or any limited theory, in terms of the rich background in the womb of which it alone is what it is. Adequacy is thus both a stance and a context; it has both content and relationship.

The law of life in knowledge is at every point to keep all possible validity, and at the same time to increase at every point all possible adequacy. The law of death in knowledge is to make validity independent of adequacy, or to make adequacy independent of validity.[7] We need science to be science more than ever; but we also need more than science. One of the real marks of maturity in our educational scene is that such an observation as this is coming to be a truism. It was not always so! validity was once almost entirely equated with knowledge. The new openness to context and significance is evident in much scientific thinking, where the relations between theory and empirical research have received thoughtful treatment.

As we shall see, philosophy and religion in much of their modern drives have been slower to accept such an ideal and such a possibility for knowledge. Even as during the last few centuries science has led us astonishingly down opening vistas of reliable knowledge, it may now lead the educational advance in this realm of expanding method, both contextually and attitudinally. The natural sciences, as a matter of fact, are generally mature and relaxed at this point, for their purposes; today some social scientists are also working with remarkable competence along the same trail. The social sciences are of course most crucial to our day and age, not only for education, but particularly for our finding the kind of co-operative seeing, distinctive in parts and yet synoptic, that shall provide the right possibilities both for education and for life as a whole.

Social science is a relatively new subject in the educational field. Robert K. Merton calls it "a fledgling discipline, anxiously presenting its credentials for full status in the fraternity of the sciences."[8] Nevertheless it is already accorded first-class and often primary importance. It feels itself to be in fact almost Messianic along such

[7] For a fuller and more technical development of validity and adequacy, and for scientific material generally, see the author's *Faith and Reason* (New York, Harper, 1946), chap. II, "The Circle of Science."

[8] "Sociological Theory," in *The American Journal of Sociology*, Vol. 50, p. 463.

lines as follows: The natural sciences do not deal with the center of the human problem; they deal with the impersonal realms, whereas our critical issue is how to deal with men. Our problems are personal and social; they therefore need to be approached on this level. The only reliable method we have, however, is science; all other knowledge is hit or miss. Religious knowledge is usually arbitrary and subjective; philosophic knowledge is generally speculative, or evasive of the more exact issues of fact.

Now, however, the social sciences can tell us—or will soon be able to tell us—what we need to know about the social realm, even as the natural sciences have given us the requisite information about the realm of nature.[9] Many of the educational foundations, too, are shifting the emphasis of their support from natural to social science. These foundations are particularly concerned about knowing human nature, especially since religion and ethics, while telling us well enough what ought to be done, have never explained how to get people to do what they should.

The social scientists themselves, of course, are usually more concerned with the knowledge of the field, for they believe that knowledge will provide the occasion for social solutions. They seem in this instance to be harboring the old illusion that education as such can save the world. Practical people, however, who want to utilize social science as they have used science to control and to milk nature, are more concerned with constructive human engineering than with knowledge as such; therefore they stress the motivational potentials of social science. Many thoughtful people, on the other hand, believe that such faith in the social sciences, whether for knowledge or for motivation, is naïve. They believe that social science is aggressive, like any newcomer who fights his way to recognition; and that much of its Messianism therefore is false—"a zeal not according to knowledge." What is the truth concerning social science, if it can arouse such needed and varied opinions?

[9] Fifteen years ago [ca. 1928], W. F. Ogburn and Alexander Goldenweiser could close the introductory chapter of their ambitious volume, *The Social Sciences and Their Interrelations,* with the words: 'Civilization, nurtured and strengthened by the natural and the exact sciences, must henceforth look for its preservation and enhancement to the sciences of society.' " Nash, *op cit.,* p. 138.

Religion has been both arbitrary and divisive; who can deny the fact? Philosophy too has been speculative, and shy of concrete counsel. In the meantime the social realm has definitely not been explored with the vigor and care that modern science demands. Social science is consequently going to fill a major need in education and in civilized life. Our own understanding of its place is that *social science represents the pole of adequacy in science as a total approach to knowledge.* Each field of science has its distinctive need for adequacy and kind of adequacy. The social sciences, however, entertain to the maximum the problems of the significance in human life and culture. This significance may be intensive, as in psychology, or extensive, as in sociology or political science; or the intensive and the extensive may meet, as in social psychology or in sociological psychology. But all the social sciences should represent adequacy in science, or science pushed to its utmost limits in the field of human relations. Our own estimation of the place and future of the social sciences is that they are of primary importance to education and culture.

The problem arises at once, however, that science is not supposed to deal with significance; science has traditionally been thought of as free from the problem of value. Significance is bound to have its subjective side, if for no other reason than that it pertains to the understanding and the affective aspect of human beings to nature, to each other, and to the realm of the symbolic.[10] How then, if such is the case, can we with a straight face write that social science represents adequacy in science, especially since it deals both intensively and extensively with the question of significance in human relations? Is social science then legitimately science, the extension of science into the field of human relations, or is it rather what Robert Redfield calls "The Art of Social Science"?[11] This author

[10] See how a psychologist feels the reductionist pull of method: "An account of man's motivation in terms of an implied final cause is understandably repugnant to the scientific mind, since final causes are not directly observable. In its extreme form a teleological theory would explain the direction of behavior in terms of goals that transcend the experience of the individual. Such a theory would make impossible any empirical science of motivation." MacLeod, *op. cit.*, p. 277.

[11] In *The American Journal of Sociology*, Vol. 54, p. 181.

holds that social science is both science and art. "Social science is essentially scientific in that its propositions describe, in general terms, natural phenomena. . . . It investigates nature. It strives for objectivity, accuracy, compendency."[12] But as an art it "consists, in some part, of perceptive understanding of some aspect of human nature, the gift or skill in making significant generalizations as a derivative of such perception, and a fresh viewpoint that questions previous views."[13]

We believe, however, that such a point of view is unnecessary. Social science is not an art. All the above-mentioned qualities are needed in natural science as well; they are needed only in a special way or degree in social science, because of its subject matter. On the very contrary, human relations in their entirety demand an art beyond all scientific methods of control. Therefore it is truer to say that social science represents adequacy in science, and validity in the art of social relations. It provides such validity for the art of living precisely by being a science. In other words, social science is the scientific aspect of the art of social relations. In this way science is kept science, within its proper scope and efficacy, while the need for an art of human relations beyond that is made clear. On the other hand, no art of human relations can be at its best unless it utilizes social science as the pole of adequacy in science, and as the pole of validity in the art of human behavior and relations.

The problem for social science has been that it has not yet discovered its own distinctive kind of scientific model. Social science needs to be a science if it is to perform its rightful duty, but it must remember that it is a *social* science. Robert Redfield, for instance, speaks of social science as describing "natural phenomena" like any other science; it deals with nature. Now on the contrary, the one thing that is distinctive about social science as a science is that it does not deal with natural, but with personal and social phenomena. It cannot classify merely as an extension of the natural sciences. The proper limit of adequacy for these sciences is natural phenomena.

A first-rate theoretician like Talcott Parsons nevertheless suggests that classical mechanics makes an ideal model even for social science,

[12] *Ibid.*, p. 189.
[13] *Ibid.*, p. 181.

because, as a science dealing with controlled phenomena, it makes prediction possible, not only of particular experiments, but even of variables that are deduced from theory.[14] He then goes on to show, however, how this model is impossible for the social scientist *at present*, because the social scientist needs a structural-functional model like that of physiology. He hankers for analytical mechanics as a model, because he wants to reduce terms of social process to their operational equivalents. Merton joins him in such an ideal integration of theory and empirical research. This hankering for social science to be a branch of natural science, however, is exactly its most serious mistake. Social scientists should not be accused of wanting merely personal certainty and professional prestige, because they too long to be rid of arbitrariness—to be in fact real scientists.

Yet science must deal with each field according to its own nature. It has no right, in the interest of methodological convenience, to falsify its problems. For the sake of distinctness, clarity, and exactness it must not simplify—and thus distort—its task. The social realm is simply not merely the natural. Even the realm of biology is not merely that of physics or mechanics. There are factors of functional purpose within the organism that refuse to be reduced to mere mechanics. The scientific ideal may be perfect prediction, but physiology cannot on this account reduce physical processes to mere chemical or structural states and conditions. Similarly, chemical regulators and organismic deficiencies play their vital part in life, but psychology cannot be true to facts and reduce motivation to physical determinism. What we know of depth psychology, endocrinology, and purpose in motivation has bearings of adequacy on psychological interpretation. Nor can physiology, *if it wants to be adequate,* rid itself entirely of psychology. Physiological process furthermore is also more than time as succession; isolated slabs of time are meaningless except in the light of the purposive process as a whole. Time is an event that involves succession, but is more than mere succession. Thus physiology is more than mechanics; biological time is not merely chronological time.

The social realm, however, including the psychological, is more

[14] Cf. his *Essays in Sociological Theory, Pure and Applied* (Glencoe, Ill., The Free Press, 1949).

than physiology. Into this realm enters the dimension of "the symbolic." The symbolic, too, is more than mere imaginative excitation; the symbolic relates to the spiritual or to the religious. The social realm involves freedom as centrally initiated motive patterns. It involves response to a spiritual realm with power to change the physical, to direct personal and social energy according to new patterns, and even to let into life new energy. The will to live, goal-directedness, is in this sense more than a physical state. It makes a difference to physiology, as any competent physician knows. Nor can psychology limit the will to live to "what happens within the skin." As reductionism was once the greatest single enemy of true science, just so it now threatens to distort and make ineffective the work of the social scientists.[15]

Let us take a concrete illustration from the social sciences. Merton has pointed out that no theory exists that allows for the prediction of variables by deduction. In a brilliant, fair minded, and remarkably competent analysis, he champions a theory for sociology where there could be "a statement of invariance *derivable* from a theory."[16] He goes on to admit candidly that "the paucity of such laws in the sociological field perhaps reflects the prevailing bifurcation of theory and empirical research. Despite the many volumes dealing with the history of sociological theory, and despite the plethora of empirical investigations, sociologists (including the writer) may discuss the logical criteria of sociological laws without citing a single instance which fully satisfies these criteria."[17] He knows of course that "approximations to these criteria are not entirely want-ing."[18] Then he goes on to indicate that Durkheim made such an approximation when he analyzed why in general Catholics have lower suicide rates than Protestants, which showed that social co-hesion by providing psychic support relieved anxieties, and that,

[15] ". . . H. A. C. Dobbs has aptly termed 'structural insight' the ability to ap-prehend relevant features which 'may well be non-metrical in the ordinary sense of applied natural science but still have geometrical or topological structure (in a general-ized sense).' " Thompson, *op. cit.*, p. 12.

[16] *Op. cit.*, p. 469.

[17] *Ibid.*, pp. 469–70.

[18] *Ibid.*, p. 470.

since Catholics excel in social cohesion, it can be predicted (or at least anticipated) that Catholics should also have lower suicide rates than Protestants.

No better example could have been taken, however, to show how sociology can seem scientific even when begging basic questions. Actually Catholics are generally far less critical about their religion, and therefore have more of the kind of faith that is taken for granted. The fear of what will happen in the next life is in our opinion dominantly what deters the most believing Catholic from committing suicide. The writer has seen Lutherans in his native Sweden shudder at suicide, convinced that those who commit it are eternally "lost" or tormented. When this faith is no longer a living world view, as it has seldom been for a long time among sophisticated Protestants, suicide takes on a different color as escape from trouble. But Durkheim omitted the efficacy of faith in the supernatural as basic motivation.

An interesting sociological investigation would be a comparison of suicide rates among fervently believing Buddhists and Shintoists. Their picture of the future life and men's present relation to it is widely different. The result seems obvious, but the study should be made. When religion, however, is reduced to a social phenomenon, explained in terms of society, it no longer commands power to account for social phenomena. In other words, the obvious explanation to the person who knows religion was simply ignored by Durkheim, and this blunder was singled out by Merton as an ideal approximation of social science to science! Social cohesion itself is thus a sociological problem. The reality of the spiritual realm was omitted by Durkheim because of a false method, due in large part to an assumed metaphysics that is defective. A narrow method arrives at partial truths!

Merton himself is aware of the danger of theory. He is afraid of what H. S. Sullivan called "precocious explanations."[19] Though he wants theory to be productive by being precise, in the sense of determinate, he also acknowledges that "in the search for precision, care must be taken to see that significant problems are not

[19] *Ibid.*, p. 468.

thus inadvertently blotted from view."[20] All the same, both he and Talcott Parsons aim at the method of the natural sciences. Parsons claims, for instance, that economics can model itself on mechanics! Economic laws, however, are mostly statistical averages of social behavior. Science does not predict who will commit suicide; neither does economics predict how far any one farmer will go in cultivating the land under conditions of diminishing return. Neither can it predict how any one family will treat an unproductive member—even economically. Nor does it indicate the precise relation between political and social conditions that can radically change economic operations. *Certain objective conditions operate in the realm of economics that can be treated scientifically as theory.* In one sense, however, economics, practically speaking, is also an art, as a personal or social value judgment. Economics can be a narrow science by treating the objective conditions that act as objective pressures on personal and social economic judgments, but, beyond such a science, economics needs to cultivate adequacy by an understanding of human nature and social conduct that can never be reduced to precise prediction.[21] Even to compare economics to analytical mechanics is to court validity at the expense of adequacy.

To discover these objective conditions that are given factors in social relations is the task of social science. These conditions are pressures on social judgments. They condition human behavior, but they do not determine it. Men are not merely natural phenomena; they are moved also by abstract ideas and by symbolic relations. Actually they are moved by the sense of right and wrong, of the proper and the good, as well as by the actually existent pressures of social conditions. In fact they are most deeply moved by religious reality. Religiously speaking, they respond to their understanding of the will of God, as well as to personal likes and social lures or forces. The problem of social science is always to find the right relation between theory and empirical research. No theory that

[20] *Ibid.*, p. 472.

[21] ". . . the most significant techniques of economic theory, for instance, are as applicable to socialist or to primitive economies as they are to capitalism. This is particularly true of what may be called 'equilibrium economics'; it is less true of the theory of economic change and development, where purely economic abstractions are less useful and a broad interpretation of history is necessary." Boulding, *op. cit.*, p. 377.

assumes a priori that natural science can account for social truth can be scientifically adequate. To neglect the problem and power of human responsibility and choice, and to treat men as social aggregates determined by external and internal forces, is to falsify the field to be investigated. Social science thereby wins spurious and expensive simplicity.

The crux of the problem is rather how to relate statistical averages to human nature. How are the objective forces that operate in social relations intertwined with personal choice and social action? The problem of deviants is not simply the problem of the psychologically or socially maladjusted; it is also the problem of the prophets and the saviors of society. It is the problem of adjustment to a Reality that goes far deeper than adjustment to actual society. The social sciences may very well deal fruitfully with the *conditions* of creativity and change, without being able fully to account for creativity or bid desirable change come forth. Social science will be adequacy in science and validity in the art of human behavior and social relations as long as it distinguishes carefully between the conditions of social action and social action itself. It may well be that these *conditions* can be reduced to operational language. There may be determinate relations of the given conditions of groups. *If so, the social sciences will describe the social fields within which freedom operates as the responsive and initiating factor of selfhood and society.* The conditions of social process may be reduced or transformed to structural language, without denying the dynamic creativity of personal and social life.

It may be that, if social science deals with the social factors that condition culture, rather than with society or persons as such, action frames of reference can be established from observational procedures that can be phrased in terms of genuinely operational concepts.[22] In such a case social science might even be normative as well as descriptive, i.e., it might be prescriptively normative based on the description of select modes of behavior that most satisfactorily fulfill their proper function. Neither personal nor social action

[22] Cf. Casserley, *op. cit.*, p. 219: "The social sciences are concerned with the analysis of those social forces which condition human existence rather than with the unravelling of the mystery of human existence itself."

would in that case be reduced to a false behaviorism, which for the sake of precision of method denies the significance of choice. Take for instance health as an illustration. Medicine can describe a properly functioning organism; from this description it can meaningfully prescribe the conditions of health. By so doing it deals with significance; it takes for granted that health is more valuable than illness. To be sure some enjoy bad health, and we have the problems of psychosomatic medicine, or even of some deeper brands of illness. Some people even violate the rules of health entirely by committing suicide. Generally speaking, in any case, health is deemed a good ideal and attainment. In the same manner social health may be accepted as a basic value judgment for the social sciences. What makes for satisfactory life in community is generally wanted; instrumental purposes become significant because of this general value judgment. Perhaps inclusiveness and integrative patterns can also become accepted as innately established by this over-all value judgment.

Merton points out how some social scientists generalize at the expense of exact knowledge, whereas others forfeit general insight by undue pressure toward precision of knowledge.[23] One side says that although they cannot prove that what they say is true, it is at least significant, whereas the other side maintains that what they say is demonstrably true, but that they cannot indicate its significance. In the integration of theory and empirical research the social sciences should be guided by truth and significance. Just as healthy specimens of physical organisms become the standard of health, even so the best functioning communities ought to be the standard of social health. The task of community building is harder than the formulation, and must combine science with art; but so does medi-

[23] "On the one hand, we observe those sociologists who seek above all to generalize, to find their way as rapidly as possible to the formulation of sociological laws. Tending to assess the significance of sociological work in terms of the scope rather than the demonstrability of generalizations . . . For the first group the identifying motto would at times seem to be: 'We do not know whether what we say is true, but it is at least significant.' And for the radical empiricist the motto may read: 'This is demonstrably so, but we cannot indicate its significance.'" Merton, *op. cit.*, p. 462. For another suggestive treatment of this problem compare Avery Leiserson, "Problems of Methodology in Political Science," in *Political Science Quarterly,* Dec., 1953, pp. 558 ff.

cine as well. A good physician is a creative person as well as an agent of science. Social science can become of utmost importance if it becomes the pole of adequacy in science and the pole of validity in the art of human relations.

Possibly cybernetics can help us as a working model. As we know, this science works with goal-directed, self-adjusting mechanisms. These mechanisms adjust their own goal-seeking in the light of shifts of direction on the part of the target. They operate by the well known feed-back device, which informs the mechanism of the need for self-adjustment.[24] Personal and social actions are not wholly determined; they are free within their field of operation, and according to the conditions of those operations. If the social sciences treat men individually or socially as automata, they err. Natural science is a false model for social science. Cybernetics, however, is an objective science that yet deals with the unpredicted conditions of the target according to the method of self-adjustment. This science to be sure is variously interpreted. By some it is used to show that purpose after all is only a mechanical operation[25]—that will is some kind of Spencerian experience of adjustment, without any real change of operation being caused by the person or the group involved. Actually cybernetics is basically the copying of the functioning of the human brain. If this is so, we are beginning to have an increasing understanding of the physical basis and operation of purpose. The fact of purpose and freedom as basic to experience remains. New models are now being worked out for their proper study; such models should also be worked out for social science.

Some social scientists go so far as to say that the implication of

[24] Wiener, *op. cit.,* Chap. IV, "Feed-Back and Oscillation."

[25] We do not claim the authority of Wiener for our philosophy of freedom. His view seems to be that the new dynamics are no whit less mechanical than the old. The writings of Karl W. Deutsch have, however, in the writer's opinion, developed more fully the philosophical possibilities of cybernetics for social theory. Compare also Rudolf Allers' comment: "It must be a great disappointment to them when they read in the concluding passages of Doctor Wiener's work, that their statistics cannot compare with those of the scientists, and that he has other methodological objections to raise, and reaches the conclusion that, in the social sciences, one will have—whether one likes it or not—to be satisfied with the 'narrative procedure' of the historian." Allers, "On Emotive Communication," XIII *Conference on Science, Philosophy and Religion.*

cybernetics for social science is that no merely objective study of social processes is enough; that the social experimenters, in order to obtain a valid observation, must involve the subjects of the experiment. If the experimenters and the subjects of the social experiment can be directed together toward the goal of a satisfactory community, the process itself can become self-adjusting to reach an ideal goal, just like the subjects studied in cybernetics. Actually, if the objective conditions for social behavior are combined with artful concern for true community, involving both sides of the social experiment, we have enacted already before our very eyes the meaning of Christian love in social theory. Such love demands the highest dynamic combination of the objective right and the subjective good; it requires the living synthesis of objective study and existential participation. If the difficult tasks of significance, of value judgments, and of the relation of the objective to the subjective can be worked out with care and productive result for theory, social investigation can become ever more fruitful.

Similarly the relation between social theory and philosophy and religion can be worked out with mutual profit. We shall not now discuss how philosophy can be of real help to social science. It can obviously help with problems of logic and of method. It can also give social science a sense of its scale of scope within the internal coherence of truth as a whole. It can help relate it both to natural science and to religion, as well as to itself. Certainly Robert Redfield is right in maintaining that "there is no longer any need to be fearful about philosophy. . . . that social scientists need to learn from philosophy, not to become philosophers, but to become better social scientists."[26] Social science can also learn more about and from religion, even as religion must continually and increasingly learn from social science. The place of faith and responsibility in life and civilization is an important one.[27] Phenomenologically it is important that this place be understood. Mature social sciences will increasingly

---

[26] *Op. cit.,* p. 189.

[27] "The behavior of human beings is never completely predictable but only probable. Political science is concerned not with that which is absolutely necessary but with that which is contingent. It deals with things which may be other than they are. And for that reason it is not a speculative science but a practical one." Hallowell, *op. cit.,* p. 388.

use the phenomenological method. The business of social science as science is to understand correctly; and each subject must be understood according to the proper conditions of its subject matter and method.

Even on the level of objective description, however, social science can learn that religion is more than a social phenomenon. It has no need to go into metaphysics or religion. It can know, however, that there is a power in religion that leads propagandists throughout the ages, when they really want to appeal to man's deepest drives, to utilize the category of the sacred. There is something in religion that works in such a way that a social phenomenon lacks equal power if it is sheared of its connection with the religious. Faith and concern are social phenomena, to be treated as such, but they cannot be reduced, in their deepest roots and highest peaks, to the level of social relations. If a false Messianism should assume the finality of its own perspective, and therefore reduce all reality apart from the physical to its own category, the philosophic and the religious disciplines must stand guard at their own gates. The social scientists who are not parochially trained or oriented, but who have depth of educational background and insight, will themselves no doubt see to it that social science lives up to its name.

Inasmuch as the Christian faith is concern for community there must naturally be a close relation between social science and Christianity. On its human side Christianity is through and through social; it must ever utilize, to a maximum degree, the social sciences in order to clarify its own nature. As responsible concern, it must promote integrity in its acceptance of the data of legitimate social science. In education naturally Christianity is more than social science; it is also an art of human living. Christianity combines the good as intention with the right of objective investigation. Both the good and the right, however, it accepts and utilizes within its own living faith and within its own more than human reality. Christianity is society with a capital S; it knows also how to spell the personal with a capital P.[28] In order to understand its own kind of com-

[28] "Human existence cannot derive its ultimate meaning from society, because society itself is in need of meaning. It is as legitimate to ask: Is mankind needed? —as it is to ask: Am I needed?" Heschel, *op. cit.,* p. 196.

munity, and in order to transform society by constructive concern it must, however, learn humbly from social science. Within its own sphere of responsibility, social science is its own master and responsible only to truth.

Science and the social sciences are of the utmost importance in education; Christian education therefore accepts and promotes them with pride and zeal. The natural sciences are now mature enough to pass more and more from the stage of using concepts by inspection to the use of concepts by postulation, having accepted concepts such as the gene or the atom. The social sciences will more and more mature away from their infant dependence on the model of the natural sciences to find their own true working model. Perhaps observation will go beyond inspection and postulation, beyond theory and induction from theory, to some more properly dynamic and open system like cybernetics. The development in any case will come from the social sciences themselves. It very likely will far surpass in creative power any tentative suggestion that we now make. The more the social sciences develop, the more they can become educationally fruitful. Their future is bright with promise.

We believe, however, to summarize—that the social sciences will always represent adequacy in the total picture of scientific method and validity in the art of human relations. Let the social sciences properly be science, but may they also always remember that they are *social* studies, not dealing with merely natural phenomena.[29] They work more with impersonal than with personal reality. The aspects of social reality with which they properly deal may be the *conditions* for society as they are exhibited by social behavior. Responsibility for the choice of conditions is then still left to mankind; it is not falsely reduced to an automaton. Society can, then, be studied objectively. Social tendencies may even yield themselves to operational, determinate concepts, without reducing humanity to a natural phenomenon. Significance and truth, then, both remain as the continual challenge and choice of education. Christian education will gear naturally into the social sciences by the fact that by its very nature it *involves concern for satisfactory community*.

[29] "As Aristotle says, 'It is the mark of an educated man to expect no more exactness than the subject permits.' " Harvard Report, pp. 66–67.

Chapter IX

History, Art, and Literature

THESE three subjects are peculiarly the essence of the humanities; no education therefore can be more than technical that does not train its students thoroughly in these subjects. It cannot even be truly vocational or professional, regardless of technical skill; for life is thin and flat without the inherited riches of man's cultural heritage. The humanities are integral to humanity. Knowledge of them may also make people better all-round men and women; it may prepare better citizens. Such knowledge may even abet vocational competence. The question, however, should not be approached primarily from this utilitarian point of view; to do so is to prostitute the humanities. The humanities are profound realms of experience and beauty that a rich life or a vital civilization cannot do without. Moral, civic, technical skills are also part of life. Training in both these branches of knowledge is needed by man and society. No apology must be made for the humanities in terms of utility, any more than we may reduce the rest of life to some sentimental service of the humanities. The depth and riches of education, however, will in a large measure be determined by the way in which the humanities are taught. Our basic question must, of course, be this: Is there a Christian way to teach them?

Human history is the story of man's life. Experience is our best schoolteacher. No education can reach depth of understanding or profound wisdom that is not rooted and grounded in history.

History, based on technical training, is a relatively new subject in man's long quest for education. Certainly there was concern with history before it became a scientific discipline. Perhaps the earliest historians were those who wrote the Books of Kings. They saw history as a pattern of success or failure according to the rulers' obedience or disobedience to the will of God. The Jewish people rooted their religion in history—in the calling of Abraham and in the deliverance from Egypt. Religion for them was a matter of God's time with His people, and of His mighty deeds within the times that He created and ruled. The Christian religion in ample measure took over this rootage of religion in history. Christ became the fulfiller of the old age, the bringer of a new one, and the final consummator of history as a whole. Christian theology and devotion have united in stressing that the Christian faith is a historic religion. Nevertheless both Jews and Christians dealt overwhelmingly with what Richard Niebuhr has called "inner history," not with objective or external history. History, whether as judgment or reward, was interpreted in the light of faith; it was not a pattern of external events, in the sense that "this is what really happened" from the point of view of the objective observer.

Herodotus wrote similar history for the Greeks. Though mixed with much incredible material it did glorify the nation, and for us it did pass on much knowledge that otherwise we should not have had. Thucydides—even though he too of course had his own presuppositions—was far more objective. In a way, however, he felt for the kind of trained interpretation of history that was to find its birth in the beginning of the nineteenth century. We need not discuss Pliny, Tacitus, Eusebius, or Bede, for all failed of the ideal of the historian—some more and some less.

Only with the work of von Ranke, at the beginning of the last century, did the historical consciousness mature—in the sense of the critical investigation of the past with aim at objectivity—like that of the natural sciences. As regards the Christian faith this kind of history undercut spurious institutional and theological props that claimed historic bases. It seemed to dissolve the historic foundation of the Bible and of Christian history. It also laid bare the indebtedness of the Christian faith to non-Hebraic sources.

Those who have read with care and actually used with critical diligence some such work as Langlois and Seignobos' *The Study of History* must admire the skillful and diligent precautions that are supposed to be taken by the critical historian in order for him to become thoroughly objective about the discovery, interpretation, and use of facts. Obviously much of this early "scientific" history was naïve as to its own presuppositions, blind as to its metaphysical arbitrariness, and overenthusiastic about many of its "findings," which were often mostly the rationalization of contemporary points of view in the name of critical history. Be that as it may, history as a trained subject had arrived with power to stay.[1] It will ever be of immense worth if it is given its proper chance to contribute to the educational process. No discipline is born mature.

Our own century witnesses political pressure on all fields of knowledge that can be helpful to the winning of ideological wars. The comparative peace of the preceding century gave objective knowledge much more of a chance. In many parts of the world there is, or has been, pressure even on natural science to accord with ideology. Social science is of course continually prostituted in the service of propaganda; psychology, for instance, lends itself to "psychological warfare." No wonder that history is being mauled! There are courses in Americanism—not to find the truth of American history, but to confirm our faith in our history and destiny. History is similarly abused in most countries. "Inner history," such as that of the Hebrews and of the Christians, is today victorious over the objective kind of historic interpretation, such as that of the scholarly world. This shaking of faith in objective history is obviously not due to political pressure and atmosphere alone.

Relativity in physics, the model of modern science, has also had profound reverberations elsewhere, including the realm of history. If in natural science it is impossible to have accessible at the same time exact knowledge both of position and of velocity, how much less possible is it to have controlled knowledge in such subjects as history. The fuller knowledge of psychology furthermore has shown us not only rationalization and collective camouflage as the natural

---

[1] Actually the nineteenth century is one of the most glorious epochs in the writing of history!

response of reason to our imperious drives, but has also shown us depths of unconscious motivation and activation beyond our most startled imagination. Disillusioned with human nature, many are now sneering or scoffing at all claims to objective history. Theologically as well we have discovered the power of sin beyond all psychological explanations in any determinate sense; sin infests every thinker. Sinners certainly do not think straight about such personal and social matters as history, whether our own or the history of others.

The two questions a Christian teacher of history must answer consequently are: (1) Is an objective history possible, in any sense? and (2) Should a Christian teacher try to teach history objectively, or with a Christian "bias"? Be it admitted at once that every human position is finite and fallible; be it also acknowledged that we who distort the truth are sinners. We are pressured both by self and society. Nevertheless, if the study of history is merely the occasion for self-glorification or self-justification, it has no place in the curriculum. Is it then more than that? History is a matter of objective conditions modified by subjective decisions; these decisions, when once made, become facts. These facts cannot be empirically verified, because history can neither be repeated with exactness nor controlled within laboratory conditions. History accordingly can never be a natural science, nor model itself on natural science. History is an art in education. It is part of the humanities rather than of the social sciences. But history, in one of its aspects, has an objective basis that can and should be treated scientifically in the sense of objective description. There are, for instance, public records that make for a real degree of public verifiability. These records, to be sure, cannot be compared with the original events; and therefore history is mostly the description and comparison of testimonies, consciously or unconsciously recorded.

History is thus not a science, but an art, which uses as far as possible the scientific technique. Archaeology similarly discovers historic objects, such as ancient ships or furniture, which up to a certain point give objective evidence, but never give us the total historic nexus of which they are a physical example. Even the comparative study of language and literature are but avenues that lead toward knowledge; they are never the objective knowledge of the total historical situation. The study of history is therefore an art of understanding the past, and its meaning for each new present. The organic relation of each new present, its reconstitution of the past that is contained within it as the objective conditions for its decisions, the selection and interpretation of data from the past, the pressure on each present to interpret the past in line with its needs and wants, and the presuppositions of each new age of interpretation, must also be kept in mind. History is an art that uses scientific techniques and scientific data. The historian's technique commands respect, and the chance for scientific data is usually not inconsiderable.

The very purpose of the study of history is to learn from the past. Objective material is at hand. Nevertheless, what of the subjectivity that we mentioned? What of man's finitude and sin? The answer to finitude is the most careful training and technical mastery possible; the answer to sin is forgiveness and the objectivity of the grace of God. The Christian faith centers in the truth of love and in the love of truth; agape and logos are inseparable partners. The more love reigns, the more there is a disposition to come under self-judgment. The more grace is present, the more readiness there is to abandon self-glorification and self-justification. Attitude, to be sure, needs the best possible implementation of technical training, and of scholarly habits and attitudes. Love that is rightly at work therefore insists on such self-discipline, and covets vocational competence for the glory of God. No Christian teacher dares to be biased in a Christian direction. Christianity eliminates as far as possible both personal and group bias. Christianity is the strongest possible antidote to both incompetence and sin's distortion.

The more Christian a teacher is the more he will love and teach the truth. The more Christian he is, the more he will unite concern for people with concern for truth. His faith will not be split in two between what he feels ought to be true and what is in fact true. The Christian teacher need not prefer his stance of faith to his scholarly understanding. His speech is yea, yea, and not equivocation. Whatever of faith and fact he cannot reconcile in his own life and seeing, he is willing to admit to himself and to acknowledge to others; he has no pretense in the matter. Only thus can there be integrity in the scholar and trust in the student. The Christian faith stance seeks always to be congruent with truth. The hesitancy of faith is not whether to accept fact, but whether what is declared to be fact is so in truth. We are Christians because we have become convinced of the truth of Christianity. As teachers and students, however, our allegiance in education must be to truth—wherever it takes us. If a truer faith stance than the Christian can be had, we have no right to be Christian educators; in such a case we must choose to teach the truth with integrity.

The whole conception of Christian "bias" in teaching is misconceived. This misconception, alas, is not limited to the teaching of history. Although no one can prove his faith, he has no right to be arbitrary or dishonest about it; certainly it must accord with fact as far as possible. The writer is convinced that the Christian faith has nothing to hide from critical history; he thinks rather that the faith is confirmed by the fullest combination of critical and constructive interpretations of history. Christian "bias" is a term that betrays a non-Christian presupposition: the relativism of ultimate nescience.

One more problem is left for us to consider: Is there a Christian meaning to history? If there is such a meaning, is this reached from the study of history as such, or is it imposed on history from the context of Christian faith? There is a Christian meaning to history. Christianity is a historical religion; it knows nothing about God, the supernatural, or the eternal that is not made known in history. Therefore if there is no Christian meaning in and for history, there is also no Christian faith. The meaning of the Christian faith—though its center is beyond history—is in and of history. The Christian faith, to be sure, centers in God and in God's history. Nevertheless God's plan for our history, namely, to create a community of love within the reality of His own Presence in Christ and in the Holy Spirit, is neither imposed on history nor read into it; it can be studied in history, and must indeed be reached from such study. The Christian faith alone can discover and use the master key of historical interpretation: God's love in Christ for the eventual fostering of the eternal fellowship. Christ as the event of events in history, and Christ as the nature of the ending that alone can become the right end for history, lays bare the unifying and universal meaning of history. Since the Christian community is mostly a matter of future realization through history, the meaning of history though discovered in history is yet also mostly beyond history. Without eternity as God's history, and without our history's being fulfilled only within and by eternity, there can never be any genuine understanding of the meaning of history itself.[2]

This meaning cannot therefore be understood and proved from within history alone. When through the disciplines of philosophy and theology this meaning of God's will to community becomes clear, it will be seen that it also gives the truest pattern of interpretation for history as a whole. It is comparable to but not limited by Lorentz' transformation in physics, with respect to which the laws of the field are invariant, to the ideal co-ordinate system of mechanics or to the catalyst of chemistry. Our critical faith judgment therefore is finally not about history, but about God. Eternal reality cannot be demonstrated from historic fact, no matter how true. Therefore, apart from externalistic credulity, the Bible cannot give us the meaning of history, nor can Jesus or the Church. The meaning of history is the God who is love and works in love by means of history to effect His community in and beyond history. The Bible, Jesus, and the Church are both partially and potentially the exemplifiers and witnesses to the reality and meaning of God's love that makes for community. This love as such, however, constitutes the regulative pattern of history. The pattern of this love, more than anything else, can receive the kind of confirmation in experience on which may be built reliably our unavoidable faith judgment about the ultimate meaning of existence. Truth in life, truth in thought, and truth in history, in this way belong together; to separate them is to court arbitrariness and insecurity.

[2] "The goal of historical knowledge and philosophy is not natural but supernatural." Nicolas Berdyaev, *The Meaning of History* (London, Geoffrey Bles, The Centenary Press, 1936), p. 19.

Elsewhere we have indicated how the key to history is God's self-disclosure in Jesus.[3] God has pushed us together from behind, as it were, by means of physical, social, and spiritual needs. Intensively, He has used the family structure; extensively, He has used the political order; in between, He has used various economic, social, and communal organizations. In any case he has made our living together a necessity of life. The growth in man's modes of togetherness, up to today's need for one world, has resulted largely from man's dependence on physical nature, and the resulting—or at least interdependent—development of technology. Our line of thought recognizes, as one aspect of historic truth, Marx's analysis regarding the close connection of history with economics, as well as his creative pioneering in the sociology of knowledge. To match this side of historic advance—which we have called "the push of progress," and which, since it is morally neutral, is only *the occasion* for community, whether good or bad—there is also "the pull of God's purpose," all the way from altruism in animal life, through outgoingness in personal, aesthetic, and social relations, to the sacrificial living and dying of Jesus, who is history's center, dividing point, and agent of the new age of final fulfillment.

This love is the latent meaning of all community, as well as the content of God's self-revelation. Response to it comes in terms of concrete decisions in history. These decisions are not rational, in a philosophic sense, but have to do with the peculiar challenges of particular historic configurations. Life is not logic; the logic of faith consequently is only indirectly related to historic interpretation and decision. History is a matter of community, and as such is the stuff of the ultimate. History therefore cannot ever be reduced, in time or eternity, to rational meaning or moral prescription. The Christian impact on history is through the confluences of choices and circumstances that come together within the indirect lighting of faith's meaning as this is abstracted, for help in decision, from other communities, and supremely from the Christ and the best exemplification of His community. The seeing of such meaning, however, is both an objective possibility and yet a call for constant cleansing of the

[3] See the author's, *The Christian Faith* (New York, Harper, 1942), chap. III.

scholarly eyes through Christian concern. Only a trustful commitment to concerned truth, to truth and love, can consummate the truest interpreting and most competent teaching of history. We need such teaching, for history is the only reservoir that contains concrete illustrations of the Word made flesh. History is the stuff of community, and Christ is the standard for right community. Truth therefore is in essence historical, as stuff, standard, means, and goal. Simple is such a saying; but complex as history itself is the meaning and the moral of this relationship.

Obviously, if history is the confluence of God and man's decisions it is neither determined nor free. God takes the sovereign initiative, and conditions history by the way He has made us, nature, and the laws of social behavior. Perhaps cybernetics especially may become the clue to the large-scale tracing of man's history. Harbison and Shinn,[4] for instance, are then right in their Augustinian espousal of open patterns, neither determined nor random, while men like Toynbee and Butterfield are also right—if we may so combine them—about the ultimacy of challenge and response in terms of the Incarnation. In any case, today we need creative historians, pioneers like the authors of the Books of Kings, who are also trained in the disciplines of history. Soon should come a great day for the interpretation and the teaching of history; and most fortunate is the historian who is also a Christian believer—provided, of course, that he is also a man of genuine integrity and scholarly competence.

Is there, furthermore, a Christian interpretation and teaching of art? Art is a touchy subject. The autonomy of art is not only a watchword but a battlecry: Art is for art's sake. To talk of the meaning or the use of art is to prostitute it! Perhaps, however, if we have the right understanding of both art and faith, there need be no such fear. Perhaps the theologizing of art need no more defile it than its being sold to a museum. The concern of our entire study

---

[4] E. Harris Harbison, "History," in Fairchild, *op. cit.,* pp. 67–97; Roger L. Shinn, *Christianity and the Problem of History* (New York, Scribner, 1953), and "Religious Faith and the Task of the Historian," in Wilder, *op. cit.,* pp. 56–77.

is to see each subject distinctively for itself, while also within the total context of truth.

Art exhibits many universal meanings as well as individual forms. Art is one form of the celebration of life. Whatever is not festal[5] is not art, regardless of subject matter. The most commonplace girl or ordinary worker, if portrayed by high art, becomes representative of life. A photograph may give exactness of detail and accuracy of representation, but it becomes art only if the subject conveys the celebration of life. "Celebration" means immediacy of apprehension and enjoyment. Much of life is wishing for the future or planning for it. Much time is spent in regretting the past or trying to substitute it for the present. Much immediacy is also humdrum; it is not experienced for its deeper meanings and veiled beauty. Thus becoming, doing, changing, regretting, hoping, striving take up much of our attention. Or we see little of what is right before us, even when our eyes are open! Art, on the other hand, is the immediate awareness and enjoyment of reality. Whether the form of it be representative or without tangible meaning, whether it be still, as in a painting, or moving, as in music, the experience of art is the immediate grasp and enjoyment of beauty. Such matters as composition, balance, tactile values, and movement are secondary to this main experience of art as the celebration of life.

In this sense art is close to religion. Religion is secondhand, apart from the immediacy of experience that is primary to its nature. Perhaps to see God and to enjoy Him forever needs to be complemented by the vision of God and the serving of Him forever. Such service, however, if needed, must be within the perfect freedom of love's vision of God. Seeing comes before service in the scale of reality; the vision of God fulfills our obedience. Art, however, also constitutes an aspect of immediacy, with no reference to service and without a direct vision of God. Ecstasy as such is not art. Art is seeing things as they are *in the light* of eternity. Art apprehends

[5] I can find no word for my meaning. No such word as "numinous" or "reverent" will do—they belong to the religious realm. Art is experience, seen not in an everyday, but in a special way. Art suggests, symbolizes, gives depth, but I am feeling for a far richer word.

life and the world in their deepest reality. Hence art is celebration, or it is not art. Art is not the seeing of the Creator in the creature, but the seeing of the creature in the light of God's creation. It is seeing creation as potentially redeemed, the actual within the real, the present in the fulfilling future. Art is no shunning of the actual. It is no idealizing or sentimentalizing of the commonplace. It is never the presenting of evil as unreal or weak; to do so would be not to celebrate life, but to falsify it. Art knows no facile or merely theoretical solution. Art sees truly what is, but it sees deeper than what is.

Art is not preaching; art is not teaching; art is the celebration of life as it is in the light of the fuller reality. The drama of art is existential in its immediacy, even while dialectic in its comprehension. That is the reason that art cannot be prostituted without a fatal violation of its virginity. The purity of art is protected by its direct relation to reality. The dialectic nature of actuality is existentially experienced. Art and religion are both forms of worship. While religion, in order to be real, refers its experience to the ultimate, art remains on the level of its actual focus. For religion, the Creator is seen behind and through all creation, the unconditional within all that is conditioned. For art, the focus is cut down to the creature, but without loss of the divine glory that is present in the picture. For religion such concentration on the divine aspect without reference to God would of course be idolatry. In art it is all right; not so in religion. A narrow zeal for religion as the all of life, therefore, must necessarily persecute art. Though the history of religion includes the production of art, religion has also dreaded art. The prophet is always soft-footed or ironclad when he approaches the realm of art; he is defensive or aggressive. In any case he is at least apprehensive. To equate religion with the prophetic tradition is consequently to jeopardize art. Art has seldom flourished within evangelical gardens; it has thrived rather within a more relaxed kind of faith. When art is used for spiritual exhorting or for moral instruction it withers and dies. When faith is genuine enough to dare to enjoy not only God but also the beauty of His creation, then art blossoms into beauty.

The temptation of art of course is to become a substitute or rival for religion; then the austerity of God's presence and the severity of moral requirement are lost. Art can then become the occasion for unbridled sensuality. The sensuous then becomes sensual. Art as religion means the loss of spiritual power and the weakening of the moral nerve. Art must be art, not religion. Yet part of mature religion is always the celebration of life—not only as the worship of God, but as the immediate acceptance and enjoyment of beauty. Creatures live mostly within the level of creation; they seldom rise to the worship of God. In this regard the duty of the Christian interpreter and teacher is to understand the autonomy of art within the totality of life, neither prostituting it nor isolating it from the full context of life. It is the duty of the Christian to see to it that religion does not rob art of its rightful place in experience; it is also to watch out lest art become the substitute for high religion. Beauty is a kind of being and experience that cannot be reduced to any other kind; but no height of beauty can ever take the place of the beauty of holiness. The central focus of beauty is God. Perhaps as an aspect of religion—or of total experience—we may say that we see God in the ecstatic saint. He alone has an immediate experience of God, and therefore an opportunity to apprehend and to enjoy directly the vision of God. Our apprehension of the beauty of God, however, is enriched by the beauty of creation. Art is the celebration of the eternal beauty of life within the immediacy of experience.

Art, however, is more than the celebration of life, the immediate apprehension and enjoyment of beauty; it is also a fount of creativeness. Like right religion, art is "a well of water" springing up within the human spirit. The human spirit thirsts for creative expression. Art ministers to this need. Art is, besides, the realm of the creative imagination. It may be objected that the creative imagination is also used in science, religion, literature, and in fact in all of life. Whatever part of life or thought is thus creative, however, partakes of art. There is art in science, in so far as the scientist creatively imagines and apprehends the new. Science, however, as such is basically a method for testing truth. The intuitive, imaginative construction of hypotheses is not controllable by science, in any sense of being bid or predicted. There is therefore art in science on its creative side; there is in truth art in all creative going beyond what is seen as actual, whenever the veil of the deeper truth is pierced by the imaginative spirit. Life is not all compartmentalized! Art, as we have said, is the existential apperception of the dialectic nature of created reality, where everything is more than it seems. The existential in art is the experience of the dialectic of actuality apart from the review of the intellectual, the command of the ethical, and the organizing wholeness of the eschatological. Wherever the creative imagination lays hold directly on the full presence of reality within a limited focus without reference to the full scope of reality, such imagination is the work of art. There are eyes of faith to pierce the darkness that veils the throne of God; there is also aesthetic vision to see the glory of a flower that far surpasses common sight. Moses met the glory of God in a burning bush; an artist beholds the true glory with which God has invested every bush. If the experience is focused on the God who created that glory, it is religious; if it is focused on the glory with which the bush has been endowed, it is aesthetic.

Art is also the creative imagination at work in co-operation with God; it creates new worlds out of old. Art extends the actual world by creative imagination. Fancy, of course, is not art. Art deals with genuine possibilities inherent in the materials at hand. These of course come from God's creation. Art is never primary but always secondary creation. It is the release of potential beauty. It is the creative freeing of form that is already yearning to become actual. Art sees glories not at hand; it endows created substance with creative glory. Phidias takes a slab of rock and leaves it a Parthenon relief. Giotto takes a wall in Santa Croce, or Masaccio takes a Santa Maria del Carmine Chapel, and the cold walls speak with color and meaning. Epstein hews a "Lazarus" and Oxford's imagination is stirred by what a creature has created. Beyond representative art creation is even more evident. Mendelssohn may use known motifs in his *Reformation Symphony,* but whence Brahms' *Fourth?* The answer cannot be adequately formulated in terms of only technical knowledge of harmony and counterpoint, of mathematics and intellectual requirement. Out of the vast potential filled with unknown glory come the great symphonies, adding glory to God's creation. The poet and the dramatist may use thoughts or history, but the more beautiful the poetry and the play as literature, the more they are works of art. The lyric is therefore in this sense more likely to be good art than is the epic; the lyric has less history and fact than the epic, and thus depends mostly on its artistic expression. Art always succeeds in its courting of beauty. Whatever is ugly in physical substance, form, deed, or suggestion fails thereby to be art— except of course as the ugly is merely the presentation of the actual for its transfiguration. Plato was puzzled by the idea of the creation of dirt. Some of us may wonder at the crocodile and the rhinoceros! The Christian knows, however, that behind all life lies the Eternal Purpose. Therefore an eschatological sheen envelops all creation with the sun that shines through the creative imagination—even in the dark. The eyes of art nevertheless may be opened, from time to time, by such Christian insight concerning what is ugly in God's creation. Man's creation, however, in order to be art must be beautiful. Cacophony is not good music, and hence not art, except as atonality may enrich harmony by dialectic tension. When man uses the creative imagination he may not evade, only transcend, the actual. This world without evil is not our actual world. Art therefore never develops a blind spot for evil. Art, however, always sees more than is actually present. Art sees the hidden glory even of the reprobate, and of the bird with the broken wing. There is art in the relentless tragedy of Hemingway's *The Old Man and the Sea,* because a broken body and a broken career only reveal the unbroken spirit of man in his fight with nature. Such a novel creatively extends man's actual world by an imaginative experience that though evil, is evil that reveals courage, persistence, and the beauty of character within the tragedy of circumstance. Creative imagination therefore gives man the unfathomable grace of creating with God.[6]

[6] Outstanding examples of such use of tragedy are of course the works of Shakespeare and Browning. Though there is no substitute for the reading of the original writings, Edwin Mims has provided us with excellent interpretations of religious literature in such books as *Great Writers as Interpreters of Religion* (Nashville and New York, Abingdon, 1945), and *Christ of the Poets* (Nashville and New York, Abingdon, 1948).

A third great realm of art is that of symbolic reference. Whitehead has made explicit the crucial nature of symbolic communication. Most of experience is through the human body as a whole, coming from the past. We experience without thought the pull of the moon and the tides, and all the great welter of the world as it forms the hidden background of our lives. We experience, on this deeper level especially, the settled hand of our own past, such as inherited tendencies, traditions, and so forth. This is the region where the depths of our convictions form and continue. They form a mighty stream of life, which—to use Groddeck's expression—almost "*live*" us." Direct experience, according to Whitehead, is infallible. In its immediacy the experience is dependable. We also experience, however, the flickering of conscious attention. This is the realm of conscious continuity—whether of rationality, morality, or aesthetic enjoyment. In its immediacy this experience too is infallible. Error, distortion, rationalization, and falseness or falsification, of whatever kind, therefore enter in at the point where we relate this conscious experience to its deep unconscious foundation. Perhaps shallowness is even a worse fate than falsification; and is exceedingly common. Such error, falsification, and shallowness, furthermore, cannot be overcome by means of rational communication. The point is therefore that we need some way to unite the rational with the depth of life, the existential.

This uniting can be done most effectively by means of the symbolic, which is really physical communication that conveys depth meaning. The sacrament is more than the moral or rational word. It is more than form; it is based on matter. It is art in worship. Depth of feeling is focused by such symbols, and reality is conveyed at a depth beyond words. Such symbols consequently demand integrity; they are violated when used for ulterior motives. They speak by being; they teach by being. Art more than enriches; art plumbs the depths of reality and of the human consciousness. No higher education can be Christian, in the sense of expressing truth and concern, which does not, to its fullest understanding and power, promote both the appreciation and the creation of art. Because art possesses existential immediacy that apprehends the depth dialectic of actuality, it can serve as the symbolic reference that unites the conscious and the unconscious levels of experience with reference to the level of creation. On the religious level the Holy Spirit does so unite man; but even here He is helped by such art as is expressed in the sacraments and similar uses of physical focus in worship. Some religiously harassed souls have found spiritual stillness by the playing of the piano. Other have sat for hours in art museums. Still others have been healed by drama. They cannot explain the experience. Explanation for some part, however, lies in the fact that art, par excellence, is the medium for symbolic reference.

One of the oldest interpretations of tragedy of course is that it serves as a catharsis; the art form of tragedy is a means of purgation. It can be such a means with peculiar effectiveness, because it uses indirection and vicariousness. The objectification of an experience by an object of art, like Rembrandt's "Prodigal Son," or in a great drama like Ibsen's *Peer Gynt*, means the confrontation of experience without that confrontation's becoming a living experience. A person is therefore freer to face himself in the fact of art; he is not directly threatened by another person. When an individual can enter into his own experience through the experience of others, without the tension of direct confrontation that usually makes the self take cover, he can understand and accept himself more easily. Self-acceptance and self-forgiveness are aspects of moral and spiritual purgation. Often a person hides most assiduously when he is confronted most directly with God. Art usually confronts man with God in an indirect manner. Art remains on the level of creation. Even in the case of art that points to God, God is not seen as He is, but through the created medium of matter and form. To stand in Copenhagen before Thorwaldsen's "Christ," or in the Sistine Chapel before Michelangelo's "Creator," is somehow to face God very much indirectly through the created medium. Catholicism has been blamed for its use of statues; many are convinced that such use is the essence of idolatry. The Reformation smashed them to the glory of God; direct access to God, the heart of the Reformation drive, could endure no such obstruction and obfuscation. Religious dancing and drama have similarly been dubbed impious. To be sure in such cases we stand not only on holy, but on also the most difficult ground. Nevertheless a strong case can be made for art as the indirect and vicarious way to reach the inner citadel of life and civilization. A Christian college should explore all possibilities, both for the teaching and the creating of art that reveals life to itself. In those people who are most depraved the sinner can see his own lost glory and set out to find it. Art is preaching and teaching by embodiment and enactment, without moral exhortation. Jesus combined the emphasis of wisdom literature with the prophetic. Art is no substitute for religion, but can and should serve to enrich it.

Art then is the celebration of life, the creative imagination at work either as the receptor of created beauty or as the cocreator with God, the means of symbolic reference whereby the depth of the united self can be achieved even as symbolic communication becomes effective, and the purging power of indirect and vicarious representation. The Christian college cannot honor God in creation without a strong emphasis on art. Because it is religious it should know how to teach art without becoming "arty" or idolatrous.

Perhaps we may mention a theological foundation for art. God Himself, of course, is the supreme Artist, and here as elsewhere we learn from God, the great Pedagogue. His love bestows freedom on men to become fulfilled according to His image in them. Man is never fulfilled, now or in eternity, until he develops the creative imagination in terms of which he can see the deeper realities of life by means of which he can truly celebrate life. Even as God creates furthermore because of His overflowing love, so also He covets for us the joyful release of creative experience. Art is adventure. Art is magnificent mystery stirring the slumbering spirit to the revelation of potentiality by means of creative activity. Art is sharing the creative, ever-outgoing life of God. As children of God His beauty is ours, not only to enjoy but to express through creative expression.

The fact that art delimits the perspective of its experience to creation apart from God is itself the outcome of the great love of God, whereby He wants us to enjoy life on our own level without the need for constant reference to Himself. God covets our freedom, and wants us to be real enough to enjoy the glory of creation for itself. God creates, and knows that what He creates is good. It is in the nature of the aesthetic experience to be nonpossessive; a great picture or statue we long to share with others. The reason we do is the working of God's image in us, which is altruism.[7] Beauty in creation both expresses and reflects the beauty of the Creator. A most important aspect of this reflected beauty is the beauty of holiness in a created being, who longs for others to share the beauty that enriches his own life. God the Lover is also God the Artist. He wants to share the joy of His experience of beauty. But He does not always want us to have His company. A good father who has drunk deep of art does not want to be with his child every moment of his viewing it. He may share some of his own insights and enjoyments with his child; but in the end he goes away in order to enable beauty to fill to the depths the soul of his child. Even so God, though knowing that we need definite experiences of His companionship, yet walks away as the glory of His creation penetrates our lives. High religion and great art are wed eternally.

Literature is high art. It celebrates life, bathes in the creative imagination, uses symbolic language, and helps to purge man's spirit by revealing him to himself. In a peculiar way literature also, like art, exemplifies the indirect and vicarious means of teaching that are characteristic of God's pedagogy. Take for instance the story.[8] Jesus himself taught by using stories. He who knew the heart of man and needed no one to tell him about man, knew also the power of the indirect method. Kierkegaard, who today pierces the modern mind with his profound philosophical and theological analysis, relied a great deal on the literary method; it was used as a means of "wounding people from behind." Today a New Testament theologian like Paul Minear, too, has championed

[7] Cf. the author's *The Christian Understanding of God*, pp. 44–45.

[8] "To know a story and why it is a story and why it cannot be translated into exposition and remain the same, and that the rarest and mightiest possessions of the human spirit can be discovered only by means of story and by no other process of thinking—to know all this and to have it as your own is to have much." Chalmers, *op. cit.*, p. 77.

the story as the best means of communicating the Gospel. Bishop Stephen C. Neill, in a popular lecture series at Harvard on religion, spent a good half of each address on English literature; and after doing so went on to reach deep into the religious needs of the academic community. Without again developing the indirect and vicarious method of teaching, it may well be pointed out how literature fills the prescription for those approaches with unusual precision. Poetry, prose, and drama—there are art forms and moods to fill every need. Human experience is registered in literature with the utmost sensitivity; human history is made beautiful and memorialized. Dumb art here finds a voice.

To be sure, literature can also speak with prophetic directness, as in the Gettysburg Address. Conscience can come clean within a beauty of words that facilitates the reception of the message of literature by the reader. In a way therefore even the directness of literature has the key to the secret entry of the human heart. Conscience can come clean, but not naked of content. Sir Richard Livingstone has maintained that philosophy and theology are the subjects by which the Christian faith can be taught directly; that the two great fields where the faith is taught indirectly are history and literature.[9] The depths of history, however, as far as man's most meaningful experience goes, are best taught in the history of man's literature.[10] To know with empathy the range and depth of a people's literature is to know in the best way possible the nature of that people. Some have made at this point a profound personal discovery; external history became living for them only after a thorough study of internal history by means of literature. If to learn from God is to use His method with all possible diligence, the Christian college should take special pains to teach great literature.

Literature combines peculiarly meaning, morality, and beauty. It is not too much to say that in this respect it expresses what

[9] *Op. cit.*, p. 117.

[10] Donald Davidson has lately made a strong plea that literature be recognized as dealing with all of life, that there be no cleft between literature and truth. Compare also Chalmers' "The first question about a thing or an incident to be answered by a poem is: what is it, really?" *Op. cit.*, p. 72.

is fullest and best in the life of God and man—to whatever extent, of course, this experience can be externalized. The fact that literature gives voice to meaning *in the sense of articulated communication* need not be argued. The meaningless is never literature, no matter how beautiful it may be. Therefore literature is not art; the artistic is rather an aspect of literature. Art need not articulate meaning; literature must. The meaning may at times be cryptic, esoteric, or hidden in lesser forms of literature; great literature, on the other hand, expresses universal experience and meaning. As a matter of fact, literature is the articulation of experience in the beauty of words. Philosophy as such, the essence of meaning, is not literature. When depths of insight rise to beauty of language, philosophy can be literature; Bergson rightly gets the Nobel Prize for Literature. Theology, as such, is not literature; but when Jesus utters the parable of the prodigal son, the depth of theology reaches the height of literature. All knowledge is enriched for being literature.[11] Alfred North Whitehead used to exclaim on the good fortune of Socrates to have had for disciple a poetic soul like Plato, who could turn Socrates' intellectual experience into literary form. Epicurus was fortunate to have had his Lucretius. Great meaning spreads the faster, lives the longer, and is learned more pleasantly and easily if expressed through great literature as well! The problem of evil has received scant systematic treatment throughout history, but who has not read Goethe's *Faust*? If the meaning were not prismed by clear beams of beauty, it might fascinate the sophisticates, but it would not speak to the world's wider needs. Melville's *Moby Dick* or Kafka's *The Castle,* though recognized by scholars, are not so accessible to vital grasp by most readers as is Shakespeare's *Hamlet* or Dickens' *David Copperfield*. Dostoevski's *The Brothers Karamazov* speaks deep and essential truth that is yet generally comprehensible to the human heart. Even a somewhat clumsy, pioneering novel, like Fielding's *Tom Jones,* catches rich human meaning within the charm of story.

Meaning is rather obvious and generally accepted as part of literature, but what of morality? Is not moralizing the death of

[11] "The oldest work of Greek literature begins with an address to a goddess." Bellinger, "Classics," in Fairchild, *op. cit.,* p. 147.

literature? Can anything be more distasteful than to have a moral tail wagging or, even worse, in need to be severed from the body of literature? Moralizing has no part in the writing or the teaching of literature; when a moral has been tacked on to a story, the unity of experience has already been sundered. The moralistic use of literature Poe called "the heresy of the didactic"! Let us, however, not dismiss morality in literature on account of moralizing. Morality is rightness. Law, in the moral sphere, is a matter of right relations. Has not form, indeed, been called the essence of morality? Morality is good form; immorality, bad form. There is a form of religion, a form of experience, and a form of literature. Bad form in literature spoils its very structure; bad form in experience stultifies it; bad form in religion alienates man from reality. Great literature is not only meaning; it is meaning that matters.

It matters because what is actually portrayed is implicitly set up against the standard of reality. If reality is not understood or accepted, literature suffers from being touched with futility. Some writers of literature, in their creative loneliness, may have been perverts; we cannot deny the fact. The history of the great writers is amazingly divergent from the history of the saints! But because they struggled with evil in the depths of experience, and wrestled for a beauty in imagination of which they had been cheated by life or which had been forfeited by them in life, these writers nevertheless worked with an implicit feeling for reality. When meaning is split from morality, the unity of experience is damaged. Morality never involves sentimentalizing or idealizing. Rightness with reality is austere judgment; it is a commanding standard. Literature catches the unimaginable variations of man's attempt to come to grips with life and to rest with his conscience, under the well-nigh impossible strains of his own drives and the pressures of society. Realistic literature mirrors back the long and tragic history of man's moral failures. It portrays also the kinds of satisfactions and substitutes for success that man finds for himself. Not only meaning but moral meaning, in both the existential and the dialectic senses of that word, are intrinsic aspects of great literature.[12]

[12] No wonder that Arthur T. Vanderbilt's "A Report on Pre-Legal Education" stressed literature as a main subject.

Meaning can be dealt with by philosophy; moral meaning can be taught by ethics; only when moral meaning rises to beauty of expression do we have literature. The distinctive nature of literature is this very combination of meaning, morality, and beauty. Such fullness of experience is what makes literature a peculiarly powerful means for the teaching of living truth. Meaning apart from beauty is arid abstraction or plodding work; morality apart from beauty is a load of legalism; literature is the summit, where meaning, morality, and beauty meet in triumph. Literature is art in words, or the art of words. Such a definition, however, cannot stand by itself. Many who plague the literary garden make beauty of words the essence of literature. John Mason Brown called literature the "gift for articulation." He said that there is no difference between the writer and the common man, except for the writer's command of words to express beauty. But the capacity to articulate attractively is not more than one prerequisite for the creation of literature. Literature is beauty marbled in meaning and hewn out of moral granite. Beauty is not apart from life, but part of reality, existing for life.

The question is continually asked: Is a Christian literature possible? Is the Christian faith a cultural matrix? There is a Marxist literature. There is English and French literature. If the Christian faith, however, is as universal in scope as truth and as deep in nature as human concern, literature is Christian in proportion to its being conceived and executed with reference to reality. Whatever is of both truth and love is Christian. The question is then rather, is literature real, right, and beautiful? does it combine meaning, morality, and beauty in the light of reality? Usually what passes for Christian literature substitutes an authoritarian dogma for meaning, institutionalized moralizing for morality, and piety for beauty. Literature cannot be abused without penalty; the penalty is the loss of literature and its enriching power for all of life. No Christian theme makes writing Christian. Much so-called Christian literature is escape into idealistic fancy, or reveals the inner poverty of its characters. Literature is Christian if it faithfully portrays reality, i. e., our actual struggles, failures, hopes, and partial victories in the light of the eternal Patience who takes no short cuts to intellectual, moral, or spiritual maturity; and if this portrayal rises to beauty of expression in organic relation to the content of the writing. The Christian faith that is as deep as love and as wide as life is alien to no great literature. To be sure the Christian faith has a given direction for the kind of answer it can accept to the problems of life and literature: God's will to love as the way of life. The final answer of God's faithfulness, however, includes also, on the pedagogical level, even man's strayings; it reports his byways as well as his highways. Some pieces of literature can represent life faithfully, with its problems and depths, and still hold as its central judgment and only hope the love of God in Christ. Dickens' *Christmas Carol*, for instance, may be a case in point.

The best example of Christian literature of course is the Bible. It is very strange that Christians often object to the teaching of the Bible as literature; for it to be thus presented they take to be an insult to its revelatory character. *The Bible, however, is exactly literature*. It is the world's best seller, and deserves to be—precisely as literature. The Bible combines in an unsurpassed way meaning, morality, and beauty. Here is no book of systematic theology or of prescriptive ethics; here is no book of science or of history. Here is a book that though it is in itself a library of literary history is nevertheless the unified expression of great faith. What variations of meaning! The several authors had no one viewpoint of reality. And yet the whole gamut of life, with all its depths and heights, is portrayed in it, not merely as discrete pieces of writing, but under the total impact of the culminating faith in God's revelation in Jesus Christ.

Some writers like Gaebelein advocate the teaching of the Bible as central to the Christian curriculum.[13] When this suggestion is understood in his sense, namely, that the Bible is the source book and standard of all other truth, the Bible is wronged, and higher education is imperialistically attacked; this is parochial pleading of the first order. When Christians renounce the magic of revelation for the sake of the majesty of God's self-disclosure within the fullness

[13] *Op. cit.,* p. 121 *et passim.*

of history and literature as well as within the fullness of time and of human life, they will discover that the truth of God's love cannot be externally defended or dogmatically indoctrinated. It must be accepted, experienced, discovered by reason, and applied to all of life and thought. The Bible, when it is taught where it belongs in the total context of higher education, can vindicate its own truth. To say that the Bible is literature is in no way to deny that at its height it bears reliable and conclusive witness to the nature of God and to His will for the world. But it is to say that even as God once came veiled in flesh, the testimony to His coming is even now veiled in literature. As He once came, and still comes, in the weaknesses of the flesh, so He witnessed and witnesses to Himself within the weaknesses of the written Word. Even as the Word once came, full of grace and truth, so the Word now comes recorded within a book, full of truth and beauty. The fact that the Bible is literature, and must be taught as such, does not degrade it, but rather exalts the place of literature within the wisdom of God.

Literature is also the best medium for two of the central ways of teaching: memorization and meditation. We have already developed the need for these in effective pedagogy; later we shall return to stress them once again. What else can be memorized so importantly as life's deepest meaning set to beautiful music in words? How can our moral heritage better be inwardly appropriated than by the hiding of these great expressions of human conduct within the creative memory? Few efforts are more enriching and helpful than the learning, for permanent use, of great passages of literature. If such memorizing is also the occasion for meditation, there is no wooden learning. Learning by rote wrongs both the learner and literature. Great literature must be read over and over again with reflective alertness if it is to bear rich fruit.

The writer can give personal testimony to the fact that what he has thus memorized and meditated on has blessed him over and over again, far beyond effort or desert; whereas on the other hand he has read much that has been as futile as a sudden summer cloudburst. What, for instance, can be more rewarding than a daily memorizing and pondering of the Bible? Let such reading be supplemented by reflection on great devotional literature and the memorizing of the best passages; let these be pondered until they are inwardly digested. Add to such specifically Christian literature the profound seeing of life as a whole from many angles, put into forms of permanent beauty, and let this be appropriated through a long process of alternating intensive reflection and creative relaxation. At length there will be fields white unto harvest.

The Christian college should use, with particular emphasis, the medium of literature. In this area of study most people are the most open. The students should of course go to the originals rather than to books about literature; many secondary sources at best give orientation only. If literature is taught with integrity, and with the passion which should be engendered by the view from the summit of meaning, morality, and beauty, the Christian college can become delivered from sectarianism and imperialism on the one hand, and from the lack of effective communication with the total student body on the other.

The teaching of literature under God is the sacred sharing with Him of His own fullness of experience, which unites meaning, morality, and beauty. Literature also unites organically man's own life as summarized in history and beautified in art. Science and social science are basic tools for knowing; philosophy and religion join to test meanings and give direction to life. History, art, and literature portray experience and beauty; it is the privilege of the humanities to touch life with the divine, provided that those who teach them themselves know the experience of the burning bush.

Chapter X

Philosophy and Religion

OUR age exhibits thought in transition; our ways of thinking are exceptionally fluid. Threats to our civilization from without and confusion within make us more willing to become flexible. Much of our faith is also dying within us. This is true whether we consider faith in science, in history, in art, in literature, in philosophy, or in religion. This dying is partly due to world weariness. The future is uncertain; we ourselves are not sure where we are going or want to go. Naturally therefore frustration in life becomes registered as the disintegration of thought. But this dying is also due to a new realism about both life and thought. Our disillusionment with regard to fact, thought, and faith is partly due to a radical rejection of many soporific rationalizations. It springs not only from dejection but also from a sterner understanding of the requirements of reason. The cleansing fire makes room for new growth. Whitehead consequently observes that as a whole the unstable ages have been the creative ages. No discussion of the content of Christian teaching can be adequate that does not develop an understanding as to the critical importance of the relation of philosophy to religion. To do so, we must at one point also relate both the meaning and method of science.

To know the history of civilization is to be aware of the sturdy part played by philosophy. Who can understand the history of our Western world, for instance, apart from the work of philosophers from Thales to Aristotle? Who can understand the modern world without knowing the thought of Hume and Kant? Who can rightly appraise the modern scene of American life unless he has grasped the philosophy of John Dewey? Religion, too, has molded history; is not Benjamin Kidd pointing out the facts when he shows how the great religions have held the different civilizations together, long outlasting the well-organized empires?[1] We name our era after Jesus; St. Augustine's thoughts helped shape the Middle Ages; John Wesley put a deep imprint on English and American life. To be sure, neither philosophy nor religion exists apart from the rest of civilization; both, indeed, are partly products of it. To know history, however, we must know philosophy and religion.

Today philosophy appears to be in a state of crisis. In many circles it is being denuded, stripped piece by piece of its inheritance. To many this dismantling seems the wrecking of philosophy; to others philosophy is becoming authentic by being shorn of its false functions. In either case, viewed from the side of science, philosophy is being denied the right to fact; and from the side of religion, it is shoved out of the realm of faith. Those whose have followed changes in scientific method and attitude, as we have already observed, know that science has become more positivistic. In some circles science has become operational to the point of being functional rather than interpretative. Some think of scientific experiments and results as a matter of convention rather than of approximation to truth or reality. In other words, there has been a drastic repudiation of the metaphysical claim or assumption of an earlier period. Accordingly, fewer scientists are now reductionistic naturalists in the name of science. They are more aware, as we saw, of hidden presuppositions, of the arbitrariness of classifications, of the difficulties of method, and of the necessity of some stance as given. Those philosophers

[1] "It was in this age that, largely from religious sources, the great cultural systems of values which have guided civilization ever since took their shape. Confucianism, Hinduism, and Buddhism have provided the main frameworks of the way of life of the great civilizations of the Orient, with the one major exception of Islam, which came later but was in many ways intimately related to Prophetic Judaism." Parsons, "Sociology and Social Psychology," in Fairchild, op. cit., pp. 316–17.

who followed science have accordingly become more operational and positivistic. Many, especially in Great Britain, have now surrendered the field of fact as a legitimate domain of philosophy.

From the side of religion, moreover, philosophy has been robbed of its right to faith. Leading Christian theologians have discarded philosophy as alien to authentic faith. Some even declare that religion faces its decision in the dark, at least as far as rational knowledge goes. If religious knowledge presupposes a concrete religious perspective that is inaccessible to general rational confirmation and criticism, certainly philosophy can only trespass if it enters the field of faith. If philosophy is allowed at all, it is as the clarifier of presuppositions, and as the criticism of the implications that are imbedded within the faith itself. Thus philosophy is either being shrunk into impotence or released from bondage to alien powers, depending on the point of view; in any case, it is in hot dispute.

Is it true to say that science deals with fact, philosophy with thought, and religion with faith? Our answer is Yes, an affirmation we shall develop in this chapter, in order to show the place and function of philosophy and religion in higher education.

Philosophy is rational knowledge that deals with the analytical and synoptic interpretation of all possible experience. This, the great historic role of philosophy, is now being challenged, and Gilson is surely right that philosophy always buries its undertakers. Historically philosophy has had three main tasks: the empirical, the analytical, and the theoretical. Every creative civilization is likely to reunite these three aspects of man's inquiry. The empirical field is basically the task of science; its method is best suited to its exploration. But from Thales and Aristotle to Whitehead and Bergson the depth of philosophic penetration has never been devoid of organic relation to the world of fact. The truths of faith belong mainly to the religious disciplines, but no philosophy that lacked this dimension has ever struck deep into reality. Socrates had faith, and creation followed. Kant wrestled with it, and sparks flew into the darkness to light up new areas of inquiry.

Of philosophy's three main areas of operation, the first is the inclusive interpretation of the world of fact. There is no science;

there are only sciences. The scientific method, though unified in its general approach, is nevertheless diversive in concrete exemplification. There is real difference between the methods of geology and physics. Philosophy works as an over-all perspective, both as regards the respective methods of the various sciences and their factual results. Beyond the facts of science, however, philosophy also listens to history, learns of art, and consults with literature. Kant found there to be many kinds of reason; all need a chance to speak, if man is to form some understanding of his total experience. All deliberate effort to see the different sciences and the different kinds of experience as a whole is philosophy, no matter by what name the work may be called.

Philosophy, in the second place, carries on the work of analysis in the realm of thought; this analysis is its distinctive task, even as that of science is fact, and that of religion is faith. In one sense modern philosophy is merely finding itself in its return to logical analysis. Philosophy is rational thought. The nature of reason is to seek self-consistency. Rationalizations often hide themselves behind "double talk." There are rules for entailment. Systematic rigor presupposes logical exactness. Philosophy has an important task, both in the development of logic and in its application to systems of thought. In these it can both help to dethrone illegitimate theory and to prepare for more constructive thinking.

In the third place, philosophy is heir to the speculative extensions of knowledge. This task is today frowned on mostly because of an unphilosophic wedding of thought to sense. The minimum hypothesis in science has actually become translated into the philosophic dictum that truth is proportionate to public verifiability. Emphasis on verification has reduced thought factually to inventory, and formally to suppositional systems of logic; at least the overwhelming tendency has been toward such reduction. Concentrated concern with fact and form as such has also tended to split knowledge in two, with experimental science at one end, and logical positivism or linguistic analysis at the other. Such words as "value," "reality," and "synoptic seeing" have lost status. Thus reason has been destroyed at its roots; its reliability as personal seeing, social vision, and constructive theory has been undermined—often to the point of paralysis. But no civilization can be steered creatively that drifts without purpose or goal. Ethics as mere analysis helps to cut the nerve of obligation; when morality becomes conventional, its will is cut. Art also becomes arbitrary. However short of full truth man's theoretical reason may fall, civilization droops from confusion when the way of seeing is exchanged for the way of drifting. To steer present process mankind needs at least approximate goals that have passed through the scrutiny of rational criticism.

There are two main objections to our view of philosophy as engaged in this threefold task. The first is to the effect that any such concept as the whole of experience or the whole world of knowledge is meaningless; no one ever knows or can know the whole. The knowledge of the whole, however, is not dependent on the totality being known in an inclusive sense; we can know the salinity of the ocean without knowing all of the ocean. This salinity, however, has more than local reference! We can pass laws for all citizens without knowing them all, either together or as persons. The human heart beats the same the world over, and the human spirit wherever it may be must face or evade reality. Eating and drinking, living and dying, rearing children or looking at the sun are common experiences the world over. Wondering about the meaning of existence and finding certain wisdom about it knows no geographic boundaries. The choice is not between knowing all about everything and knowing nothing about experience as a whole; the choice is between arbitrary and disciplined thinking, between individual fancy and the community of inquiry, between mere inventory and philosophy, between drifting and steering in the best light available. There is no more subtle danger to thought and civilization than from the perfectionist presumption, which disregards responsible, rational decision because we cannot know correctly and fully all the truth there is. The philosopher who is in fact a frustrated scientist is a sorry sight!

The second objection is that reason is pressured by self and society to the point of distortion. Science deals with objective fact, but philosophy, in so far as it attempts to deal with any meaning of existence, becomes subjective. Metaphysics is thus held to be a matter of faith, and not of rational knowledge. Facts are interpreted within a presupposed context, viewed from a perspective that cannot be rationally demonstrated. The position we take for interpreting experience synoptically is not the result of factual interpretation or objective thought, but depends on some dominating interest within which the facts are organized. So run the arguments that are raised as objections to our definition of philosophy.

Let us admit at once that this objection must be for a very large part sustained. Metaphysics never escapes the problems of a faith stance,[2] as we have seen in our chapter on religion, and shall see in our discussion of religion in its relation to philosophy; but faith, if right, is not set apart from rational criticism. Practically no decision we make in actual life can be conclusively demonstrated factually or rationally. Certainly most of our decisions do not wait for such objective investigation. And yet reason is the capacity for a moment of weighing; it is the chance for delayed response. In some sense the self transcends the situation. Any field theory of freedom requires such constructive and critical understanding of reason. We have to make decisions to live. Most of the time reason, reporting through memory, operates in the form of a general route of decisions that lack critical, objective analysis. Such are the requirements of life. Similarly, civilization moves, for the most part, along its accustomed way, making decisions without adequate rational examination.

Neither life nor civilization can fully know its presuppositions or

[2] "It is not by any means true that we needs must believe this metaphysic when we see it. . . . On the contrary, we may, if we will, reject it, but if we do so we must face the consequences of such a rejection. *The only way out of ultimate relativism lies through metaphysics*" (italics ours). Casserley, *op. cit.*, p. 114.

"Nothing is more likely to infuriate some philosophers than to be told that philosophy, regarded as a serious human enterprise, is itself an expression of man's religious aspirations, and that every philosopher is, at least in his ultimate concerns, religiously oriented. Yet it is hard to avoid this conclusion if religion is broadly and basically defined as man's perennial attempt to probe into reality as deeply as possible, to root himself in this reality as completely as possible, and to adapt himself to it as realistically and vitally as he can." Theodore M. Greene, "Philosophy," in Fairchild, *op. cit.*, p. 139.

rationally determine its points of view. Nevertheless, just as life profits from its bit of possible objectivity by means of reason as delayed response, and, ideally, as critical and constructive evaluation, even so civilization can steer more wisely if its faith is submitted as far as possible to the methodological criticism of philosophy. Problems there are aplenty; we have no wish to hide them. Philosophy is both partial, and pressured by self and society; nevertheless we are well advised to seek whatever reason is possible in life, and whatever philosophy is available for civilization. Without them life is ruled by passion without rational purpose, and civilization by power without moral ends.

Philosophy is presently in crisis; religion always involves the permanent crisis of mortal life. Philosophy espouses rational thinking; religion is facing the full judgment of reality and reaching decisions concerning it. The historic crisis through which we are passing makes us more conscious, if anything, of the need for religion. External threats, such as that of communism, may endanger religious institutions. The crisis of life and death, of the meaning of individual existence, of the nature of human fulfillment, remains. The transiency of life haunts us, whatever be the theology, ideology, or Utopia in which we believe, and under whatever form of government or social organization we may happen to live.

For man must live by faith. He needs to know and to use facts; he has need of rational disciplines; but he must *live* by faith. Life is continually a venture of faith. Life mostly goes on, demanding acceptance beyond proof. To be sure, it is in relation to facts and the accumulative interpretation and managing of fact; it is always, to some extent, examined by thought and directed by it. But to live is to believe. When fear predominates, life declines; when anxiety is uppermost, the nerve of clear decision is cut. Fear frustrates life; it shrinks it and undermines it. As science is for the realm of fact with laws of its own, as philosophy is for the field of thought with laws of its own, even so religion is for the power of faith with laws of its own.

In particular, religion deals with the ultimate, the unconditional, that which is permanently real, true, right, and good. This region is not mostly the receding island of the unknown; religion does not shrink with the advance in knowledge. It is man's highest and total perspective on what is real and good. This master motive, which issues from man's central stance, cannot be arrived at by any increase in knowledge, whether of fact or of thought. It is the assumption of some presupposition that cannot be proved in terms of something more ultimate, without itself ceasing to constitute man's ultimate allegiance. It is the living of some point of view within some particular context of life that eludes precise appraisal. It is a riskful decision with relation to a deep ambiguity. Only insecurity can blind us to the truth that sound, normal living requires faith; faith is the daily bread of creative living, in all dimensions of life. All dimensions, too, run together within man's basic problem of the total meaning of life, both on the part of man and of mankind.

We may break down this general description of religion by the use of a few specific words. Religion is *existential*. It is not a matter of factual or rational knowledge, but of concrete decision. The existential nature of religion registers man's inescapable involvement in choosing situations that do not wait for fuller inquiry. To live is to keep deciding. To postpone choice with respect to ultimate commitments is in fact to live by some other choice. To refuse one faith is to allow another; to reject one stance is to stand in another. Man is free to choose within the measure of his capacity, and according to the possibilities of any situation. Moreover, he is forced to employ some measure of freedom. He cannot choose not to choose his primary responsibility in responding to the field of forces in which he is caught; he must face or evade reality. And he must choose how to face or how to evade reality.

Nor can man fall back on factual or rational knowledge, because real mystery veils man's ultimate stance or living center. Reality does not come with a clear face, but comes hid within various historic interpretations. Man's arms are also too short to take hold of the ultimate for the sake of any close examination of it. And besides, there are the pressures of self and society, conscious and unconscious, that make choice hazardous. Again, a close examination of the world as we know it gives us, we believe, no simple or single stance that can be proved to be correct with factual or logical rigor. Man must choose his living perspective; facts and reason can and should be consulted; but man's final choice is at its innermost a matter of faith. Religion is thus existential; religious thought and theory are the elucidations of concrete faith.

Religion is also *eschatological*. Religion seeks deliverance from evil; it affirms faith in some order that will end evil. This ending of evil may be an individual matter, or may be conceived of as some great historic consummation. At the heart of religious experience, in any case, is the recognition that the present order of life is wrong, that there is a better order, and that this better order can free the worshiper from the evils that beset him. In more mature religions like Buddhism and Christianity the ending determines the ends of life; present living prepares for things to come. It may be some eightfold path to salvation, or some conversion to a community of salvation, but whatever the form of expectation, the ending molds the goals. Eschatology is the determiner of ethics. Eschatology may be rooted in some past event that foretells the nature of the ending; it may be grounded in the impact of the eternal on the present, which thereby receives some eschatological dimension of experience; or it may be centered in some future event that will be the consummation of present hope. The transiency of life, however, focuses experience on a concrete ending. Reality gets interpreted most deeply in conjunction with our conscious or unconscious response to reality as putting an end to earthly life. Last things are realities that last. The ending of the evil order basically shapes our understanding of the central reality that determines our ends.

Religion is also *organismic*. It is more than a heuristic device to order experience. Life is steering. The present contains and fulfills the past; it contains frustrations and fulfillments. The past conditions present possibility into limited potentiality. The past is a strong stream, with the momentum of a given direction; steering is with respect to this stubborn fact. Yet the present is open within conditions; new decisions help alter the total direction. At some points in life, too, the stream can be radically redirected; this is so because the whole of the past is organically involved in each present. A basic decision in any present therefore constitutionally involves the reintegration of the total past.

Not only are the facts of experience organically related within the whole of life—with whatever resisting tendencies—but our thinking too is basically the elucidation of our central direction. As a miner's light in the middle of his forehead is thrown in whatever direction he turns his head, so reason is the flashlight that illumines present decisions. Most of the time the direction of that light is straight ahead. We see what we want to see. But the head can be turned, and the self can change its direction. When it does so, however, the whole self has to go along, whatever resistance may then be offered by frustrated drives. Religion is man's main stream of life;[3] it is his steering into ever unknown tomorrows by the light of the past and by whatever light he may find overhead. It is the total organization of life, which refuses to remain the same except as life becomes frozen stiff through fear and clings dyingly to the wreckage of its own past.

Religion is also *dialectical*. It lives necessarily within two discourses of meaning and motivation; it alternates between the real and the actual world. The two worlds must be held together in some way—at least practically. Religion can seek to transcend the world, to affirm it, to transform it, or to renounce it. Whatever main road it takes, or however it may combine several or all of these approaches, there is always some tension between the two worlds that makes for some dialectical movement between them. Unless there is tension religion is not real, for religion is never simply the acceptance of things as they are. Religion thinks and feels within the tensions of the world as it is and the world as it really is and can be; it moves from one world to the other.

Religion also gives rise to *concrete communities*. Faith is not merely personal, in the sense that it does not participate in some

---

[3] "We can define man as the being that is aware of the world as a whole. Man is therefore a metaphysical or a religious being. He is religious not accidentally but essentially." Richard Kroner, *The Religious Function of Imagination*, (New Haven, Yale University Press, 1941), p. 10.

more general form. Even the reformers and founders of new kinds of religion have been related to concrete communities they have tried to modify. One way of putting this truth is that theology is the rationalization of the faith of a community. Another way of saying it is that faith grows only out of faith; that faith is extended by faith, and not by reason as rational speculation. The religious use of reason is always that of the whole man thinking as a concerned individual and/or as a concerned community; the thinker is ultimately involved in the thinking. Thinking is integral to choice—not only to personal choice, but also to the choice of worshiping communities. To be sure, mature religion is not merely community choice; it is always also personal decision. Religion is stubbornly personal, because no community can take the place of the individual in his great crises of life. Nevertheless such crises become related to the common crises of the group. Out of the need of the individual in crisis within the context of the community arise such religious phenomena as liturgy, sacraments, and institutional arrangements.

Finally, for our purposes religion, like art, makes use of *symbolic reference*. Science seeks exact formulas, measurements, equivalents, predictions; philosophy seeks clarity of rational discourse; religion seeks depth of reality. Science deals in a large measure with signs. Philosophy uses signs and symbols, but tries always to arrive at clarity; even in the case of symbols. Art uses symbolic reference to appropriate beauty of nature and of life. Religion observes signs and glories in symbols—not for the sake of rational clarification, or merely the enjoyment of beauty, but for the sake of the unification of the conscious and unconscious reaches of experience, for the sake of the transformation of life and the reformation of the world. Religion seeks to go beyond the division of head and heart, of fact and thought, of thought and faith. The use of symbol by philosophy is interpretative; the use of symbol by art is appreciative; the use of symbol by religion is motivational. Therefore Tillich is right—at least in the case of religion—in asserting that symbolic communication demands existential participation. Philosophy employs the symbol to enrich a controlled understanding of experience; art uses the symbol with no thought of controlling or being controlled; religion uses the symbolic mode of communication for the sake of becoming controlled by reality. Philosophy by its very nature makes knowing most important; religion, while also seeking knowledge, puts as its first concern our being known. The philosophic symbol expresses; the religious symbol conveys. The philosophic symbol clarifies depth; the religious symbol seeks depth beyond clarity. Philosophy lives by *seeing*; religion lives by *being*, even beyond seeing. Philosophy seeks knowledge even through the depths of symbolic reference; religion wrestles with knowledge, but above all seeks life through depth, the life which is rooted and grounded in reality.

The relation between philosophy and religion is at least thus far clear: philosophy seeks truth through rational knowledge; religion seeks truth through fullness of life. Science majors in fact; philosophy in knowledge; religion in faith. There are laws of fact; there are laws of reason; there are laws of faith. Science should have its home in fact, but must be open to the laws of thought in terms of which its method and presuppositions can be tested. Science needs also to look at each of its specialized domains in terms of the fuller relationships of the whole world of fact and form, in order the more fully to understand each separate field with its distinctive method. When it carries on this task of reflective and creative thought in the light of ever larger wholes, science is relating itself fruitfully to philosophy. Science needs also to work in an area of creative faith. Those who know best the history of science know how rapidly its results change and how radically; there is no resting place in scientific certainty. Science is a great act of sustained faith. This is increasingly true in social science. When science becomes thus daringly creative it relates itself significantly to the realm of religion. All the while, however, the main work of science is to be critically careful according to the laws of its own realm. By being humbly, openly, but determinedly its proper self it can best serve the general welfare of mankind.

We have returned to a discussion of science in order to bring out more clearly this interrelationship of science, philosophy, and re-

ligion; in order, that is, to show the place of thought in its relation
to fact and faith. Philosophy too should be unashamedly itself. For
this reason, we repeat, we hail the contemporary return to the central
function of philosophy: the examination and development of the
laws of thought. When philosophy usurps the place of science, and
tries to be the final arbiter of fact, there is trouble afoot. When
philosophy tries to replace religion, and makes metaphysics its central
function, it becomes only false religion.

The function of philosophy is mainly to develop and determine
rational method; the place of religion is mostly to develop and to be
determined by facts for faith. The metaphysical use of reason is
always religious. It involves a stance that cannot be rationally demonstrated; metaphysical claims are faith judgments. The easy and
natural thing to conclude is that therefore philosophy should abandon
the field of metaphysics. This does not follow. True, philosophy cannot be the final judge as to fact, but it becomes empty of content if
it refuses to deal with the realm of fact. On the factual side philosophy must be a junior partner in the firm of science. But it is
needed by science and by knowledge as a whole. Similarly on the
side of faith, philosophy must be a junior partner in the firm of religion; but it performs there an indispensable function of challenge
and criticism.

This work of philosophy in the realm of religion is much more
than merely checking the consistency of the claim of religion; philosophy can do more than merely developing the implications and
involvement of religious presuppositions. The work of philosophy in
religion is more than suppositional, even from its own point of view.
The task of philosophy is this, to be sure; and in this sphere it does
a hard and heavy job. Religion, in order to claim knowledge, is required to submit to this examination by rational thought—as far
at least as this can cope with the nature of religion. But at the same
time philosophy has the right and the duty to investigate to the
furthest of its ability the claim of religion to interpret fact and to
have the power to change this actual world. In this sphere it is
assisted by science. Thus all disciplines work together for the validity
and adequacy of knowledge; they are co-workers for truth.

The religious reason is the whole man thinking; it is existential. Theological reflection as such is not religious thinking; it is the work of philosophy in religion. It is secondhand; it is needed, but not primary. Mere exegesis is not thinking in the proper sense of the word. Reflection, the development of implications, the testing of consistency, and the checking of relations to fact are the task of the philosophical reason; they are the work of philosophy in religion. Metaphysical thinking involves creative faith. On its believing side it is religious; on its thinking side it is philosophical. As individual man can delay response in general, and thus think; even so he can delay his response to the ultimate—not in the sense that he escapes living a faith even while he ponders and weighs, but in the sense that his metaphysical thinking can be altered through successive experiences by means of a partial but very real methodological objectivity.

Religion in the field of philosophy, as a junior partner, is metaphysical; philosophy in the realm of religion, as a junior partner, is methodological. Both fields, furthermore, serve and are served by science. Religion alone, open or disguised, provides the creative ventures of adequate interpretation as to the final meaning of life and reality. This fact accounts for the hold that religions have had on civilizations, and for the fact that only the ages of faith, as Goethe said, are the creative ages. The form of faith may vary; it is as rich as reality. But faith alone lights the candle that dispels the darkness. Within that light mankind must then correctly appraise and arrange for the best use what it finds within the reach of its longest beams.

Today we need a new common enterprise of science, philosophy, and religion. Limited though our topic is to the field of higher education, more depends on the right direction being given our institutions of learning—which should be the mind of the world, as we shall see in the next chapter—than we can easily imagine. We glory in the progress of science; new prospects dazzle those who know. Science has not failed us; we have failed science. The world of fact can be abused by becoming the servant of unimaginable destruction. But it is there to be used for a new and better age. The world of philosophy is hesitant when it is most needed. We have faith, however, that its concentration on the world of thought, in divorce from fact and faith, is more than an escape from the unbearable burdens of our time; it may herald the return of philosophy with sharper instruments and a surer hand.

The field of religion has to face fact and thought with new creative courage, if it is to find the resources for motivation that shall make our burdens bearable. If persons today are to be mentally stable and work with creative zest and satisfaction, they need a healthy faith. They need to face and to trust reality for adequate answers to our complicated, multiplying, and threatening problems. If civilization is to become creative and free, it needs to major in faith; religion must become, in an unprecedented way, the major of education. Religion working with science, history, art, literature, and philosophy fulfills education; it is its crowning glory.

Such religion must *itself* be creative and free. It must have been willing to face the hottest fire of fact and thought—to learn humbly and honestly from science, the humanities, and philosophy. But when religion has carefully consulted its partners, its own responsibility and privilege is to find the faith that can set free, the beauty that can satisfy the spirit, the truth big enough to use the world of fact for the common good and to stretch the mind strong. To do so religion must wrestle with the dark angel until the day breaks.

Chapter XI

The University and the World

THE crisis of the university is the crisis of the world; no university can escape being adversely affected by unstable cultural patterns and unpredictable political conditions. The crisis of the world, on the other hand, is in a large measure attributable to the crisis in higher education. The world's confusion and disintegration owe much to the lack of effective steering—to use the language of cybernetics—and to the lack of dynamic leadership on the part of the universities. Is the university, then, to be construed as the world's keeper? No, but it should be the world's mind. The mind, moreover, is no piece by and for itself; the mind is the clarifying function in and for the organism as a whole, with respect to all its experience and relationship. Similarly the university should serve as the clarifying function for the world.

What, then, is the university? It is the top perspective of the educational process, not only as a whole, but in its deliberate wholeness. It is not only the highest form of education, but education at the summit of its organic unity. A university is constituted by the pursuit and propagation of all genuine forms of knowledge, separately and together, in their bearing on all of life.

What, then, is the world? The world is the entire history of humanity within the reality of the cosmos. It is made up of the total confluence and context of past human living as they condition and require present response in thoughts, feelings, and decisions, where all actual social behavior, patterns, and structures are in turn con-

233

ditioned by our concrete cosmic epoch and situation. The world is humanity as a whole, with all its problems, hopes, fears, and satisfactions.

What, then, is the nature of the crisis? It is a piling up of confusion due to the lack of a common world view, purpose, and destiny. The old gods of religious faith are largely dead or dying, having been dethroned and destroyed by science, history, and psychology. Philosophy also, as we have just seen, crouches like a suppliant invalid, and hardly dares whisper about constructive solutions as large as our problems and as wide as all human knowledge; so far it has had to speak mostly to itself. Gods of the blood and soil also squirm, because their devotees are not only frustrated from without but also from within. Their external success is limited, and their hold on the deepest in humanity is either shaken or precarious. The god of the masses grins his defiance at past and present injustice, and sweeps with unparalleled rapidity through great countries and through many jaded lives. His offer to change history for the better when the old religions and philosophies are practically bedridden, however much music may issue from their couches, at least speaks some hope to multitudes; but deep within the allegiance quavers, some turning wistfully away, some pumping up the cruel zeal of uncertainty. Wistfulness wins the larger slice of the day. What can we therefore believe that is larger than our own lives, and what can we do to enable that faith to become real to us ourselves—let alone the world? Our age is a seeking age, and our mood is a willingness to listen to positive positions.

In the meantime war, and possibly with it revolution, threaten to plunge us all into destruction and catastrophe beyond human capacity to calculate. What place in a world like this, where "muddling through" may work but not satisfy, and where too much muddling may be costly beyond our power to pay—what place, we ask, can there be for the university? How can the university do more than twiddle its thumbs, bemoan the state of the world, hope for the best, and go on with its ineffective steering and its compromised leadership? The age is open for determined and wise leadership, but what can those of us who work in universities do about it?

The university can at least begin to assume its proper function in the world. It can do so only by understanding, with cutting clarity, what its proper function is.

The function of the university in the world is, first of all, to be its mind. The mind, as we have said, is the clarifying function of the organism. The world is neither an organism nor a person, but its processes may legitimately be compared, as rough, working analogies, to both—or perhaps to a kind of halfway house between them, rather than to either of them separately. The function of the mind is to identify, distinguish, and help the person-organism to relate itself to the different items in its experience. The more mature the mind, the better it can interpret the nature and value of the various possibilities for response, and thus further the purposes and satisfaction of the person-organism. To do so requires correct analysis and competently reflective evaluation. Without a hiatus between stimulus and response, without a delay between the world as conditional cause and the act of the self as effect, there can be no chance for the weighing of consequences and for choice in the light of them. The mind clarifies the significance of the pressures of the past on the self, and thus allows for a discriminating response. The self, through the function of its mind, is thus able to transcend the mere flow of process and to alter its direction, within its scope of competence, by means of a purposeful selection for the process; and by means also of the initiation of new chains of causation or new directions of energy. A biosocial-field theory of freedom of the kind we have proposed understands that the patterning of the flow of energy is reciprocal among organism, organisms, and environment. In the light of these facts we can grasp the importance of objectivity as the identification, evaluation, and selection of meaning before response. Such objectivity operates by means of free ideas, of conceptual abstraction in order to steer and thus to control the direction of our lives within the relevant possibilities of history and of nature.

The university as the mind of the world should provide exactly such objectivity. The world rushes toward us with myriad choices. Not to transcend the world-process by means of competently reflective evaluation is to drift; it is to be driven by circumstance. Obviously some thinking always must and does take place in order for human life to survive, but the university exists as the mind of the world for the sake of providing effective steering by dynamic leadership. The ship of society as well as the ship of state drifts hither and yon, because it has neither captain nor calculator able to know the destination, nor any standard for chart and compass.

We have indicated our faith that history has a haven. Humanity has been given a ship to steer toward it; but, as we shall see, we must devise our own way there. The intelligence has been provided us as the means whereby we may navigate. In order to do so, however, we must have a captain's bridge and a steering staff. The university exists for this purpose.[1] Instead of belaboring "the cult of objectivity," therefore, and of relinquishing, for some frenzied existentialism, the calm observation and calculation based on the discerning of the signs of the time as well as of the steady procession of the stars, we ought instead to regain our confidence in the opportunity for calm steering, even when the weather outside is rough.

The trouble with objectivity is not that it is either unreal or unnecessary; there is a real chance for it, and we need it very much. The blame that rightly falls to the cult of objectivity is that it may falsify the weather chart, and declare the weather smooth when the ship is in danger of foundering; or that it may become so obsessed with right calculation that it forgets that the chance for objectivity is given in order to steer the ship—particularly in rough weather. The university that worships at the holy altar of fact, or genuflects at the shibboleth of truth for truth's sake, is idolatrous. The discovery of fact and the true interpretation of fact are both in the service of life and society. Unless the university is motivated by such concern, and focused on such a function, the university betrays its trust. The mind has a right, a need, and a chance for objectivity, but always and completely in the service of the organism. The integrity of mind and integration of life cannot be had apart

---

[1] This figure is not meant to suggest *authoritarian* command, but rather *authoritative* command of the situation by means of knowledge and skill.

from the right relation to reality. Truth, reality, life, and society belong together, and must not be pulled apart by education.

The university exists, in the second place, to find and to make clear the unity of the universe. In order that there be a universe there must be unity; and the function of the university is to ascertain its nature, and how the world can become effectively unified by rightly relating itself to it.

The unity of the universe within which the world can become organically whole is the most important field of study; all knowledge, pure and applied, gears into this most comprehensive and essential question. Not to answer it as fully as possible is like a meticulous analysis from all possible angles of the nature of a vehicle of transportation without asking where it is to go and what are the several choices for the directing of it.

The difficulty with the study of the ultimate, however, as we have tried to show, is that it not only escapes exact analysis and prediction, but that it can neither be known as a single object or field, nor competently controlled in so far as it is known. We have indeed contended that the ultimate unity of the universe creates the kind of mystery that alone makes choice real, maturation possible, and community meaningful. Our present evidence for this assertion is only, we saw, the opening paragraphs of the plot; therefore the ultimate unity does not lend itself to indoctrination, but requires experimentation. On the other hand, we need to ascertain and to be guided by the unity that constitutes what we know as a universe, for otherwise we drift and fail to achieve progress. By progress we mean development in desirable directions, particularly with regard to our organic participation as a human history in the Eternal Purpose within the reality of the cosmos. On the other hand, we cannot externally bind the mind of the world; both because the destiny of man can be freely accepted only when it is discovered by personal insight, and because there is no finished process that can even now exhibit the nature of the ultimate Purpose.

Faith alone can find the stars by which to steer the ship of society. We all steer by some star; the function of the university is to train the telescope with patient and critical care on the severally suggested stars in order to determine which ones are real and right to use. Shifting weather and changing seas will continually make the stars hard to find; and constant calculation and better methods of search will be necessary as the ship keeps entering ever uncharted seas and as new weather conditions hide the sky. There is adventure in the steering, and no settled course once for all is available. No wonder those who have long and carefully studied the ship, its passengers, and the nearby waves, grow discouraged with the lack of final prediction in the captain's cabin; but, at the pain of losing our way, we must keep steering by the stars. We dare not drift, and we must not trust the nearby observations of weather and wind. The university must seek and make known the unity of the ultimate, with critical and creative honesty and diligence. If it does so, though it will find external indoctrination well-nigh impossible, it can nevertheless provide definite goals to steer by, goals that are both true and effective, but that must ever be redefined and reconstituted.

The unity of the universe should be used to create unity in the curriculum. The curriculum needs cohesion. When every field of knowledge considers itself a law unto itself, the only result can be overt or hidden war.[2] Specialization as an escape and a dogma, beyond its obvious legitimate use, is the poisoned brew that sends the experts doped into battle. Most bitter is the inner conflict, where a guilt-laden self-idolatry denies the sovereignty of truth as a whole, and tries to ignore while it refuses to acknowledge the secret rebellion against the larger loyalty. The university sends out soldiers, defensive against other fields where defeat might lurk, and armed for battle against entrenched evil, with one arm or foot or side well provided, but with the body as a whole weak and exposed, and with

[2] "The university, like the contemporary intellectual scene generally, is a Babel. There is no common means of intercourse because the different sections dwell in different intellectual worlds. The first need is to restore communication." Moberly, *op. cit.,* p. 116.

"There is a sting in the remark of a Roman Catholic friend of mine that a State University is a 'City of God that is all suburbs'; our innumerable specialties spread around the intellectual map in formless clusters, with only the most congested trickles of communication between them, and there seems to be no center which can relate one to the other." Boulding, "Economics," in Fairchild, *op. cit.,* p. 381.

the eyes so long set in one direction that they no longer can move to consider the whole field of battle. The modern need, in a complicated world, is for the university to develop core courses that are based squarely on the unity of the universe as that must reflect itself within the coherence of the curriculum. Perhaps we can summarize our previous discussions on these subjects and bring them to a climactic focus.

Concretely this must mean a reinstatement, from a more constructive stance, of a metaphysics that roots in and spreads from the knowledge of God and of His purpose with the world, metaphysics thus adumbrating the most adequate and valid faith. Or, plainly, we need a theology based on the absolute love of God that in turn is ready to be tested for its capacity to illumine the meaning of existence and to provide a relevant context or stance—"the hidden presupposition" for all other fields. Supplementing and yet supported by such teaching of religion and philosophy should be core sources of general knowledge, worked out by long-time interdepartmental co-operation of the teaching staff as a whole, possibly mostly through its most competent delegates both in specialized knowledge and in constructive synthesis, particularly in the bearing of all the social sciences on the meaning of life and on the choices of civilization. We believe that the case method, along with group dynamics and the chance for reflective privacy, may hold the key to the needed solution.

Within the unity of the universe, reflected in the coherence of the curriculum, there should then be the pursuit of dynamic differentiation. The universe does not exhibit tame uniformity, but creative variety. Each field of knowledge is characterized by a distinctiveness that is intrinsic to its nature. A legitimate pluralism banishes such methodological monism as assumes dictatorial rights over all areas of knowledge. A theology based on truth can only learn humbly from all legitimately established facts and contexts.

In this sense each field is autonomous, and we do well to heed its findings. Only when any field considers nothing beyond its own stakes, and thereby becomes arbitrary and out of focus in the light of the fuller perspective—only then is its autonomy forfeited by being abused. The coherence of knowledge refuses to become embodied within any fixed formula, or to abide by any settled pledge. We need rather co-operation on the part of the specialist and of the synthesizer, as they together steer forward, offering suggestions and checking each other's result.[3] The coherence of the curriculum means a community for the pursuit and dissemination of knowledge where the channels of communication are open both ways, between specialization and synthesis and between research and teaching. Variety enriches unity, while unity constructively appropriates creative difference.

The university as the mind of the world functions to find the unity of the universe, and creatively translate it into the coherence of the curriculum, where an over-all harmony of meaning and direction produces and discovers enriching difference. But the mind is for the organism as a whole, and for its satisfactory operation within its total environment. The university has the chance and the need for objectivity; it can and should lead, for the most part, a basically isolated existence from the world. The mind should not try to be the body, or directly to set things right throughout the organism as a whole; yet it is nevertheless through and through in and for the entire body. The university is likewise, in the third place, altogether in and for the world—however much it may enjoy and use deliberate isolation from it. The Christian understanding of the university is that it must be motivated, at the center of its life, by outgoing concern for the world. The university as the mind of the world should seek to make available for it the unity and creative richness of the universe. By so doing it can help to steer the world; it can direct its destiny by means of a creative and harmonious purpose. This guidance and unity the university can accomplish in at least three ways.

The university, in the first place—to return to a theme of our first chapter—can help to form and to foster the individuals who are in

---

[3] "The cause of this failure of Christian scholars to relate their Christian convictions to the specialized knowledge of the academic subjects which they profess is not far to seek. It lies in the widespread but fallacious notion that religion is merely one subject among others in the curriculum of a school or college." Nash, *op. cit.*, p. 266.

large measure to shape the destiny of society. This it can do, first, by enabling them to develop creative solitude. The home and the schools—and even the church—practically always fail to provide the setting for solitariness. Without solitude there can be no depth of society; without solitariness no rich solidarity can grow. The university needs to put students squarely on their own, to stop being nursemaids to their intellects. To master a language, or to be able to take examinations on the content of specified books, is not to be educated; such drill work is the necessary preparation for education, but constitutes no education. To educate, as Jeffreys suggests, may be a term derived from *educare,* to feed, rather than *educere,* to lead out; but no amount of feeding will educate a person. Memorization is a necessity of method; but higher education, at least, comes basically through meditation. Without skill we cannot navigate the rough, uncharted seas; but to determine both personal and social destiny we need vision.

If the university can only enforce learning, it can manufacture only wooden intellects, and thus perpetuate the past, without its creative spirit that alone produces that which is worthy of perpetuation. Somehow, beyond the attainment of knowledge, the university must breed the spirit of personal insight and creative adventure.[4] This cannot be bid; it can come only as the senior members vibrate with creative thinking and contagious wisdom, born within them from the closet with the closed door, and from the lonely road with the Alone; and as the undergraduates who emulate them, touched with the same sense of meaningfulness, begin in privacy to experience the transforming power of Reality. All study must be transfigured by the present urgency and peace of living truth, or it lies like a lump of undigested learning, and causes personal and social biliousness and inertia.

The university, in the second place, can also be the stimulater of creative individuals, those with social concern and vision, by its subconscious incubation of a community exhibiting the creative unity of the universe. By enacting an open community among all its members and by developing concrete behavior patterns and

[4] For the origin of academic freedom compare Boyd, *op. cit.,* p. 283.

practices, the university can prepare individuals for the larger society.

Only a community based on the criterion of complete concern on the part of each for all and all for each, with wide-open channels of communication, can do this.[5] If the university is to serve a world that is now to be born, it must outgrow much of the anthropological infantilism that separates it both in spirit and in externals from the world it is to serve. The only mark toward which all should shoot without invidious comparison, as golfers play for an ideal score, is the attainment of wisdom and the combination of skill and vision; each helping the other, where there is differentiation of gifts, variety of functions, and diversity of fields, but one spirit withal, in all and for all. Where senior members are sharply separated externally from undergraduates, and where both are a separate species from the staff, the world as it is is too much with us, and the university reflects its faults rather than offers its remedies. First and foremost, therefore, the university should allow the unity of the universe to become operative through it; for the world, because it embodies an inclusive togetherness of co-operative living, bound together in fact by its very purpose of the pursuit and dissemination of knowledge, and beyond knowledge, of living wisdom as the appropriation of learning within social vision and performance.

Then, and only then, in the third place, may the university export its social and scientific leadership. The modern world will increasingly become so complex in its functions that only the trained can cope with its make-up. In so far as the world stands at all—as we now know it—science is here to stay, and the social sciences will play an ever more important role. Social, political, and economic leadership can no longer be the task of the amateur. An almost inevitable presupposition for competent public service in the future, and even for the highest use and enjoyment of leisure, will be advanced education. The divisive aristocracy of education based on

[5] "Not until the study of religion, in the objective and constructive spirit, is made part of the required cultural curricula of schools of higher learning will it be possible to recapture an attitude toward life in which the values of meaning, purpose, and holiness will be restored to their role of fostering the human differential." Mordecai M. Kaplan, "Religion As the Symbolization of the Values of Holiness," in *Symbols and Values, an Initial Study*. Symposium XIII, Conference on Science, Philosophy and Religion (New York, Harper, 1954), p. 195.

some financial-social situation will give way, we believe, to a functional division of labor, where those with superior ability and application will not only be afforded special opportunity to reach a quality of vision and the kind of possession of relevant knowledge that makes possible superior service but will also become motivated by Christian humility and concern. The general level of education must also, at the same time, be raised as high as possible.

Those particularly who are to lead the generally educated must prove their competence by the judicious mastery of knowledge and the wise application of it to our personal, social, and political questions. The university must be more than the incubator of character and community; it must become the final training ground for scientific, social, and political leadership. If the concern of the university is some evasive truth for truth's sake, the university is a parasite on the social organism; it is not then the mind, functioning for the world and representing the unity of the universe, which through the coherence of the curriculum facilitates social harmony and creative experience.

The university, then, will fall short of its function unless it works with constructive objectivity in the central light of the meaning of existence. Within the perspective of the most high and the most real, the university works away at theoretical truth with calm isolation from the immediate pressures of society and politics; such freedom it must have in full measure; but it should ever work for the sake of the world which supports it and of which it is an organic function. The highest perspective of truth and the fullest commitment to it are, as we have seen, the two main aspects of our understanding of high religion.

The teaching of religion is by nature as central to the university as the unity that constitutes the universe. In such teaching inheres the coherence of the curriculum. To be sure religion, which should solidify while it releases creativity, has usually caused conflict and imperiled objectivity. Obviously we are most tempted to contend concerning what is most important to us! Much actual religion, however, runs deep outside its institutional guards, precisely because we have become defensive and divisive about that which should hold us together. We have tried to control what should control us. We have doubted the innate power of the pursuit and presentation of religion as truth, and have actually named courses in it "apologetics." We have defied religious history, and clamped the cold hand of the past on the tenderest thoughts and aspirations of today; then wondered why people fight shy of our offerings. The sin that always crucifies afresh the Son of God's love is the denying the work of the Spirit of Truth in the present.[6]

Naturally we cannot escape organization. Every vital idea, or whatever reality persists through history, develops some form of institutional expression; the Word becomes flesh. Yet we can keep the Word always as the judge and user of the flesh. The Church, as we saw, is necessary to perpetuate the saving purpose of God's love through history; but the Church needs the university to check its claims, to steer its search for truth, and to test the consistency of its faith, both as for self-consistency and with all known facts. *The university should be the intellectual conscience of the Church*. The authority and function of the Church is concern for the world— primarily in relation to God, and secondarily among men under God. The function and authority of the university is entirely concern for the truth, the intellectual side of life, as this affects the world in all its dimensions.

The university therefore needs to teach religion, both as a department and in relation to all departments. Even as English literature was once taught not as a department but only through other subjects, so religion can and should be taught through all departments, as far as it is naturally implied or involved within their subject matters; but it should also be taught departmentally.

Full education should train spirit, mind, and body. The religious department should be strong for the separate training of the spirit as such. Modern education has material mastery and enormous intellectual information; what is most needed is adequate training of the life of the spirit.

---

[6] Openness to the spirit of truth is the only practicable way to avoid making the religious ultimate into a controllable object. We do well to heed Martin Buber's profound warnings concerning the false use of reason, as, for instance, in his *Eclipse of God* (New York; Harper, 1952), pp. 44–45.

The department of religion should be manned by men of the highest concern both for truth and for man; men widely read and wisely experienced in the ways of the world. Those who teach in this field must not only know the field and facts of religion and be generally well-informed and balanced, but, more, they must themselves, in humble honesty and in retentive openness, embody in their own lives the attitudes and behavior of the religious perspective and force. They must themselves be touched and inwardly healed by the unity of the universe, while also being ready to widen out along with it into creative difference. Side by side with them should stand philosophers with wide vision and practical concern. Around all these, and on the same level, should work the scholars of all the fields that make the university what it is, the highest summit of the most comprehensive perspective; and together they should all live and love the truth, both as an objective quest and as a means for the practical guidance for the world.

As far as constructive leadership goes, the university needs a new lease on life in order to strengthen the total impact of truth on a confused and anxious world. Some intellectuals are now looking to religion; and right they are. But our traditionalistic religion has failed the university as well as the world. The simplest formulation of the all-inclusive love of God for men, and of our need for childlike faith in Him, in some such manner as we have tried to set forth in this volume, is yet the profoundest truth by which we must be led and can be healed.

When men of integrity dare to apply this truth to all of life, both in thought and in deed, then shall the university find the unity that translates the name into reality, and thereby also provide precisely for the world both help and healing. The crisis of both the university and the world comes from the unity and validity of a Purpose confronting them that cannot be by-passed; it can only be faced and solved. The solution is there for the finding; the finding is there for the willing. Higher education, in order to climb in the direction of its own summit, needs to become resolutely Christian. To make it as Christian as possible is as profound a task as has ever been offered to man by God.

Index

Set in Linotype Granjon
Format by Edwin H. Kaplin
Manufactured by The Haddon Craftsmen, Inc.
Published by HARPER & BROTHERS, *New York*